PASTORAL THEOLOGY

PASTORAL THEOLOGY

Norbert H. Mueller
George Kraus († 1989)
Coordinating Editors

Publishing House
St. Louis

ISBN 0-570-04249-6

0 78777 04249 3

Copyright © 1990 Concordia Publishing House
3558 S. Jefferson Avenue, St. Louis, MO 63118-3968
Manufactured in the United States of America

Library of Congress Cataloging in Publication Data.

Pastoral theology/Norbert H. Mueller, George Kraus, general editors.
      p.   cm.
   ISBN 0-570-04249-6
      1. Pastoral theology—Lutheran Church. 2. Lutheran Church—United States—Clergy. 3. Lutheran Church—Missouri Synod—Clergy.
I. Mueller, Norbert H., 1926–   . II. Kraus, George, 1924–1989.
BX8071.P37 1990
253—dc20   89-38014

1 2 3 4 5 6 7 8 9 10   99 98 97 96 95 94 93 92 91 90

Contents

ABBREVIATIONS

LW–American Edition of Luther's Works
(Philadelphia and St. Louis, 1955–1986)

References to *The Book of Concord*
(Philadelphia: Fortress Press, 1959)
AC–Augsburg Confession
AP–Apology of the Augsburg Confession
SA–Smalcald Articles
SC–Small Catechism
LC–Large Catechism
FC–Formula of Concord
SD–Solid Declaration of the Formula of Concord
EP–Epitome of the Formula of Concord

Foreword

Since the founding of The Lutheran Church—Missouri Synod in 1847, three textbooks have shaped students preparing for pastoral ministry in that church body: C. F. W. Walther's *Pastoraltheologie* (1872), John H. C. Fritz's *Pastoral Theology* (1932), and *The Pastor at Work* (1960, multiple authors).

Today's issues, however, have created the need for another pastoral theology textbook, yet one still based on sound theological principles. Because of the complexity of these issues, the coordinating editors determined from the outset to address current issues by enlisting the assistance of theologians with special competencies. The contributors represent parish pastors, district officials, synodical executives, and college and seminary professors. Each has had broad experience in the pastoral ministry, and each addresses the task with a pastoral heart.

Contributors to the text are David Bush, Eugene Bunkowske, Charles Evanson, L. Dean Hempelmann, Arthur A. Just, Charles Knippel, Philip Lochhaas, Roger Pittelko, Gary and Shirley Schaper, Richard L. Schlecht, Randall Shields, Rex Spicer, George Wollenburg, George Kraus, and Norbert H. Mueller. The latter two also served as coordinating editors.

Numerous people contributed substantially by reviewing the original manuscript and various revisions of it. Those who typed the original copy deserve special mention: Dawn Bates, Beverly Castator, Dorothy McGill, Brenda Schamber, and Doris Walther.

Although this textbook is designed to provide principles and guidelines for future pastors of The Lutheran Church—Missouri Synod, all Biblically committed pastors may find it useful as a review and as a manual of suggestions.

George Kraus
Norbert H. Mueller

UNIT I
INTRODUCTION TO
THE PASTORAL MINISTRY

Pastoral Ministry
in Perspective

What a challenge to fulfill God's purposes through the public administration of the means of grace! What a thrill to deal with the mysterious power of God at work in water, bread, wine and earthen vessels! No wonder some have called the pastoral ministry the highest office!

The honest pastoral candidate knows that the office, not he himself, should be on a pedestal. Even before serving in the ministry, he senses his personal inadequacies. He contemplates both the limitless possibilities as well as the numerous demands that the ministry will place upon him. He is simultaneously overwhelmed and encouraged by the comprehensiveness of the pastoral ministry:

—providing a kerygmatic and eschatological-pointing ministry;

—responding to the caring concerns of contemporary congregations;

—combining an understanding of God's revelation to man with contemporary insights;

—providing therapeutic pastoral care;

—knowing where to look for long range and immediate theoretical as well as practical resources; and

—artfully bringing a theological and insightful wisdom to the lives of people who seek to remember that although they are in the world they are not of it.

In a sense, there is little if anything which is new in the canons of pastoral theology. Pastors have always been called upon to apply the means of grace, in corporate and individual settings, to the needs and conditions of the people of God entrusted to their care.

What has become new is that certain aspects have assumed a greater need to be addressed. The church and its people seem to be becoming increasingly worldly; secular values, priorities, and standards of success or failure are being adopted by the church more and more. People in and out of the church increasingly dismiss the church as though it has no significance whatever in addressing the complex ethical and moral issues confronting society—much less the ultimate questions of life and death, sin, guilt, and forgiveness. The world, it seems, is setting the agenda.

The world's acceptance of abortion on demand, the right to practice homosexuality, serial polygamy, and similar customs related to morality are not only sanctioned but openly supported by certain communions within the church family. And people find in this ambivalence an excuse for behavior which they realize stands at variance with God's clear Word and will.

The modern church is also being affected by the shift in the role of women, with its concomitant effect on the stability of the home, child rearing, and the roles of husbands and wives.

The growing moral neutrality causes great perplexity, especially with regard to life issues and human sexuality. The life issues are many. At life's inception, abortions and the complications and the misuse of technologies such as amniocentesis confront the believer. At life's close, increasingly, the acceptance of euthanasia is being urged. The right to life and the right to die, by no means simple issues, are publicly debated.

Concerning the questions of human sexuality, present capabilities in reproductive technology simply boggle the mind. Facing the pastor and his people are such practices as artificial insemination, in vitro fertilization, surrogate motherhood, sex determination, genetic manipulation, and cloning.

Overall advancement in technology evidences a richly-endowed and highly-blessed society. By and large, except for a small percentage of the populace who do suffer profound poverty, no people has ever been so abundantly blessed with material gifts and wealth. It is a society so impressed with its own capabilities that it believes that there are no problems so great that it cannot solve them. At the same time, the society is adrift and at loose ends. It is so insecure that it seeks answers to the ultimate questions from sources—even purportedly spiritual sources—that can never provide the solutions in any lasting or meaningful way. The people of God, irrespective of age, are tempted by the New Age, astrology, eastern religions and philosophies, pseudo-Christian cults, and various sects incorporating mysticism, reincarnation, and spiritism.

People today sense a lack of purpose and meaning to life. How else can one explain substance abuse, the abuse of family members, marital infidelity, and divorce so prevalent that it becomes serial polygamy? We are a lonely, bored, anxious, and guilt-ridden people.

To be Scriptural and personal—those two words summarize the pastoral ministry. John R. W. Stott, in his book *Between Two Worlds*, says that "a true sermon bridges the gulf between the Biblical and the modern worlds and must be equally earthed in both."[1] What he says about the preaching task is no less true of the pastoral ministry in general.

The novice may envision a time when he will have arrived as a pastor; the veteran knows ministry means always striving, never arriving; he is thoroughly committed to and enjoys the daily and continuous striving as he personally grows in faith. He may be perplexed, but he will never despair; he may be hard pressed, but never crushed; persecuted, but never abandoned; struck down, but never destroyed (2 Cor. 4:7–9).

The Gospel Ministry

The only effective power for the ministry is the Gospel. Only through the Gospel are people brought into a new, saving, living relationship with God. Only through faith in Christ Jesus and his Word are ultimate answers found, sins forgiven, eschatological therapy received, eternal destiny assured, anxieties relieved, despair turned to hope, and selfishness turned to service. Only through the Gospel can the church come close to being the salt, the light, and the leaven it is intended to be (Matt. 5:13ff.; 13:33). The Christian pastor, as minister of that Gospel and steward of the mysteries of God, is committed to the faithful administration of the means of grace. As *Augustana* says,

> To obtain such faith God instituted the office of the ministry, that is, provided the Gospel and the Sacraments. Through these, as through means, he gives the Holy Spirit, who works faith, when and where he pleases, in those who hear the Gospel. And the Gospel teaches that we have a gracious God, not by our own merits but by the merits of Christ, when we believe this. (AC V 1–3)

As the pastor leads the flock of Christ also in a life of Christian

---

[1] Grand Rapids: Wm. B. Eerdman's, 1982, p. 10.

growth and service, he must remember the inseparable connection between faith and works summarized so succinctly by John, "We love because he first loved us" (1 John 4:19). Article VI of *Augustana* explains,

> It is also taught among us that such faith should produce good fruits and good works and that we must do all such good works as God has commanded, *but* we should do them for God's sake and *not place our trust in them* as if thereby to merit favor before God (AC VI 1; emphasis added).

And the Formula of Concord reiterates,

> As St. Paul expressly and earnestly reminds us, "Working together with him, then, we entreat you not to accept the grace of God in vain." This is to be understood in no other way than that the converted man does good, as much and as long as God rules him through his Holy Spirit, guides and leads him, but if God should withdraw his gracious hand man could not remain in obedience to God for one moment (FC SD II 66).

Effective ministry depends totally upon the means of grace which alone create and sustain life in Christ. Any appeal, overt or covert, that casts the believer back to any degree upon his own efforts cannot in any sense be considered pastoral. True, human skill and effort may serve more effective communication, but they cannot produce conversion to saving faith, which alone bears the fruit of Christian living. Therefore, observable manifestations are not in themselves valid criteria for success. The pastor is to be wary of adopting uncritically secular methodologies, pragmatic expediencies, and, worse yet, resorting to gimmicks in attempts to effect success in his ministry. Justification and resulting sanctification come only through the faithful administration and use of the means of grace. Only the Gospel—Word and Sacrament—sustains the people of God in saving faith and equips them to live as the people of God.

Pastoral Ministry: The Art of Applying God's Word

The source of ministry is God himself, and its standard is God's own Word,[2] which the pastor cannot approach in "academic freedom" as the modern world understands it. The pastor, a man of God, finds God's will and teachings in the Scriptures alone. He steeps himself in Scripture until he *thinks* theologically. He yields his will to God's and so measures the world's condition from God's

---

[2] 1 Tim. 6:3; John 17:20; Eph. 2:20.

point of view—and proclaims God's solution.[3] Luther's dictum, *So steht's geschrieben* ("Thus it is written"), guides all pastoral ministry.

God alone is the source of the ministry of reconciliation and has justified the world by grace through faith.[4] Therefore, since he provides his self-revelation only in Scripture, Scripture norms ministry by its testimony of the crucified and risen Christ.[5]

A people-oriented pastor must also understand the setting of the ministry in God's world. As Paul said, "I have become all things to all men so that by all possible means I might save some" (1 Cor. 9:22). The rigid, inflexible pastor who works out of some real or imagined "practical rule book" cripples his ministry.

The Lutheran Church in Germany has an old word for the man who knows his flock and applies the Scripture to people's lives: *Seelsorger*, a "curate of souls." The Lutheran church in this country has elected to use the Biblical word "pastor" (shepherd). Regardless of the term, all theology must have this spiritual task as its goal and purpose.

The latter half of the 20th century has witnessed the pastoral ministry adapt more and more to sociological-psychological models and methods. While Christians take every thought captive for Christ (2 Cor. 10:5), pastoral ministry is more than sociology or psychology; it is based solidly on the revelation of God in Jesus Christ and his Word. Here the Christian pastor finds his authority, power, and direction.[6]

Nathan's confrontation with David over the Bathsheba-Uriah event illustrates a pastoral care based on the Word of God (2 Sam. 12). Nathan gave no room for the "how" or the "why"; he allowed no self-justification, no excuses, no sharing of blame with parents or environment. He accepted no psychological theory as a mitigating factor, no sociological model or cultural pattern as a way of glossing over the act. The prophet of God confronted the king with a simple accusation: "You are the man!" David's confession likewise elicited from Nathan no discussion of future resolutions but the simple, direct absolution: "The Lord has taken away your sin." In Nathan, God has provided the pastor with a role model in applying Law and Gospel for the glory of God and the salvation

---

[3] Is. 8:20; Luke 16:29–31.

[4] Rom. 1:16; 5:1; 2 Cor. 5:19–20.

[5] 1 Cor. 2:2; Rev. 5:9; 2 Cor. 5:15.

[6] 1 Tim. 5:21; 6:13–14; Ezek. 3:17; 2 Tim. 2:25.

of all people.[7] When the pastor proclaims Law and Gospel, the Holy Spirit is at work in the heart of the hearer.[8]

Pastoral ministry, then, is the *art* of applying that living Word (the Book that is "God speaking") to the human heart in all its varied conditions. Listen to C. F. W. Walther in his volume *The Proper Distinction Between Law and Gospel*[9] on the art of applying God's Word to the hearer:

> *Rightly distinguishing the Law and the Gospel is the most difficult and the highest art of Christians in general and of theologians in particular. It is taught only by the Holy Spirit in the school of experience.*

> . . . But at the present time we are studying the *application* and the *use* of this doctrine. The practical application of this doctrine presents difficulties which no man can surmount by reasonable reflections. *The Holy Spirit must teach men this in the school of experience* [emphasis added]. The difficulties of mastering this art confront the minister, in the first place, in so far as he is a Christian; in the second place, in so far as he is a minister.

In applying himself to this "most difficult and highest art," the minister of the Gospel may find himself in tension and indecision. The all too familiar clergy "burn-out" frequently finds its cause in the wear and tear of seemingly insoluble people-problems in the congregation. Yet by the study of the Word, his own pastoral experience, the advice of brother clergy, and the guidance of the Holy Spirit through the Word, the pastor will learn and mature and even find strength and joy in this glorious art.

---

[7] 2 Sam. 12:9–12 (Law), 13 (Gospel); 1 Cor. 10:31–33 (mission goal).

[8] Jer. 5:14; 23:29; Ps. 19:8; Rom. 1:16.

[9] 14th printing, 1986, copyright 1929, 1986 by Concordia Publishing House, St. Louis, pp. 42–43.

UNIT II
THE PASTOR, THE OFFICE
AND THE CHURCH

1
The Office
of the Public Ministry

We are all equally priests, that is to say, we have the same power in respect to the Word and the Sacraments. However, no one may make use of this power except by the consent of the community or by the call of a superior. (For what is the common property of all, no individual may arrogate to himself, unless he is called).[1]

The Office of the *Public* Ministry has been instituted by God and is to be distinguished from the ministry that God has given to all Christians: the Office of the Keys—the privilege and duty to proclaim the good news of salvation, the authority to forgive or not forgive sins, and the responsibility to administer those means of grace called the *sacraments.* Peter calls Christians "a chosen people, a royal priesthood . . . that you may declare the praises of him who has called you out of darkness into his wonderful light, . . . offering spiritual sacrifices acceptable to God through Jesus Christ" (1 Peter 2:5–6).

With that in mind, Luther commented that if a Christian "is in a place where there are no [other] Christians, he needs no other call than to be a Christian called and anointed by God from within . . . . even though no man calls him to do so."[2]

---

[1] *The Babylonian Captivity of the Church,* LW 36:116. See also *Concerning the Ministry,* 40:34.

[2] LW 30:310. See also LW 40:18–34 and Martin Chemnitz, *Ministry, Word*

God, however, has not called each Christian to exercise the Keys *publicly*. Scripture clearly refers to God's establishment of a special office for that purpose: Acts 13:2–4; 20:28; Rom. 1:1; 10:15; 1 Cor. 3:5; 4:1; 12:28–29; Eph. 4:11; 1 Tim. 4:14; 5:22; 2 Tim. 1:6; 1 Peter 5:2.

The Lutheran Confessions, Chemnitz, and, later, Walther maintained the distinction:

> The public ministry of the Word and Sacraments in the church is not entrusted to all Christians in general (1 Cor. 12:28; Eph. 4:12). For a special or particular call is required for this (Rom. 10:15).[3]

> It is taught among us that no one should publicly teach or preach or administer the sacraments in the church without a regular call (AC XIV).

> The holy ministry of the Word or pastoral office is . . . distinct from the priestly office which all believers have.[4]

> In order that we may obtain this faith, the ministry of teaching the Gospel and administering the sacraments was instituted. For through the Word and the sacraments, as through instruments, the Holy Spirit is given, and the Holy Spirit produces faith, where and when it pleases God, in those who hear the Gospel (AC V, Lat.).

No General Call to the Public Ministry

A distinction must be made between the general "call" that every Christian has and the "call" to hold the public office of the ministry. Every Christian has a calling to live out his or her life as a Christian, to bear witness in every situation to the truth of Jesus as our vicarious atonement. (Unfortunately, many Christians defer to the secular view that their means of gaining a livelihood is their sole vocation, forgetting that their first calling is that of Christian. That unfortunate view has grave consequences for the Christian's faith and life.) The call to hold the office of the public ministry, however, is the specific invitation and assignment given by God through the church for a man to exercise the Keys *publicly* (i.e., to serve on behalf of the church, answerable through it to God).

While some people talk of a man feeling that he has a call from God to study for the ministry, such a use of the term "call" can

---

and Sacraments, trans. and ed. Luther Poellot (St. Louis: Concordia, 1981), p. 29.

[3] Chemnitz, op. cit., p. 29.

[4] C. F. W. Walther, *Walther on the Church*, trans. John Drickamer (St. Louis: Concordia, 1981), Thesis I, p. 73.

be confusing. Strictly speaking, only two types of calls exist: the calling that all Christians have and the call from God through the church for a man to hold the office of pastor.

Of course, those who would be pastors need to be convinced in their hearts that God, working through natural means and events, has led them to commit themselves to full-time service as pastors; that through a congregational call God will extend to them the specific call into the pastoral ministry; and that they will be equipped for the pastoral ministry if and when that call comes. They need to meet God's requirements as set down in 1 Timothy 3 and Titus 1. But until God calls them through the church to hold the office, they have no call into the pastoral ministry. (Cf. Unit II, 3.)

Terms and Functions of the Public Ministry

While the New Testament contains a number of terms that describe the function of the parish pastor, perhaps none describes his primary function as well as the name for Jesus Himself: *Rabbi* (teacher), who is also the model. Some 58 passages in the Gospels use a form of the word *teach* to describe Jesus' activity. The title is given to Jesus already at his baptism, and it is used consistently by his disciples and others. And, lest some separate the function of *teaching* from that of the pastoral ministry, note that in Eph. 4:11 the common article links the two together as "pastor-teacher."

Bishop, Elder, Pastor: While some denominations have sought to differentiate between these terms, Scripture uses them interchangeably. For example, in Acts 20:28 the elders (*presbuteroi*) are told that the Holy Spirit has made them overseers (*episkopoi*) and has commanded them to shepherd (*poimainein*) the flock (Lat., *pastor*, "shepherd"). In 1 Peter 5:1–2, the elders (*presbuterous*) are encouraged to "be shepherds [*poimanate*] of God's flock that is under your care, serving as overseers [*episkopountes*]."

Each term, however, denotes a particular emphasis and will help in understanding the context of the passage in which it appears.

Episkopos was applied in the secular world to public officials of Athens who were sent to the colonies to supervise Athenian interests, enforce decrees, and to collect revenue. The title indicates responsibility for oversight.[5]

---

[5] For a more complete understanding of *episkopos*, see Gerhard Kittel, *Theological Dictionary of the New Testament*, trans. and ed. Geoffrey W. Bromiley (Grand Rapids: Wm. B. Eerdmans Publishing Company, 1965), Vol. II, pp. 611f.

Presbuteros ("elder") seems to have originated in Hebrew communities. In Ex. 4:29–31; 12:21; and 19:7, elders (older and mature people, based on their wisdom and judgment) represent the people. After the occupation of Canaan, the elders had more responsibility and even legal powers (Deut. 19:11–13; 21:1–9; 22:13–21; 25:5–10). At the time of Jesus, elders were responsible for religious guidance (Matt. 15:2; Mark 7:3, 5). *Pastor* (Lat.) is another synonym for *elder* and *overseer* (Acts 20:17, 28–29). Most laity do not know the Latin background for *pastor*, yet prefer its warm and personal connotation. Any Biblical term is appropriate.

Many people use the term *minister* to refer to the person occupying the office of the public ministry. Though used in common parlance, care must be taken to differentiate between the office of holy ministry and the general ministry of all believers.

To reiterate, the term in vogue matters little. The importance lies in the fact that the pastor publicly administers the Gospel through the means of grace.

Lest this "specialness" of the public ministry be taken to an extreme, note that the office is not synonymous with the office which the disciples/apostles (including Paul) held.

First, Jesus himself personally and immediately called the apostles to their special position. As Paul repeats in Eph. 4:11, they were gifts of the ascended Lord to the church. In Eph. 2:20 he combines the apostles with the prophets as "the foundation" of the church, together "with Christ Jesus himself as the chief cornerstone." And in Rev. 21:14, John describes the heavenly Jerusalem as built on twelve foundations with "the names of the twelve apostles of the Lamb" written on them.

As personal representatives of the Lord, the Twelve had a special, once-in-history duty: to deliver the revelation that they had received. They were the ones God himself had chosen to witness personally that Jesus was, in fact, the Messiah who had died for our sins and had risen from the dead. This fact they were to transmit without alteration (1 Tim. 6:14); and what they transmitted was to continue to be transmitted by their successors without alteration (2 Tim. 2:2).

Clearly, the apostles occupied a unique office, directly commissioned by the Lord, entrusted with the revelation of the mystery of Christ. As his representatives, the apostles are the teachers of the church for all time (John 17:6, 8, 20–26).

Following the apostles, calls to the public ministry have been through the mediation of others, though the calls are still from God. So, for example, Paul reminds Titus to appoint elders (pastors) of the congregations on Crete (Titus 1:5). Because the church alone has been given the power of the Keys (cf. above), God calls

men to the office of the public ministry only through the mediacy of the church. Thus, "where the true church is, therefore, the right of electing and ordaining ministers must of necessity also be" (Tractate 67).[6]

Installation/Ordination

The rite of installation publicly declares the new relationship entered into by pastor and congregation. During the candidate's first installation (i.e., ordination), he declares his intention to make the office his life's vocation. However, the rite *per se* does not admit him into the ministry. Note the words of the officiant in the rite of ordination, first from *The Lutheran Agenda* and then from *Lutheran Worship Agenda*:

> The Lord pour out upon you his Holy Spirit for the work committed to you by the call [i.e., not "by ordination"].

> Dear brothers and sisters in Christ, _____ has been called by the Lord of the church into the office of the public ministry.

The Roman Catholic Church and others hold that ordination raises the candidate to permanent priesthood. In contrast, the Lutheran Confessions teach,

> These words apply to the true church which, since it alone possesses the priesthood, certainly has the right of electing and ordaining ministers. The most common custom of the church also bears witness to this, for there was a time when the people elected pastors and bishops. Afterwards a bishop, either of the church, or of a neighboring church, was brought in to confirm the election with the laying on of hands, nor was ordination anything more than such a confirmation (Tractate 69–70).

Nevertheless, the ancient custom of ordination was practiced already in apostolic times (Acts 6:6; 13:3; 1 Tim. 4:14; 5:22; 2 Tim 1:6) and should not be arbitrarily omitted.

On the other hand, ordination does recognize and announce that the candidate is available for service to the whole church.

> In a synod of congregations bound by a common confession and loyalty, good order demands that admission into the pastoral office or into its closely allied auxiliary offices is not the act of

---

[6] Regarding the immediate reception of the Keys by the church, see (e.g.) Fritz, *Pastoral Theology* (St. Louis: Concordia, 1933, 1945, Heritage edition 1977), p. 35f; and Luther's comments as quoted in Ewald Plass, *What Luther Says*, 2967, 2970 (St. Louis, Concordia, 1959, Eighth printing, single volume, 1986), pp. 946–947.

a single congregation or agency. . . . This transparochial nature of the office of the public ministry and its auxiliary offices is important because a person called to one congregation is recognized by the whole church and, by virtue of ordination or commissioning, is eligible to be called by other segments of the church.[7]

Therefore, although a pastor may not be serving in a parish because of some other called service or because he has (for valid reasons) resigned from a parish and is awaiting another call, he is still recognized as an ordained pastor in the service of the church and is accountable to it—and legitimately may perform pastoral functions when asked by a parish.[8]

Valid, Legitimate Calls

Since the public ministry is a divinely established office, those called to serve in it are "servants of the Lord Jesus Christ" (Rom. 1:1; James 1:1) who have been set apart for the role(s) and position(s) of the office of the whole church's public ministry. Therefore, a call to serve in that ministry must be both valid (*rata*) and legitimate (*legitimata, recta*). This means that the call must be extended by those who have the authority to do so and that the one called be accountable to them (i.e., be valid); and the call must be properly extended (i.e., legitimate).

An invalid call, for example, would be one extended by a small group of individuals for a pastor to serve them privately in their homes. Of this, Luther commented in his letter to the " 'neun Männer' Zu Hervord" of April 1532,

> It does not follow that every citizen may establish a congregation in his house; that is not permissible. There is a great difference between a common and public gathering of people, and a family circle; for what a citizen does in his own home is of a private nature.[9]

He also stated,

> If two or three citizens were to ask me to preach, I would not

---

[7] *The Ministry: Offices, Procedures, and Nomenclature* (September 1981), The Commission on Theology and Church Relations (The Lutheran Church—Missouri Synod), p. 30.

[8] Ibid., pp. 20–21.

[9] Luther, *Sämmtliche Schriften*, Vol. XXIa (St. Louis: Concordia, 1903), p. 1741; translation from Fritz, *Pastoral Theology*, p. 41.

follow such a private call; for this would open the window to the ministers of Satan.[10]

This practice (under normal circumstances) would be an act of separation and would contradict the Biblical concept of the congregation as the assembly of believers in a given area who are gathered by Christ around the saving and strengthening Word and Sacraments.

Challenges to a Call's Validity

The congregation, not individuals, makes the call valid. This principle applies whether or not another pastor (vacancy or circuit counselor) was present, whether or not any other called ministers in the congregation gave their approval, whether or not the congregation has any internal problems not mentioned in the call document, whether or not the call is temporary or permanent, or even whether or not the call vote was unanimous. On the other hand, these issues ought not be summarily dismissed. The church still needs good order.

A congregation does well, for example, when it follows the precedent set in the New Testament era of the church when one or another apostle was present as an established congregation called a minister (Acts 1:24; 6:3; 14:23). A vacancy pastor or circuit counselor can help maintain good order and can help the vacant congregation grow in understanding the office of the ministry, the call process, and the congregation's unique situation. (At the same time, he will be careful to avoid asserting himself unduly.)

So, too, when a congregation has (e.g.) a "senior pastor," his views about when and whom to call as an additional minister(s) should be considered. Although the congregation possesses only one office of the ministry, more than one person can occupy that office—and the congregation alone has the authority to determine if/when an additional pastor should be called in order that the office of the ministry be fulfilled in its midst.

Nor do internal problems within a congregation invalidate its call. Though a congregation may have treated its former pastor shamefully, or though it is presently burdened with serious internal problems, such a congregation's call still is valid because the congregation still has Christians within it. As the Apology of the Augsburg Confession states,

There is an infinite number of ungodly within the church who

---

[10] Comments on Gal. 1:1, LW 26:19.

oppress it. The church will abide nevertheless; it exists despite the great multitude of the wicked, and Christ supplies it with the gifts he has promised—the forgiveness of sins, answer to prayer, and the gift of the Holy Spirit (Ap VII and VIII 9).

Even a call extended by a heterodox congregation is valid; the people extending the call are doing so because they are Christians, not because they are members of a heterodox church.[11]

Nor does a call's permanency affect its validity. Some calls, by their very nature, include a time limit—e.g., the military chaplaincy and establishing a mission. Thus, the Synod's Commission on Theology and Church Relations has specifically stated, "There is no Scriptural evidence to indicate that all calls are necessarily permanent or tenured."[12]

And, finally, a less-than-unanimous vote does not negate the call's validity. On the other hand, objections should be raised and resolved when the list of candidates is presented and discussed. No pastor should be faced with an opposition party from the outset of his ministry; nor should any member be of the opinion that the new pastor is coming without having been guided by the Holy Spirit. Thus, following the election of a candidate by the majority, the voters assembly ordinarily approves a subsequent resolution to make the choice unanimous.

If a pastor has serious doubts that the vote truly was unanimous, he should counsel with the calling congregation. If he in good faith accepts the call only to discover that he was not the choice of some and that their objections did not receive a fair hearing, he can overcome their concerns through love and faithfulness and gain their confidence.

Transmitting the Call

To be legitimate, a call must be properly extended. As part of that, good order requires a congregation to forward its call by means of a diploma of vocation (a call document) along with supporting data and information about the church and community. The diploma of vocation states that the congregation requires the pastor to accept the Holy Scriptures as the inspired Word of God, to regard the Lutheran Confessions as a true exposition of them, to preach and teach accordingly (Titus 1:9), and to shepherd the people of the congregation and conduct his office in a manner that will be a credit to his high calling. If a special need of the congregation is to be a priority, the call document should indicate

---

[11] Fritz, op. cit., pp. 42f.

[12] *The Ministry*, p. 33.

that. The call document also contains the promise of the congregation to receive the pastor as God's servant (1 Tim. 5:17), to faithfully use and respond to God's Word of grace, and to pray for the pastor.

Since the office of the pastor requires his full time and energy, the diploma of vocation assures him that the congregation will provide adequately for his physical needs (e.g., salary, fringe benefits) so that he and his family will not suffer hardships (1 Cor. 9:6–14; Gal. 6:6). All matters relating to the financial support of the pastor are to be resolved at the time the call is extended. The circuit counselor can help the congregation to understand its responsibilities and make arrangements to provide adequately for the pastor's need. The pastor should be able to live according to the average living standard of the members whom he is called to serve.

> It is a disgrace and a sin if the church that is able to pay its minister a living salary compels him, in order to make ends meet, to earn additional money at some other occupation. On the other hand, it is a disgrace and sin, if a minister whose congregation pays him an adequate salary nevertheless spends the time he ought to give to his congregation, and for which his congregation is paying him, in doing other work in order that he may get more money. Such a minister is greedy of filthy lucre and unworthy of the holy office, 1 Tim. 3:3; Titus 2:7.[13]

Delegating the Authority to Call

The right and responsibility to call a pastor to the public ministry has been given to the congregation, but Scripture nowhere delineates how the congregation is to carry out this task. Thus, delegating the selection of the pastor is permissible.

Under ordinary circumstances in the parish, the congregation delegates to a church council or board of elders only the authority to select and present a few candidates from a larger list. Past experience advises against the members delegating all of their rights as spiritual priests. Each and every member of the congregation has the solemn responsibility to call the pastor, and grievous repercussions often develop when the choice of a few has not found favor with the whole congregation.

On the other hand, when congregations band together to carry out a public ministry (e.g., in a hospital ministry, at a synodical educational institution), good order dictates that they do delegate to others the authority to call.

---

[13] Fritz, op. cit., p. 54.

The very existence of the Synod indicates that the church must do some of its work jointly. The Synod is not an alien organization. It is the whole confessional fellowship of congregations. In this case, by common agreement, certain offices are filled by the Synod or its commissions through authority delegated from the congregations.[14]

Summary

God . . . reconciled us to himself through Christ and gave us the ministry of reconciliation: that God was reconciling the world to himself in Christ, not counting men's sins against them. And he has committed to us the message of reconciliation. We are therefore Christ's ambassadors (2 Cor. 5:18–20).

---

[14] *The Ministry*, p. 31.

2
The Pastor as Person

The pastor as person—always a popular topic—continues to be in the spotlight, partly because the electronic church has exposed its preachers to intense scrutiny based on a popular image of what a pastor "ought" to be and act like—and a human glee when "the mighty are fallen." The parish pastor may feel uncomfortable under prying eyes; yet that age-old, fault-finding propensity prompted Paul to counsel Timothy and Titus that Christians (especially pastors) should "set an example for the believers in speech, life, love, faith, and purity" (1 Tim. 4:12) "so that God's name and our teaching may not be slandered" (6:1). The Christian pastor should be a "workman who does not need to be ashamed" (2 Tim. 2:15) "so that no one will malign the Word of God" (Titus 2:5). He should "set them an example" (2:7) "so that in every way they will make the teaching about God our Savior attractive" (2:10). Paul is not concerned about ego (his own or that of Timothy or Titus) but about "those who would believe on [Christ Jesus] and receive eternal life" (1 Tim. 1:16).

Within that context, Paul recognizes that all Christians have a vocation (Eph. 4:1) as members of the royal priesthood (1 Peter 2:5, 9)—but that not all have the qualifications which are required of the man whom a congregation calls as pastor (1 Tim. 3:2ff; Titus 1:6). Simply put, those qualifications call for the pastor to *image* the perfect model, Jesus Christ. Paul wrote: "Be imitators of God, therefore, as dearly loved children and live a life of love, just as Christ loved us and gave himself up for us as a fragrant offering and sacrifice to God" (Eph. 5:2). As Luther put it, we are to be "little Christs" to our fellow human beings.

At the same time, the pastor cannot model Christ perfectly. In spite of the mistaken, even popular notion, that "a bishop must be blameless" to the point of perfection, no one is without sin. Even the pastor's life is troubled by spiritual, emotional, and physical traumas. He is a sinner, yet a new person in Christ—*simul justus et peccator,* as Luther put it. The church does not seek a sinless pastor but one who is of good report and of a strong and mature faith, a man who strives publicly and privately to model Christ before all. In short, his life should be a credit to his high calling.

Numerous Scripture passages characterize the ideal Christian. These, coupled with passages specifically directed to the pastor, profile the model. The passages speak of his personality traits, gifts and abilities, and lifestyle.

Personality Traits

Dealing with eternal verities and matters of life and death is serious business. The pastor must be a *sincere* Christian who believes what he preaches. He lives and breathes his faith, formally and informally, in the pulpit and everywhere, even in his home. Genuineness that automatically creates respect is best linked with a discerning sense of humor rather than with a sanctimonious and pietistic (as opposed to pious) manner that no one likes and that is ultimately counterfeit sincerity. The pastor who laughs at his own foibles preaches an effective sermon on the doctrine of man. Humor, of course, cannot be at the expense of *dignity.* The test is whether the pastor can freely shift roles to become a competent comforter, counselor, or preacher. His manner will always reflect a *cheerfulness* appropriate to the occasion that comes from the Gospel message.

Sincerity leads to *humility* and *unselfishness*—traits that the Gospel alone can produce. Parishioners may tolerate but will detest a proud and conceited pastor because, in effect, he is preaching that his gifts are his own and not from God. Self-promotion weakens the respect and dignity he needs as pastor, which can only be earned and not demanded.

A sincere and humble pastor who has been transformed by the Gospel will be *faithful* and *conscientious* in the performance of his duties—ultimately the only demands the Lord places on him, regardless of how gifted he is. He will also be *patient* and *tolerant,* willing to suffer wrong rather than err by dealing unkindly or inflexibly with people.

The pastor will have to cultivate *tact* if he does not have it. Once again, the Gospel can remold a person, and the pastor needs to be conscious at all times of the image he projects.

Other desirable traits mentioned in 1 Timothy 3 and Titus 1 are related to or can be subsumed under those already mentioned: temperate, not overbearing, self-controlled, not quick-tempered, disciplined, not violent but gentle, not quarrelsome.

Abilities and Competencies

Like every professional person, the pastor needs the capacity to acquire knowledge, to impart it, to think analytically, to lead, to inspire confidence and trust, and to convince others of his position.

The pastor is also expected to be a leader, an evangelist/missionary, and *Seelsorger* (a curate of souls, one who can help people individually). These roles defy clear definition because they require skills or techniques and a knowledge of how to use them. More than that, they call for practice and a kind of sixth sense for anticipating results. (For further discussion on the pastor's role in various situations, see Units IV through VI.)

The Educated Pastor

Knowing the Scriptures, church doctrine, and church practice is basic. Formal training for public ministry begins at the Seminary, where the necessary basic information, tools, and skills are acquired. The pastor's education does not end with his graduation from the seminary. Every conscientious professional person constantly "renews his license" through some form of continuing education. The value of knowing the Greek and Hebrew languages is obvious for recognizing shades of meaning, idiomatic expressions, and nuances not conveyed by a translation. Knowledge of the Bible is essential. Bible history, personalities, the basic thrust of each of the 66 books, and the location of important passages to illustrate Biblical doctrine can be learned through systematic, perhaps brief but conscientiously followed, periods of study. Generally speaking, the more the pastor can commit to memory (including sermon content), the more effective he can become in his various roles.

The pastor cannot be conversant in all disciplines, but an inquiring mind and a lively interest in all extra-Biblical fields will help him to listen understandingly, to relate the Gospel to the world of his parishioners, and to interact with non-Christians. The mere evidence of his craving for knowledge may on occasion make his conversation about Christ and salvation all the more credible.

31

The Pastor as Teacher

Most of the pastor's activities call for teaching the Word of God in some way. Therefore, he must be "apt to teach" and learn to enjoy the varied opportunities for teaching. The Scriptures as they speak to us (2 Peter 1:20; Titus 1:9), not the pastor's private interpretation or his presuppositions, will inform the essential content of his teaching. That first step must be followed by learning to impart knowledge.

The pastor should understand and appreciate effective teaching methods. He must develop the ability to spell, to write and speak correctly and clearly, to organize subject matter, to outline, and to prepare tests appropriate for the circumstances. He need not be conversant with all aspects of education, but he should have an interest in it, be able to listen, and want to learn as he relates to the educational staff which he is to lead—Christian day school teachers, Sunday school teachers, or the director of Christian education (Cf. Unit VI, 4).

The Pastor's Lifestyle

In Gal. 5:22, Paul lists the "fruit of the Spirit"—not as qualifications for being a Christian but as a result of the indwelling Spirit—"love, joy, peace, patience, kindness, goodness, faithfulness, gentleness, and self-control." These qualities are the gift of God the Holy Spirit and certainly are qualities to be cultivated by the pastor through "daily contrition and repentance." Perhaps with this list in mind, Paul directs Timothy and Titus to consider the man chosen to be the Christian flock's "overseer"/elder/pastor—the one who needs to exemplify the fruits of the Spirit if he is to help others to grow in the grace of the Holy Spirit.

In 1 Timothy 3 and Titus 1 Paul notes that the pastor's lifestyle should be temperate, not overbearing, self-controlled, not quick-tempered, disciplined, not violent, gentle, not quarrelsome, hospitable, not a lover of money, not pursuing dishonest gain, not given to drunkenness, and in general respectable with a good reputation. Paul, of course, does not present an exhaustive list or laws for a pastor's life. Rather, he highlights those general qualities that can guide the selection of the one who is to serve the flock of God.

How the pastor lives out these qualities is a matter of judgment. He needs to be cautioned that negative traits crop up in subtle ways. For example, he may avoid physical violence yet resort to verbal abuse, mistakenly assuming that his status as pastor gives him the right to lord it over other people (1 Peter 5:3; 1 Tim. 5:2).

Hospitality—a love for people, especially strangers, and interest in charity and community causes—preaches a powerful sermon: All people are creations of God; all have been redeemed; there but for the grace of God go I (Matt. 25:35; Rom. 12:13; Heb. 13:2).

The pastor always will be tempted to be a "lover of money," to seek an increase in salary, to meet the standards of the secular world, to consider unnecessary spending of an organization's funds as less sinful than taking financial advantage of individuals, to treat wants or wishes as needs, and to assume that what "everyone else is doing" in financial matters justifies it for the pastor. A balanced view should include the ability to manage personal finances and to avoid indebtedness that realistically cannot be paid and that gives the pastor a bad reputation.

A "respectable" (1 Tim. 3:2) lifestyle embraces many common-sense considerations. For example, for the sake of his office, his personal reputation, and his personal health, the pastor should resist a lifestyle that leads to excessive fondness for alcoholic beverages. He will avoid slovenly dress, unkempt hair, and indifference toward personal hygiene. He will avoid consistent overeating so that excessive weight will not diminish his pastoral effectiveness. He will walk or follow exercise routines, not for reasons of vanity but because physical fitness contributes to general alertness and productivity. He will be polite, show common courtesy, and be aware of how others are responding to him, a common-sense style that rules of etiquette cannot supply.

To be "temperate" (1 Tim. 3:2) in all things, including all of the traits mentioned, is a desirable goal. At the same time, the pastor cannot be so humble (falsely so) that he becomes docile and unassertive or that his love for people degenerates into self-love because he lacks the courage to stand up for what is good and right.

Spiritual Maturation and Growth

Paul very interestingly notes (1 Tim. 3:6) that the pastor "must not be a recent convert," presumably because an effective ministry depends upon a firm faith growing out of a mature understanding of the grace of God. A shepherd of souls will want to nurture and enjoy a daily relationship with Christ through prayer and meditation on God's Word in addition to the regular preparation for a sermon or teaching a Bible class. This calls for self-discipline and time management in all matters, a common-sense use of his time. A personal devotional life, a proper family relationship with his wife and children, and even adequate time for recreation are legitimate aspects of the pastor's call to serve. Abandonment or neglect of family, friends, and one's own spiritual development signal a faltering ministry. Congregation members soon sense when their pastor is in emotional, spiritual, or even physical trouble.

All of the foregoing calls for a balanced view of what is expected of the pastor. Recognizing the pastor's dependence upon God and man's need to use the gifts and means of help at his disposal, C. F. W. Walther, in the opening sentence of his *Pastoral Theologie*, speaks of a *habitus practicus theosdotos* (a God-given practical aptitude) whereby the pastor can carry out the ministerial office. Perhaps Luther's well-known advice better than any sums up what goes into the making of a pastor: *"Oratio, meditatio, tentatio faciunt theologum"* (Prayer, meditative study, and experience or testing make the theologian/pastor).

The Christian Parsonage[1]

The Pastor's Wife

Luther strongly believed that God endorsed marriage for the pastor. He himself married at the age of 42, contrary to the church's practice of priestly celibacy, and established the parsonage. He believed that marriage would eliminate much of the scandalous life among the clergy and would help pastors empathize with the traumas, difficulties, and joys of their parishioners. However, marriage is not a prerequisite for the ministry. Consecrated celibacy is an option (Matt. 19:12) whose advantages Paul points out (1 Cor. 7:32–35).

The relation between the pastor and his wife should be balanced, with neither making all of the decisions or the demands. His wife is not the assistant pastor nor even the chief social organizer for the congregation, though she is expected to provide support for him and his work, just as any husband and wife share mutual love and concerns, ask questions, offer constructive criticism and make positive suggestions. In that spirit the wife can be most helpful to the pastor (and—let it not be forgotten—he can be most helpful to her). But she should not be expected nor required to participate in church activities more than other women, as though the pastoral call includes her.

Therefore, the choice of a helpmeet is of great consequence. The ideal spouse in any marriage is the person for whom each can do the most for the other. Husband and wife must have some

---

[1] For additional discussion on the pastor's family, see Unit V, Ch. 2, "The Pastor Relates to the Married."

mutual concerns and interests, the same general intelligence level, and gifts that both complement those lacking in the other and reinforce some that both have. Among the latter would be a firm faith in Jesus Christ and a desire to bring others to the Christian faith. The pastor's wife who is a member of another denomination will find it difficult to help convince the congregation members of the importance of being in a denomination in which the Gospel is purely taught.

The pastor should consider his wife the most precious gift, next to his salvation in Christ Jesus, that God has given him for this life. She is his helpmeet in every way—spiritually, emotionally, and physically. He in turn must love, nurture, and respect her in every way. The husband is to view his wife as Christ sees His church—one for whom he sacrifices and serves.

The Pastor's Children

The pastor is expected to "manage his own family well. . . . If anyone does not know how to manage his own family, how can he take care of God's church?" (1 Tim. 3:4–5). He should rear his children in the Lord and train them to be respectful and obedient (1 Tim. 3:4), not "open to the charge of being wild and disobedient" (Titus 1:6), standards that equally apply to his parishioners.

Children are precious gifts of God to be enjoyed and appreciated. No pastor should make himself so busy that he has no time for his wife and family. Pastors who opt out of familial obligations deceive themselves and are poor models for their own family and for the congregation. Families demand time—and the pastor needs ingenuity and careful planning to provide it, for time is the only way to build strong relationships and meet the God-given obligation.

The pastor's children are criticized for their conduct more often then other children, and they resent it. The congregation needs to remember that all have been redeemed; all are righteous before God; therefore no one is better. But all are sinners, subject to temptation, and "daily sin much." To expect a pastor's children to be "better Christians" is to deny the fundamental Biblical doctrine of man.

The Divorce of a Pastor

Divorce has become far too frequent in America, also among the clergy. Any man who has been unfaithful to his wife and has caused a divorce can be forgiven, but he is no longer suited to hold the pastoral office. Service in the pastoral ministry is a privilege, not a right. Very rarely can the restoration of a divorced pastor to the public ministry be justified. Declaring the pastor to be the innocent party does not solve the problem. Is either party in a divorce ever innocent? Even if the divorced pastor takes a call to a different congregation far away, can the divorce be kept a secret? Is it possible for the pastor to carry out an effective ministry after such a traumatic experience, whether or not he is the party less responsible for the divorce?

Later comments concerning divorce (Unit V, Ch. 5)—how to deal with it and how to prevent it—apply to the pastor himself, but with some added concerns. A pastor is apt to be driven by the mistaken notion that the work of the Lord is so important that he dare not create time for his wife and family. A second misunderstanding is the view, also held by Augustine, that sex in itself is sinful, a concession to human weakness and only for procreation purposes—especially for the pastor. Quite the opposite, Luther recommended a vigorous sex life to be enjoyed as a gift of God for the success of the marriage. The pastor may agree, but he may need outside help in working through problems that have grown out of his background. Obviously, many a pastor's marriage breaks up because the pastor fails to practice the very doctrine he preaches: that man is a sinner in need of giving and receiving daily forgiveness because of Christ. That stands at the heart of most problems.

The Pastor's Friends

A good general rule for pastors has been, "Be friendly with all, intimate with none." Becoming too intimate with parishioners may later place the pastor in awkward circumstances. Yet the pastor may find no one else within reasonable distance whom he can treat as a friend. The same holds true for the pastor's wife. In social gatherings with members, neither the pastor nor his wife should divulge confidential information, and, to the extent possible, they should avoid discussing other members, certainly negative criticisms of them.

The Pastor's Pastor

The pastor often finds he is lonely, even alienated. Though he may go to his wife for sharing, counseling, and also confession, sometimes he needs another pastor in whom to confide or "talk shop." He should be circumspect in what he discusses and with whom. He is fortunate if he finds a fellow pastor, perhaps a veteran of several years, in whom he can trust and confide almost everything. Like clinical psychologists and psychiatrists, the pastor cannot confide in one of his "patients" (i.e., parishioners). The district president and even the circuit counselor may not be the person in whom to confide, since both have official administrative roles that may conflict with confidential sharing. A respected retired pastor with no aspirations or personal goals for the ministry may be of greatest help. The example of David and Nathan illustrates the value and importance of confession. As Scripture urges, "Confess your sins to each other, and pray for each other, so that you may be healed. The prayer of a righteous man is powerful and effective" (James 5:16).

3
The Pastor Relates to the Church

The Augsburg Confession defines the church as "all believers and saints" (AC VIII 1) in whom the Holy Spirit has worked faith "when and where he pleases, in those who hear the Gospel" (AC V 2). Thus, strictly speaking, the church, which is God's work and his creation, is the assembly of all believers and saints. Although human eyes cannot see the church (since faith cannot be seen), its presence on earth can be recognized by certain external marks: the preaching of the Gospel and the administration of the Sacraments. Since no one is brought to faith without the external Word of the Gospel (AC V 4; Rom. 1:16; 10:17) and since God's Word does achieve its God-intended purpose (Is. 55:10–11), therefore, where the Gospel is, there is the church.

The Sacraments are included as marks of the church because they, too, are Gospel; in them God gives forgiveness and grace. In Baptism, the Holy Spirit is received (Acts 2:38), we are united with Christ's death and resurrection (Rom. 6:4ff.; Col. 2:12) and made heirs together with him (Gal. 3:27, 29), and we are given salvation (1 Peter 3:21). In the Lord's Supper, a communion or participation in the body and blood of Christ (1 Cor. 10:16), we are given the forgiveness of sins (Matt. 26:28) through the blood of the covenant (Mark 14:24), and we proclaim his death and his coming again (1 Cor. 11:26). Therefore, although we cannot identify those who truly believe, we can know and identify those who use the means of grace (Word and Sacrament) and profess the Christian faith.

The Local Congregation

"An Evangelical Lutheran local congregation is an assembly of believing Christians at a certain place among whom God's Word is preached purely according to the Confession of the Evangelical Lutheran Church and the holy sacraments are administered according to Christ's institution as stated in the Gospel, in the midst of whom, however, there is always an admixture of spurious Christians and hypocrites, and at times even public sinners."[1] (Cf. Acts 8:1; 11:22; 13:1; Rom. 16:1, 5, 23; 1 Cor. 1:2; 4:17; 11:18; Phil. 4:15; 1 Thess. 1:1; Rev. 2:1, 8, 12, 18; 3:1, 7, 14). The congregation derives its authority from Christ himself (Tractate 24–27) and not from the whole church or any part of it. Therefore, the local congregation is bound only by the Word of God and is bound to it.

The mysteries of God, i.e., the Gospel and Sacraments (the Office of the Keys), are entrusted to the congregation. "All the rights of an Evangelical Lutheran local congregation are embraced in the keys of the kingdom of heaven, which the Lord gave to his whole church originally and immediately and in such a way that they belong to every congregation in equal measure, the smallest as well as the largest."[2] As a result, all of the congregation's doctrine, teaching and life (and the materials used in those activities) must conform to the Spirit-inspired Scriptures. Human traditions and opinions dare not replace the pure teaching of the Gospel; for, as Paul wrote, "Even if we, or an angel from heaven should

---

[1] C. F. W. Walther, *The Form of a Christian Congregation*, tr. by John Theodore Mueller (St. Louis: Concordia Publishing House, 1963), p.1.

Scripture also describes the church as
  • God's elect or chosen people (Matt. 25:31–46; Mark 13:20; Rom. 8:33; Eph. 1:4; 2 Peter 1:2; 2:4, 9);
  • holy and blameless before God (Eph. 1:4);
  • the pure and holy bride of Christ (Eph. 5:25–27; 2 Cor. 11:2; Rev. 21:2);
  • the children of God (Matt. 13:38; Luke 20:36; John 1:12; Rom. 8:14, 16–17; Gal. 4:5–6; 3:26; Eph. 1:5; 1 John 3:1, 10; 4:4);
  • the household of God (Eph. 2:19);
  • saints (Rom. 1:7; 1 Cor. 1:2; 2 Cor. 1:1; Eph. 1:1; Phil. 1:1; Col. 1:2, etc.);
  • his holy temple (1 Cor. 3:16–17; 2 Cor. 6:16; Eph. 2:21–22);
  • sheep of the Good Shepherd (John 10:4–27);
  • the flock of God (Acts 20:28; 1 Peter 5:2–3);
  • the mystical body of Christ (Rom. 12:5; 1 Cor. 12:12–27; Eph.1:22–23; 4:4; 5:30; Col. 1:18, 24; and
  • God's holy people and royal priesthood (1 Peter 2:9).

[2] C. F. W. Walther, *The Form of a Christian Congregation*, p.13. This book by C. F. W. Walther is a valuable resource regarding the responsibility of a congregation to God and its members.

preach a gospel other than the one we preached to you, let him be eternally condemned" (Gal. 1:8). Paul applied the same standard to everyone: "I urge you, brothers, to watch out for those who cause divisions and put obstacles in your way that are contrary to the teaching you have learned" (Rom. 16:17).

In order to exercise the Office of the Keys, the congregation has not only the right but also the divine command to call a suitable man according to God's will to the office of the public ministry (AP XIII); no human authority can take that away (Tractate 67). Because the congregation entrusts to its pastor as its representative the responsibility of publicly teaching the Gospel to itself and others and of administering the Sacraments in its midst, he is accountable to the congregation (yet through it to God); and the congregation always retains the right to remove from office a pastor who is an unfaithful servant of Jesus Christ.

To repeat: Scripture alone provides the norm for everything the congregation does. Yet, because of the wide variety of ways in Christendom to understand Scripture, those congregations that call themselves Lutheran have subscribed to the understanding expressed in the Lutheran Confessions (the Book of Concord) because (*quia*) they are a true and correct exposition of the Word (and not in so far as, *quatenus*, they are in agreement). Obviously, the Lutheran pastor also pledges a *quia* subscription.

Note that this subscription pertains to doctrine, not to rituals. The Augsburg Confession declares, "It is not necessary for the true unity of the church that ceremonies instituted by men should be observed uniformly in all places" (AC VII 3); and the Formula of Concord declares that the congregation has the right to reduce, increase, or change ceremonies that serve the purpose of good order and the edification of the church (FC SD X 9). Nevertheless, the congregation may require that its pastor ordinarily use the ceremonies of the Lutheran Church and that he not arbitrarily introduce ceremonies according to his own whims.

The Pastor in the Congregation

As Teacher

The Reformation made every effort to restore the pastoral office as a teaching office (cf. Unit VI, 5.). For Luther, teaching was the essence of the pastoral office:

> Whoever has the office of preaching imposed on him has the highest office in Christendom. . . . Afterward he may also bap-

tize, celebrate mass, exercise all pastoral care. . . .[3]

If the office of teaching be entrusted to someone, then everything accomplished by the Word in the church is entrusted, that is, the office of baptizing, consecrating, binding, loosing, praying, and judging doctrine.[4]

As Overseer

The pastor, an overseer (*episkopos*) charged with tending the Gospel in the congregation, must be equipped with the Word in order to protect the flock from without and within (Matt. 28:20; Acts 20:31–32; 1 Tim. 4:1–3, 13; Titus 1:9).[5] His authority as overseer comes not merely from the congregation but because he is a slave (*doulos*) of Jesus Christ and the Gospel (Rom. 1:1; Gal. 1:10; 2 Peter 1:1).

As one practical application of this principle, the pastor, who is responsible for all teaching in the congregation, may delegate the teaching task to others, but only to trained and (as necessary) supervised persons.

"Overseeing" includes the process of excommunication. However, the authority to pronounce a person excommunicated belongs to the congregation (cf. Unit IV, 10). This ought not be coldly done by a simple, majority vote hastily cast. The congregation should be convinced from the clear Word of God that the sin has resulted in a loss of faith, shown by the person remaining obstinately impenitent.[6] Yet, the congregation should maintain the goal of spiritually restoring the erring (2 Tim. 2:25).

Finally, as an overseer, the pastor dare not exercise tyranny over his people (1 Peter 5:3; Mark 10:42–45; Luke 22:22–27). Foolish quarrels can lead to a despising of God's Word. Therefore, the pastor should avoid disputes over non-Biblical matters, and he should not impose his own personal opinion on his people. In fact, if the pastor does not yield in nonessential, nonspiritual matters for the sake of love and peace, he may need to be rebuked

---

[3] "That a Christian Assembly or Congregation Has the Right and Power to Judge All Teaching, . . ." LW 39:314.

[4] *Concerning the Ministry*, LW 40:36.

[5] To *tend* means to apply oneself to the care of—to cultivate or foster—to have charge of—to manage or oversee the operation of. The pastor as one who has been appointed by God through the church is to give himself to the care of the Gospel that it may not be distorted but used as God intended.

[6] Walther, op. cit.: "In difficult cases a congregation should seek the council of one or more sister congregations; or, if asked for, it should be ready to advise others as well as it can." Ordinarily such counsel from other congregations would be sought through the office of the district president.

(1 Tim. 3:3; Titus 1:7). Gentleness and patience without compromise are always in order.

As Administrator of the Sacraments

Administering the Sacraments (cf. Unit III, 3, 4) means more than simply performing the ceremony. It includes the instruction of the congregation concerning the right use of the sacraments and, at times, the decision who may not receive the sacraments. In his instructions for parish visitors (1528), Luther stated, "Whoever . . . does not know why he should receive the sacrament is not to be admitted to it."[7] He further advised that those who continue to live in open sin after repeated admonitions and are unwilling to amend their ways should be denied Holy Communion.[8]

As Confessor and Absolver

The privilege to hear confession and then absolve the troubled belong to both the pastor (cf. Unit IV, 2 and III, 4) and the congregation members in order to restore relationships with God and within the church. The goal is to create a new spirit among all members, all redeemed sinners who can, therefore, freely forgive and accept one another.

Information disclosed to the pastor in confession is, under no circumstances,[9] to be disclosed by him, not even to his wife. Nor is he to use such matters as illustrations for sermons or teaching lest he destroy the trust that people have in him. In hearing confession and pronouncing absolution, he is but the confidential ear and voice of God.

As Counselor

Unless so trained and certified, the pastor is not equipped to be a professional counselor as commonly understood.[10] Rather, the pastor counsels in the Biblical understanding of the term: he strengthens and encourages people in their faith. He teaches and brings the Word of God in every kind of setting, public and individual—to the sick and the dying, to families grieving over death, to those hurting spiritually, to those needing spiritual support (cf. Unit IV). The pastor learns to rejoice with those who

---

[7] *Instructions for the Visitors of Parish Pastors*, LW 40:296.

[8] Ibid., p. 311.

[9] See Unit IV, Ch. 2 for a discussion of hearing the confession of a criminal offense.

[10] Cf. Unit IV, Ch. 3.

rejoice and to mourn with those who mourn—even as Jesus did (John 2:1–10; Rom. 12:15).

As Administrator of the Congregation

Scripture gives no specific direction regarding the organization of a congregation. While the office of the public ministry is Biblically mandated (cf. Unit II, 1), the congregation may create any additional offices to meet its needs (cf. Unit VI).[11]

For example, the congregation may establish an evangelism committee, concerned not for numbers but the eternal salvation of all for whom Christ died. A committee, however, does not replace the concern and efforts of all members to witness to Jesus as Savior.

Christian education ordinarily occupies another important department of congregational structure. Again, though, the concern and effort should occur within *every* organization, committee, and part of the congregation. (In some congregations that requires considerable ingenuity by the pastor.) The value of the day school, weekday religion classes, Sunday school, confirmation classes, and vacation Bible school is evident. Yet, Christian education (broadly speaking) should happen also in quilting groups, bowling teams, on hayrides, and during the youth car wash. In these situations the spiritual thrust will be less prominent and more casual, but should be evident, nevertheless, to the group members.

The stewardship program/committee, likewise, should undergird the reason for the congregation's existence. Properly designed stewardship activities produce *spiritual* growth that reduces fund-raising schemes to a minimum.

Most congregations also include a variety of organizations to meet the needs of identifiable groups (women, men, youth, etc.). They provide opportunity for Christian fellowship and growth in Christian knowledge and service and complement the congregation's program. They should be adequately supervised so that they do not form cliques or control the congregation's program, and they should report on their activities to the whole congregation. While the pastor will work with these groups, he should enlist the help of qualified members so that he does not devote too much time to these auxiliary aspects of the congregation.

While any structure can be helpful in administering the affairs

---

[11] Already in apostolic times churches established the office of deacon—which is the model for the office of elder in Lutheran congregations today—called "lay ministers" in some parishes.

of the congregation, the existing one should be reviewed from time to time to evaluate how well it contributes to the church's overall purpose and work.

The Pastor in the Denomination

As in apostolic times, a common understanding of fundamental Biblical doctrine brought together in 1847 the organization of congregations and pastors today known as The Lutheran Church—Missouri Synod. As expressed in its constitution, the Synod was organized to

> Conserve and promote the unity of the true faith (Eph. 4:3–6; 1 Cor. 1:10), [to] work through its official structure toward fellowship with other Christian bodies, and [to] provide for a united defense against schism, sectarianism (Rom. 16:17), and heresy.[12]

In addition to concern for doctrine, the constitution of the Missouri Synod (the popular sobriquet for The Lutheran Church—Missouri Synod) lists other purposes for the organization, e.g.,

- the joint sending of missionaries at home and abroad;
- joint recruitment and training of pastors, teachers, and other church workers; providing them support as well as supervision; and providing for their general welfare while active or retired, and their families in the event of illness, disability, special needs, or death;
- providing a variety of resources for the congregations in carrying out their work of worship, evangelism, stewardship, Christian education, etc.; and
- joint service in meeting human needs.

The smallest congregation can share in these projects, and together the denomination can do what each congregation cannot do by itself.

Although the Synod possesses no legislative powers over its pastors and congregations with respect to their self-government,[13] nevertheless, congregations, having joined the Synod, agree to honor the resolutions of Synod and should feel obligated to abide by them for the sake of love and peace. Therefore, pastors and congregations need to be well informed about the regulations and

---

[12] Constitution Article III, *Handbook of The Lutheran Church—Missouri Synod* (The Lutheran Church—Missouri Synod, St. Louis, 1989), p. 9.

[13] Ibid., Article VII, p. 11.

resolutions of the Synod and should participate actively in the legislative process. When, on occasion, a nondoctrinal resolution does not fit its circumstances, the congregation will use its best judgment in response. Doctrinal statements and resolutions, however, are to be honored and upheld because they restate God's Word (which God, not the congregation, controls).[14]

As a member of the Synod, the congregation owes financial support to it—not as to an outside agency, but as within a bond that the congregation has established with other congregations to carry out joint efforts. Such support should be willingly given out of gratitude for the many blessings that God works through that bond called "Synod."

The Pastor and Other National Lutheran Organizations

Some auxiliary groups in a congregation have a national counterpart that supports the work of the congregation as well as the Synod. The Lutheran Laymen's League, the oldest in the Missouri Synod, sponsors "The International Lutheran Hour," "This is the Life," and a variety of other programs designed to proclaim the Gospel. Likewise, the Lutheran Women's Missionary League has an impressive record of missionary support. The synodical Board for Youth Services sponsors Lutheran Youth Fellowship.

In addition, Synod recognizes various types of additional organizations: Lutheran family and social agencies, nursing and retirement homes, and homes for the mentally disabled—some quasi-synodical, some under district sponsorship, and others with various kinds of organizational sponsorship. The synodically recognized and listed service organizations usually are printed in the official roster of the Synod: *The Lutheran Annual.*

The pastor ordinarily will encourage his members to participate in and support these organizations (as well as secular organizations in the community) that strive to meet a variety of needs (Jer. 29:7).

---

[14] Ibid., Bylaw 1.09, p. 21.

4
The Pastor Begins His Ministry

Few experiences reach so deeply into a pastor's life as when he receives a call. He feels humble that the Lord has counted him faithful and has led him to consider serving in another parish.[1] He is torn by the thought of having to choose between a new parish and the one which he has nurtured and loved as his spiritual family. He realizes that whether he moves or stays, the two congregations as well as his family will be affected by his decision. Yet, its reception dictates a number of mundane but important responsibilities.

A Valid and Legitimate Call

Only very rarely would it happen otherwise, yet the pastor/candidate should be convinced that the call is valid and legitimate (see Chapter One of this Unit). Both the calling congregation and the pastor who receives the call have the burden of keeping it legitimate. Neither party should resort to "back room" maneuvering for its own gain. A pastor should not impose himself on a vacant congregation because he covets its call. Nor is it proper for him to urge friends and relatives within that congregation to in-

---

[1] Calls to serve in nonparish ministries (e.g., at a college, seminary, or other institution, as a military chaplain, on a district or synodical staff, etc.) deserve similar fair and sincere consideration; they, too, are calls from God to serve (cf. Unit II, 1).

For additional reading, see Oscar H. Reinboth, ed., *Calls and Vacancies* (St. Louis: Concordia, 1967); and Armin W. Schuetz and Irwin T. Habezk, *The Shepherd Under Christ* (Milwaukee: Northwestern, 1974).

fluence others to vote for him. Such activity on the part of both pastor and congregation raises questions about the legitimacy of the call, ignores the very nature of a divine call, and degrades the sacred office itself. Luther counseled that

> we should carefully see to it that there is no evil design, that no one in any way obtrudes himself as a preacher, either to get a livelihood or to gain honor. For this is dangerous; nor will it ever turn out well. If you are learned and understand God's Word well and think that you would present it to others faithfully and profitably, then wait. If God wants it, he will have no trouble finding you. My friend, do not let your ability burst your belly. God has not forgotten you. If you are to preach his Word, he will no doubt call on you to do so at his own time. So do not determine the time limit or the place for him.[2]

The increasingly popular system of interviewing prospects frequently smacks of improper maneuvering. The procedure (whether in person and/or through questionnaires) can lead to serious problems. First, the committee may disqualify a candidate unaccustomed to the tensions of the interview process, but who may be highly qualified and might even serve with distinction. Second, the same can be said for a candidate who conscientiously declines to be interviewed or who chooses not to respond to questionnaires. Third, since a pastor who participates and "passes" the screening process is considered to be willing to accept the call if received, the congregation is often left confused and bewildered if he declines—which results in discredit both to the man called and to the office itself.

On the other hand, congregations with very special needs may require more extensive information about candidates than is normally provided. While interviews or questionnaires may be appropriate in such special circumstances, these matters might be resolved through the guidance of those elected to oversee the overseers (i.e., district presidents, counselors, etc.). Normally, guidelines available from district presidents (1) ensure that the entire voting membership can exercise the divine privilege in which each member shares equally, and (2) provide safeguards against thwarting the operation of the Holy Spirit through the entire process.

The church is the Lord's. Since he alone provides suitable pastors to carry out the church's ministry, the church seeks his guidance. Only the Holy Spirit, working mediately, can empower

---

[2] Quoted by Ewald Plass, *What Luther Says*, 2950 (St. Louis: Concordia, 1959, 8th printing in one volume, 1986), p. 939.

a congregation to choose a pastor according to the Spirit's will, based on information about the candidate and on the congregation's understanding of its mission and ministry.

Reaching a Decision on the Call

When a pastor receives a call, he immediately acknowledges its receipt and assures the calling congregation that he will give it serious and sincere consideration. His response acknowledges the honor that has been conferred on him and the respect he feels for the office. He informs the calling congregation when it may expect his decision. If more information is needed, the pastor-elect should feel free to request it.

Ordinarily, three or four weeks should be sufficient for reaching a decision; a call held too long can be harmful to people, for time is very important to a vacant congregation. It can be very disheartening for its call to be treated lightly. Should the pastor-elect procrastinate and yet accept their call, his arrival at his new parish could be received with much less than full enthusiasm.

The pastor also promptly notifies his own district president and his circuit counselor (and, if he is serving a mission congregation, the mission executive). In this letter he simply informs them of the call and solicits their counsel and prayers.

As soon as possible, the pastor-elect informs his present congregation that he has received a call to serve elsewhere. He may want to contact the president of his congregation and the chairman of the board of elders and arrange for a convenient time to discuss the call. Notification of members may be done by a mailing to every home, thereby notifying all members at the same time, or by an announcement at the close of a worship service. (The latter, though common, carries the disadvantage of not notifying the members who are not present.)

Some pastors decline a call without informing their congregation that they have received it because they fear the response of their parish and/or the possible assumption that they have been "fishing" for a reason to leave. Others return the call out of hand, not wanting to suffer the trauma of making a decision. Since the membership will eventually learn of the matter, the pastor should discuss every call with his people. A sincere regard for God's process of calling pastors requires that each call receive fair and thorough consideration, openly and honestly, by pastor and people.

The deliberating process provides the opportunity for both pastor and people to care for and serve one another in a most critical period for both as they (1) weigh their individual responsibilities; (2) deliberate on one another's welfare; and (3) evaluate the work of the whole church in contrast to their own personal and parish needs.

As the pastor seeks the counsel of his congregation, he should be prepared for varied reactions. Some people struggle to express their feelings. Others will react openly, with expressions running from shock to sweeping promises just to keep their pastor with them, from brutally honest to beautifully honest comments. And the voters assembly usually passes a magnanimous resolution to support the pastor during his time of deliberation. All reactions should be received as well-meant counsel to assist the pastor in reaching a decision.

A visit to the calling congregation may be in order. However, before accepting such an invitation (especially if at the expense of the calling congregation), he should be quite certain that the visit is justified—i.e., that it will provide a better understanding of the needs of the congregation.

Ultimately the pastor himself must make the decision, understanding that no divine command orders him to accept every call. God often uses a vacancy and returned call(s) to strengthen a congregation.

The best advice in the deliberation of a call is to let the wisdom of God and the guidance of the Holy Spirit guide the decision through reflection, conversation, and prayer. The following questions (although not exhaustive) may help:

- Where does God want me to serve?
- Is the need of my present parish less than the need of the calling congregation?
- Would my gifts and experience be more effective elsewhere?
- Am I so comfortable in my present parish that I no longer see the growing needs of my people?
- Would I grow by my experience in a new challenge?
- What are my family needs? the state of our health?
- Because the public ministry calls for selflessness, how might I apply the words of Paul as he warns against those whose God is their stomach and whose mind is on earthly things (Phil. 3:19)?

If there is still doubt, consider Luther's advice: "If one doubts that God has willed him to do a certain work, he had better not undertake to do it."[3] *The Pastor at Work* adds, "One of the fundamental requirements for a successful ministry is a good con-

---

[3] Quoted by Fritz, *Pastoral Theology* (St. Louis, Concordia, 1932, 1945, Concordia Heritage Series 1977), p. 47, and by Albert Schwermann in *The Pastor at Work* (St. Louis: Concordia, 1960), p. 112—both without reference.

science. . . . Therefore, no pastor should decline a call if his conscience tells him to accept; nor should he accept a call if his conscience presses him to decline."[4]

Announcing the Decision

The words used to announce the decision are most important because emotions, both positive and negative, will abound. Whatever the decision, the Gospel of God's grace for all needs emphasis.

If the decision is to decline the call, the pastor immediately notifies the calling congregation by phone. The diploma of vocation should be returned immediately, along with a letter declining the call and requesting that the decision be honored. (A copy of the letter is sent to both district presidents and any other church authorities affected by the decision.) The reasons for declining need not be stated in the letter, but the pastor should assure the calling body that the call has been given sincere and prayerful consideration. He offers thanks for the honor bestowed upon him, and he assures the calling group of his prayers to the Lord in its behalf. (The formal letter of declination should never be used to advise the calling congregation of any objectionable features of its call, nor to counsel the members what to do before extending another call. If something must be said, direct it in confidence to the respective circuit counselor and/or district president in a fraternal, pastoral, and evangelical manner.)

If the decision is to accept the call, the pastor should not show disregard for his present parish nor degrade it as he offers his reasons for accepting. Rather, he should considerately and pastorally share what the Holy Spirit has led him to do and request their concurrence by granting him a peaceful release. If a congregation, out of love for its pastor, declines to grant a release, he may follow his conscience. If the reason is other than love, he will want to resolve any problems before asking again for the release. The parting of a faithful pastor and a loving congregation should be a time for praise and thanksgiving to God for the blessings received because of each other.

After accepting a call, the pastor-elect immediately notifies his own district president of his decision (also the mission executive if he serves a mission parish) in order that arrangements may be made for (1) a vacancy pastor; (2) the transfer of his membership if the call is to another district; or (3) if the new parish is in his present district, for authorization of his installation.

---

[4] Ibid.

Arrangements should be made for his farewell service, moving, and the date for installation in his new parish.

If the call is to another district, the notification to that president also requests authorization for installation. When setting the installation date,[5] the needs of the new congregation should be favored; however, sufficient time should be allowed for a wrap-up of duties before moving. Ordinarily, four weeks should be quite adequate.

Before leaving one parish for another, the pastor arranges to have all church records in proper order, meets with all boards and assists them in planning their ministry during the vacancy, makes final visits to the sick and shut-ins, and prepares for a farewell service that terminates the work of his present call.

The farewell sermon is not the time to chastise a congregation nor to play on the emotions of people. The final service should be the best and the clearest presentation of the Gospel coupled with a commendation of the flock to the Shepherd and Bishop of the church.

Beginning the Ministry in a New Parish

Because the call creates a sacred relationship between a new pastor and congregation, a good beginning is important. The image the pastor wishes to project should permeate his initial activities and set the tone.

The Rite of Installation/Ordination

According to church custom a pastor begins his ministry when he is ordained or installed in the presence of the congregation that called him—usually the first Sunday after the pastor's arrival. For the sake of good order, the bylaws of the Synod assign the responsibility for the rite of installing pastors to the congregation's district president or his representative.[6]

The nature of ordination urges that a candidate be ordained in the presence of the congregation which called him. The growing custom of ordaining seminary graduates in their home congregations to please relatives and friends conveys a wrong understanding of the nature and purpose of ordination.[7] As a more

---

[5] Christmas, Easter, and other special days in the festival half of the church year are not suitable for the farewell sermon or installation service, for their focus on the life of Christ should not be diluted.

[6] 1989 Handbook, The Lutheran Church—Missouri Synod, Bylaw 2.13b, p. 27f.

[7] Fritz, op. cit., p. 70.

meaningful and proper involvement, the home congregation might conduct a prior service of "Farewell and Godspeed" for a candidate for ordination (as suggested by the *Agenda of Lutheran Worship*). However, Synod's bylaws allow that "the appropriate district president may authorize that the rite take place in the home congregation of the candidate, or other appropriate congregation with the permission of the calling congregation or other entity."[8]

When a missionary or chaplain is commissioned or installed, the service is essentially identical to the service of installation/ordination and is conducted by those in whose name he will serve.

Preaching the Initial Sermon

Ordinarily the new pastor delivers his initial sermon on the first Sunday after his installation. The occasion will be most important for him and will provide the congregation with a first (and often lasting) impression of him as a preacher.

The first sermon should present most clearly both Law and Gospel, applied to what both pastor and people can expect of each other. Focus on the new relationship, which is to magnify the Lord and advance his kingdom. Do not announce a platform of goals and objectives (as is done in politics and secular callings; no pastor knows his new congregation well enough to announce such changes). Nor should a new pastor discuss any internal problems that may be fracturing the congregation. Rather, the focus should be on the heart of Scripture: the Gospel of Jesus Christ.

Getting to Know the Parish

Visiting Every Home. As soon as possible, the new pastor will make every effort to acquaint himself with every member of his new parish (Acts 20:20). He will set up a plan for visitation—and follow it, even if the size of the congregation requires spreading the plan over years. For an effective ministry, he needs to observe his flock in its homes and community environment—to diagnose and evaluate the spiritual life of the congregation—so that he can effectively apply Law and Gospel.[9] These initial calls will build a trust in himself and in his commitment as the shepherd of each individual. (The new pastor should give first consideration to the sick and the homebound, who cannot actively participate in mutual service or corporate worship of the congregation.)

---

[8] *Handbook*, op. cit.

[9] Knowing the membership and relating to every individual also will help prevent back door losses.

In today's complex society the home is often no longer the center of family life. An every-member visit may be nearly impossible. Under such circumstances, a pastor may arrange an "Evening with the New Pastor" program. The agenda needs to be clear, the size of the group limited, and sufficient opportunity for conversation provided.

Do not permit members to air grievances against the former pastor or tell tales about fellow members of the parish. After listening to hurts, tactfully reflect the Gospel of forgiveness in Jesus Christ, and redirect the conversation.

Show no partiality. Visit the careless and the spiritually indifferent, the poor and humble, the rich and distinguished, regarding each person as an equal among equals, loving each the same as the other (James 2:1–9).

Background Information. In the first week after his installation, the pastor acquaints himself with the articles of incorporation/constitution and bylaws of the congregation, the church records, and the minutes of the preceding year's voters assembly and the leadership council. Prior to the first council meeting, the pastor can benefit by meeting individually with each board. These organizations and the council are the pastor's most helpful resources for understanding the congregation and will help him discover any needs/weaknesses within the congregation.

If the congregation maintains a Christian day school, the new pastor arranges for an early meeting with the principal and his staff. He supports those who work with him, always remembering that their common mission is to save and nurture God's people; and he visits the school regularly (not only when an immediate problem requires it).

In addition to the general background of affairs, the new pastor needs to discover any particular changes that will make his ministry more effective. Sometimes a congregation may expect change when a new pastor arrives and sometimes requests him to make the needed changes. Common sense dictates caution and first gaining the confidence of the people. Thereafter, the new pastor can expect the support of the people for change.

Expanding the Staff. When the pastor is called to the office of the public ministry, he almost always quickly checks whether professionally trained people are necessary to help him carry out the responsibilities of the office. Growing numbers may require the new pastor to plan for expanding the existing staff. Planning for additional staff, developing clear job descriptions, and taking steps to be sure that good staff relationships are established and maintained—and much more—is a part of good administration (see Unit VI, 2).

Leaving the Office

A man who has been called to the pastoral ministry should not forsake that office merely for purely personal reasons. However, a pastor may resign from a particular call for valid reasons. For example, serious illness may prevent a pastor from performing all of the responsibilities of his call; and out of concern for the congregation he may resign from the call he has and retire from active service. Or he may conclude that he cannot do what is required of him and, (having resigned from his call) await another call that is more suited for his abilities. Or advancing age may bring the pastor willingly to recognize that the Lord is nudging him to retire from active service. (Regrettably, a pastor occasionally fails to realize his inability to function as pastor and forces his congregation to urge his retirement due to declining mental or physical abilities.)

Leaving by Forced Resignation or Defrocking

Unfortunately, the change may be forced by tactless, legalistic, and unwise decisions. If so, the services of the circuit counselor and/or district president may be needed to bring peace. Such counsel is needed *especially* when the criticisms against the pastor are not personal but are directed against his faithful preaching of Biblical doctrine.

A Christian congregation, of course, has the right to depose its pastor or ask for his resignation—assuming the action is according to God's will. (The irony is that the pastor is the one who has taught the congregation what God's will is.) Biblical reasons for removal from office are (1) teaching false doctrine (Titus 1:9); (2) ungodly conduct (1 Tim. 3:1–7); and (3) willful neglect of duty (1 Cor. 4:1–2). Since the principles of admonition and church discipline (cf. Unit IV, 10) apply to the pastor as well as anyone, the aid, counsel, and support of the transparochial church and ministerium should be sought. In the Missouri Synod, the circuit counselor and/or district president should be informed and should assist so that proper procedures are followed.

As more and more stress affects the relationship between pastor and congregation, both are tempted to treat problems with non-Biblical means and to use the power and authority of the secular courts. Yet, both problems and punishment can be God's means of bringing about confession and repentance. Following that, the Gospel can renew, heal, and restore both the pastor and the Christian congregation.

5
Pastor to Pastor Relationships

Relationships with Brother Pastors

The call to become a pastor is a joyous and God-empowered responsibility. Of it Luther writes,

> It is an astounding assignment for a frail man. Our Lord God fills his high office in an odd manner. He entrusts it to preachers, poor sinners, who tell and teach the message and yet live according to it in weakness. Thus God's power always goes forward amid extreme weakness.[1]

Luther echoes the words of the apostle Paul,

> We have this treasure in jars of clay, to show that this all-surpassing power is from God and not from us. (2 Cor. 4:7)

As "frail men" and "jars of clay," pastors need each other. They should make time for cultivating Christian relationships with each other. God calls upon pastors just as much as other Christians to live out their lives in peer relationships by

- loving one another;
- visiting one another and discussing problems;
- sharing joys and sorrows, successes and failures;
- studying and working together; and,
- with loving confidence bearing one another's burdens.

Within The Lutheran Church—Missouri Synod, district pastoral conferences and the more casual circuit conferences (*Win-*

---

[1] Plass, Ewald, *What Luther Says, II*, p. 950, 2982.

kels) help establish and maintain this intimate fellowship. They give opportunity for pastors to be drawn close to one another, to grow spiritually as they study the Word, to grow professionally as they discuss the practical aspects of ministering, and to be actively involved and interested in the mission of the church at large.

In order to maintain a Christian, fraternal relationship with his fellow clergy, the wise pastor recognizes that, because his fellow undershepherds of "God's flock that is under your care" (1 Peter 5:2) also have a responsibility, there are times when the pastor himself does *not* have responsibility—(1) When dealing with the parishioners of a sister congregation; and (2) when he has resigned from his own parish (e.g., to accept a call elsewhere or to retire). As Fritz points out, a pastor who interferes with the official responsibilities of another pastor is a busybody in other men's business.[2] Drawing away the affections of members of another parish invites the label of sheepstealing. Even in secular professions, similar activity is regarded as unethical.

After a pastor has accepted a call to a new parish, he usually closes his present ministry with a farewell sermon. Whatever the final act, he no longer serves the old parish as the undershepherd. The privilege now falls on the vacancy pastor and, subsequently, his successor. The former pastor should not continue to advise the congregation through correspondence or personal contact. While he cannot be deprived of the cherished friendships which were developed over the years, he must divorce himself from any activity that would interfere with the ministry of his successor.

The same principle applies to a pastor who retires—and therefore the suggestion that he normally not remain a member of the parish lest members seek his counsel and services. His successor needs to have the opportunity to build his own ministry and relationships among the people. (For the same reason, a retired or nonparish pastor will not usurp pastoral roles or functions within a congregation—although he could become the subsequent pastor's closest and most helpful friend.)

Relationships with Sister Congregations

God looks for his people to serve together in the spirit of mutual respect and love. Thus, a faithful pastor leads his congregation to seek its own welfare as well as that of other congregations in the unity of faith. He leads his people to pray for all the saints (Eph. 6:18) and to agree with one another, perfectly united in

---

[2] Fritz, John F. C., *Pastoral Theology*, p. 57.

mind and thought, so that no offense will be given and no dissensions develop among neighboring congregations (1 Cor. 1:10). And when a neighbor parish has a critical need, both pastor and congregation provide counsel, assistance, and financial support as the situation may require (2 Cor. 8:1–14). Should a pastoral vacancy occur or should a small congregation be unable to maintain the office of the ministry by itself, a neighbor congregation permits its pastor to serve as needed.

In spite of the best fraternal efforts, tensions between parishes in close proximity can arise. Sometimes people switch church membership seemingly with little regard for the body of Christ. The specific reasons vary, but the common denominator is some dissatisfaction with one congregation and hope for better conditions at the next. Rather than feed on any possible competition and/or jealousy, the respective pastors need to talk together about how the members, the congregation, and the Gospel are best served.

As a general rubric, members who wish to change congregations (from "A" to "B") should ask their own pastor for a transfer. Keeping that responsibility with the members keeps everything in the open. It also affords the pastor of "A" the opportunity to do an exit interview and the separation to occur peacefully. In cases when members are under any form of church discipline, no transfer can be authorized until the offense is resolved in the Gospel of reconciliation.

Generally speaking, people who want to transfer out of church "A" feel uncomfortable speaking the truth to their own pastor. Therefore, the pastor of congregation "B" will be the one to apply the above principle—not legalistically, but as an opportunity to help the member come to a better understanding of the body of Christ, the nature of local churches, and to deal with any sin that may be hidden in the heart.

In summary, a Christian pastor and his congregation will strive diligently to maintain a close relationship with sister congregations, "to keep the unity of the Spirit through the bond of peace" (Eph. 4:3).

Ecumenical Pastoral Relationships

The teaching of the Lutheran Confessions on ecumenism has been summarized by The Lutheran Church—Missouri Synod's Commission on Theology and Church Relations in these words:

> For the sake of preserving the preaching of the Gospel according to a pure understanding of it, we seek, by faithful and perpetual confession of the truth, to promote through Christendom full

agreement in all articles of faith so that peace and concord may prevail within the unity of the church.[3]

Concord among Christian churches must be our sincere concern and endeavor. It is Christ's will that his church be one (John 17:20–21), that his church continue in his Word (John 8:31–32), that it hold firmly to the trustworthy message (Titus 1:9), and that it contend vigorously for the faith that was once-for-all entrusted to the saints (Jude 3). However, where faithful adherence to the true doctrine in the preaching and teaching of the church does not exist, the basis for God-pleasing altar and pulpit fellowship does not yet exist.

How the above should be applied on the denominational and congregational levels is thoroughly discussed in a number of documents developed within the Synod.[4] The test of the pastor's "art," however, will come as he is called upon to apply the principles to individual situations.[5] Well-intentioned couples of mixed faiths will ask to have both pastors officiate at their wedding. A pious shut-in may ask permission for a non-Lutheran chaplain to administer private Communion. A staunch and faithful member may ask that his non-Lutheran brother-in-law pastor be allowed to preach on a holiday. Members who are civic leaders may express dismay at the "standoffishness" of the pastor who declines to participate in the community Thanksgiving Day worship. Unfortunately, under such circumstances, some members may not care about the correct Scriptural and confessional doctrine or church

---

[3] *The Nature and Implications of the Concept of Fellowship*, The Commission on Theology and Church Relations (The Lutheran Church—Missouri Synod), pp. 13–16.

[4] Only a few such documents are listed here:
- *The Nature and Implications of the Concept of Fellowship.*
- *A Lutheran Stance Toward Ecumenism.*
- *Theology of Fellowship.*
- *A Brief Statement.*

Luther's advice (FC SD X 31) is noteworthy: "Churches will not condemn each other because of a difference in ceremonies . . . *as long as they are otherwise agreed in doctrine and all its articles* and are also agreed concerning the right use of the holy sacraments" (emphasis added).

[5] As a *Seelsorger*, the pastor may face situations in which the principles ought not be rigidly applied. The Synod has recognized this and has affirmed the pastor's responsibility and authority, for example, to commune persons not in fellowship with us "in situations of emergency and in special cases of pastoral care" (Resolution 3–12, "To Encourage CTCR to Complete Its Report on Communion Practices, *Convention Proceedings: 52nd Regular Convention; The Lutheran Church—Missouri Synod; Dallas, Texas; July 15—22, 1977*, p. 133). These situations, of course, are exceptions and not the norm.

fellowship and may reflect the attitude, "I've got to follow my own conscience."

The care of souls must be the pastor's first concern; and within that general care stands his responsibility for the souls in his flock. To that end, he ought not project a judgmental, harsh attitude but understanding and compassion for those who come to him.

While members are assumed to have faith in Christ alone as their savior, not all understand the principles involved. Lead them gently to understand not merely the errors in heterodox churches but also the witness that unionism[6] gives to one's self, one's family, one's congregation, and one's community. Help the members appreciate their faith so much that they willingly choose not to compromise or denigrate it through their actions. Build up their zeal for the Gospel.

None of the above implies that the Lutheran pastor should refuse to have contact with pastors or people belonging to heterodox churches. Members of the *Una Sancta* can be found throughout all denominations.[7] Lutherans may participate in those activities that do not imply that there is complete doctrinal agreement between respective church bodies.[8] Such activities may include bringing relief to victims of disaster or poverty, cooperating in World Relief efforts, supporting the forces that battle drug traffic, pornography, abortion on demand, alcoholism, and all immoral customs and events that defame the name of God among us. Lest his participation send a confusing signal, the pastor will help his members as well as others to understand that such activities do not imply doctrinal unity or church fellowship. The pastor's example along with his public and private instruction will help his flock to appreciate, hold dear, and proclaim the pure Gospel to all.

Other Relationships with the Community

The pastor proclaims the Savior from the pulpit, in the classroom, and through the activities within the congregation as well as in his work within the local community. In the latter arena, the public looks upon him as a man of God and respected rep-

---

[6] Defined as "joining in religious worship or in religious work or in both by such as are not in doctrinal agreement" (John H. C. Fritz, *Pastoral Theology* [St. Louis: Concordia, 1932, 1945, Concordia Heritage Edition 1977], p. 211).

[7] See, for example, Ap VII and VIII 10; and Tractate 16.

[8] CTCR, *A Lutheran Stance Toward Ecumenism*, pp. 15–16. See also the CTCR documents *Guidelines for Crucial Issues in Christian Citizenship* (April 1968) and *Civil Obedience and Disobedience* (January 1967).

resentative of the church and of his denomination.

In approaching the community, the pastor remembers the words of Micah, "What does the Lord require of you? To act justly and to love mercy and to walk humbly with your God" (6:8). Just so, the pastor can lead the congregation in showing mercy and doing justice in the community—and, in its broader context, in the state, nation, and world.

The pastor's leading begins from within the Word. Through discussion, workshops, and seminars the pastor enables the congregation to apply the Gospel of Jesus intelligently and appropriately to today's issues. As God's people become sensitized to human needs and respond to the Gospel by word and deed, they will support those who suffer because of intolerance and injustice.

This Christian action, however, has the potential of the believer confronting civil/secular authority. And the committed Christian may wonder how to balance the ideals of Acts 4—5 (especially 5:29) with Romans 13. The pastor can help by pointing out the difference between *rebellion* and *disobedience*. Rebellion, a type of disobedience, pits itself against the government and, hence, against God. Disobedience, however, need not include rebellion. Peter and John exercised civil disobedience for the sake of the Gospel, but they did not rebel against the God-established authority. So today, for example, responsible Christian citizens may actively oppose the sin of abortion even though government policy and law permit it under certain conditions. But to burn abortion clinics or kidnap abortionists constitutes unacceptable rebellion against authority and, therefore, against God.

In short, love for God, prompted by the Gospel, motivates the Christian to render to "Caesar" the honor, respect and obedience due to him. Love for neighbor leads the Christian to make full use of his rights as a citizen and work for justice through the established legal framework (social action) and to help the victims with personal aid (social ministry).

6
The Pastor Relates to Secular and Quasi-Religious Organizations

Americans join organizations in numbers unlike anywhere else in the world. More than 30,000 formal organizations claim over 150 million members. Thousands of local clubs and ad hoc movements attract a large number of followers.

Several explanations have been forwarded to explain this phenomenon—e.g., that the groups provide acceptance and identity, fellowship with one's own "kind," shared interests, business advantages, community service opportunities, group protection through job security or insurance benefits, vocational or avocational study opportunities, a feeling of exclusiveness, the elation of pageantry, and even a religiosity that provides quasi-spirituality.

Service Clubs and Similar Organizations

Almost every community of more than a few hundred people includes at least one civic club or service organization that meets weekly for a luncheon or dinner and features a speaker and/or entertainment. These clubs commonly promote community improvement, patriotic endeavors, charitable support, encouragement of scholarship among students, and other worthwhile projects and programs in the community, without discrimination. These differ from lodges and fraternal orders (to be discussed later)

in that they have no religious tenets and make no spiritual pronouncements. Their beliefs and purposes, including their forms
for receiving members, are open to prospective members and other
inquiries. Guests may be brought to any of their meetings, including those designated for receiving new members.

In recognition of the existence of God and humanity's responsibility toward him most of these clubs open their meetings
or begin their meals with prayer. Any member may be called upon
to pray, and all understand that such prayer represents the beliefs
of only the one praying, not the members individually or
collectively.

Scouting organizations and youth vocational clubs, like adult
civic clubs, generally recognize the existence of God and encourage
regular worship in the church of each member's choice. They usually make provision for such an opportunity when members are
away from their home church on camping or training weekends.
These organizations have been most cooperative with the
churches in adopting tenets and in designing programs that are
not offensive to confessing Christians.

Fraternities and sororities number more than a thousand national organizations. They range from nonreligious to Christian-
sponsored to those based on pagan mythologies to some that are
very similar to the lodges after which they have patterned themselves. However, most professional fraternities and sororities have
rid themselves of religious involvements. Because of the wide-
ranging types of groups, each must be evaluated separately on the
basis of its ritual and religious content.

In general, the Christian's participation in such service clubs
and similar organizations may be decided by his or her own com-
patibility with the members and programs of the organization,
and in some cases, by the general reputation of the club in the
community, especially in its social activities.

To Join or Not to Join?

Many committed Christians join a variety of organizations
(such as those previously discussed) without compromising their
profession of faith. To be sure, some of these groups mention God
in their charters and/or public pronouncements. However, a careful distinction must be drawn between recognition of the existence of God and the actual worship of him and/or the making of
definitive pronouncements in spiritual matters. America's trea-
sured national documents, her coins, pledge of allegiance, and
national anthem all recognize the existence of God. Yet none of
these *establishes* religion.

On the other hand, some organizations oblige Christians to blunt their witness and to deny outwardly the character of their faith. Racist or criminal organizations espouse principles contrary to God's Word, as do the organizations that require their members to profess a religious platform contradictory to Christianity, even though such organizations may espouse noble purposes and carry out commendable programs. Christians cannot be associated with such organizations.

The Christian must avoid those organizations that make spiritual promises contrary to Holy Scripture, require calling upon God to witness a frivolous oath or uncertain oath, promise eternal life as a reward for virtue, regard the Bible as only one moral code among many, practice quasi-sacramental rites of religious significance, pronounce all religious concepts valid before God, or require prayer but do not permit the free exercise of it.

No doubt some organizations intend to do no more than recognize the existence of God, but in fact establish religion in the above matters. Many of these are to be commended for their moral standards, patriotism, charity, and service; regrettably, they must at the same time be considered objectionable from the Christian perspective because of their universalistic religious pronouncements. Refusal to join an organization that promotes a non- or sub-Christian religion may cost the believer certain business, social, or recreational advantages, but the Christian's life cannot be compartmentalized into that which relates to faith and that which does not (1 Cor. 10:31).

In the final analysis, the Christian ought to follow but one standard of evaluation for contemplating membership in an organization: "Will my participation glorify God, maintain the distinctive character of the Gospel, and promote a Christian witness?" (Gal. 2:20–21; 1 Peter 2:9; 3:13–15.)

The Lodges

The popularity of the lodges as "male hideaways" has declined greatly in recent years. The lodges that perpetuate this image are suffering membership losses, while those that offer facilities and activities for the whole family are growing steadily. Whether family oriented or not, the better-known lodges still have spiritual pronouncements and retain religious requirements that deeply disturb conscientious Christian candidates for membership.

Among the most disturbing religious involvements are (1) the promise of access to God outside of Jesus Christ, and (2) the pronouncement (implied or overt) that all sincere members of the organization will be reunited for all eternity on the basis of the virtues that the particular lodge has chosen to extol.

Behind these two religious involvements looms a universalistic-unitarian posture, especially in regard to four cardinal Christian doctrines: *Scripture, God, man,* and *salvation.*

When a group considers the *Bible* to be merely one of many sacred books and restricts its use to that of moral prescription, the Christian cannot give assent or lend support, for the very foundation of his faith has been subverted.

When a group teaches that every concept of *God* is valid no matter how he is visualized, the object of the Christian faith, God, has been diminished to human whimsy.

If the group assumes *man* to be perfectible (either through a process of initiation or a charitable disposition), the work of Christ is made of no effect.

When the group promises *salvation* on the basis of virtue and heaven as the result of earthly brotherhood/sisterhood, then the group itself discriminates against and excludes men and women of Christian convictions.

Meeting Objections to a Biblical Stance

"The Lodge Promotes Public Morals." As America appears to drift toward moral and spiritual bankruptcy, concerned citizens grasp at anything that promises to keep them afloat. Anything bearing a religious stamp appears noble in comparison to the immoralities that surround them. Even pseudo-Christianity seems better than no religion at all. Yet, imitation Christianity carries with it a particular tragedy, for its possessor builds security on a sham. True Christianity is more than a defense against immorality, more than works of benevolence, more than brotherhood based on mutual membership. True brotherhood, true morality, and true charity are created and sustained by atonement through the blood of Jesus Christ and sanctification by God's Holy Spirit. Only that which testifies to God's grace in Jesus Christ is spiritual truth; identification with a spirituality less than this betrays the truth.

"There's No Conflict." All of the prominent lodges assure candidates for membership that "nothing will be required that conflicts with your religious opinions." However, this is totally meaningless, for these lodges refuse to waive or delete those oaths and ceremonies which do conflict. In addition, since only the candidate can know what might conflict with his religious convictions, the lodge cannot logically or morally assume to declare otherwise.

"It's Only a Social Membership." Occasionally a *local* unit of one of the lodges may recognize that religious conflicts do occur.

Moreover, many local lodge members have no interest whatsoever in the rituals and ceremonies of the lodge and offer unapproved "social membership" (much to the dismay of their national lodge).

Surveys list the following reasons as most common for joining a lodge: the social-recreational facilities, the restaurant maintained by the lodge, the inexpensive (or only available) golf course, the only (or only segregated) swimming pool, the only legal bar open after certain hours, a prominent avenue for doing charitable work, or the best place to entertain business clients.

"Social memberships" officially do not exist; they have no uniform membership requirements, method of joining, or privileges of membership. According to lodge officials, offering such a membership breaches the civil charter by which the local lodges are franchised and is, therefore, illegal. They insist that every member, "social" or otherwise, is held responsible for subscribing to all the tenets of the lodge. Obviously, a Christian who accepts a "social membership" contributes to the violation of civil contract as well as identifies publicly with an organization "with crossed fingers" (in a lie).

The Pastor's Role

In public ministry, the pastor must reflect his calling as one who cares for souls, not as one who sits in judgment. His whole demeanor must breathe love for the individual and an earnest desire to be in Christian fellowship with him or her. The conscientious exercise of pastoral care will include concern that all church members and candidates for church membership—including those to be received by transfer or profession of faith—be instructed concerning the incompatibility between the Gospel and "other gospels" (Gal. 1:8–10).

Unfortunately, when asked about objections to lodge membership, some Christians (pastors included) focus on the lodges' oaths, rituals, secrecy, and closed memberships. These objections are valid only if specific elements are considered.

For example, not all *oaths* that call upon God as a witness can be condemned. In the better-known lodges, however, the candidate is required to take a sacred oath of obligation of lifelong support of the lodge before he is permitted to examine those tenets. Lev. 5:4–5 pronounces such an oath "sin" and "guilt" even if the matter is discovered to be good and noble.

Furthermore, committed Christians cannot regard a vow, made in God's name, as "merely a form you must go through" to gain certain social or business advantages. Precisely because the lodges intend the oath to be taken seriously—they insist on it being in God's name—some lodges even specifically include a pledge that the oath is taken "without any mental reservation or secret evasion of mind whatsoever."

The use of *ritual* in itself is not objectionable. Rather, the content of the ritual determines whether or not it is compatible with the Christian's confession.

Secrecy also is not objectionable *per se*. Good reasons may exist at times for an organization to keep some of its affairs confidential. However, secrecy becomes objectionable for the Christian who is required to take an oath to support that which has not yet been revealed to him.

Closed membership, too, may be maintained for valid reasons as, for example, when a hobby club limits membership to people sharing interest in the chosen hobby. The same may be said of political, cultural-heritage, professional, and many other kinds of organizations. However, closed membership becomes offensive to the Christian when membership is restricted on the basis of race or national origin, and is especially offensive when race discrimination is practiced by an organization that claims to promote a broad principle of "the Fatherhood of God and the brotherhood of man." Because of certain civil court rulings, some previously "white only" organizations have dropped that stipulation, but this does not always indicate a change of heart. A secret membership ballot with no required reason for a negative vote makes possible racial discrimination *de facto* if not *de jure*.

Again, oaths, ritual, secrecy, and closed membership are not the primary reasons for the Christian's concern with the religiously involved lodges. Those issues can be important, but only insofar as they call upon the Christian to compromise or ignore the core of faith: *sola gratia, sola fide, sola Scriptura*.

In spite of conscientious pastoral care, "lodge problems" can develop in a congregation for a variety of reasons. Experience shows that what may appear on the surface to be a lodge problem actually may have much deeper roots—a broken fellowship with other Christians, a poor understanding of the Word of God and what constitutes Christian commitment, misinformation or a lack of information from a former pastor, or a hostility toward a pastor or a fellow church member. These root problems often must be addressed first. Discussion of the lodge question itself must be "evangelical," i.e., centered in the Gospel. Tolerance of error has never been evangelical, and this is especially true when error stabs at the very heart of the Christian Gospel: salvation by grace alone. Men and women are not led to a knowledge of the Gospel by adjusting the Word of God to suit their convenience.

A particular problem will be the peer pressure put on preteen children to join a youth extension of a local lodge. Children of this age feel the need for peer approval so greatly that they often will compromise any relationship to receive it. Rather than be "trapped" into a free-for-all during preconfirmation classes, a personal visit with the child and parents together is recommended.

As long as instruction and ministry to an individual continues without procrastination and is moving toward an eventual resolution, a pastor is not guilty of negligence. His goal is always that the lodge member may resolve his divided allegiance and become or remain a communicant member of the Christian congregation.

A pastor can hardly cope with a serious problem of any sort unless he has the intelligent support of those who share his ministry in the congregation. This often requires a great deal of study of available resources on the part of church officers and boards of elders. Lodge members, too, active and prospective, should be willing to study. In doing so, some have discovered that they knew very little about the Bible and even less about the lodge to which they belonged. In fact, at times they have found that the pastor knew a great deal more about the lodge than they themselves knew!

In Summary

An endless variety of organizations bid for the Christian's affiliation—many professing a non- or anti-Christian religion. The church and pastor cannot avoid confrontation with them. The one and only Gospel is at stake. If the church does not insist on an undiminished Gospel, it has lost its purpose and direction and has defaulted on the Great Commission which has set it in motion. Certainly, the church cannot judge a person's faith, but the church can judge a public affirmation of faith—both as it is given in the church and in the world in which the church exists. The diligent and conscientious pastor will continuously put forth effort to resolve contradictory and incompatible public confessions of faith on the part of those who would be or remain in fellowship with the Christian congregation.

Additional Reading

The Lutheran Church—Missouri Synod maintains a commission that gathers and provides information and counsel concerning thousands of organizations, both objectionable and nonobjectionable from the theological perspective of the Synod. Requests for information should be as specific as possible and addressed to

The Executive Director, The Commission on Organizations
The Lutheran Church—Missouri Synod
1333 South Kirkwood Road
St. Louis, MO 63122-7295

UNIT III
THE PASTOR APPLIES
THE WORD AND SACRAMENT
WITHIN THE ASSEMBLED
COMMUNITY

1
The Pastor Leads God's People in Worship

Liturgy as the Living Expression of God's People

When the book of Genesis announces the birth of Enosh, grandson of Adam, it notes, "At that time men began to call on the name of the Lord" (Gen. 4:26). As the rest of the family of Adam was splitting apart in wickedness, the line of Seth and Enosh was coming together in public worship. Throughout the Old Testament, "calling on the name of the Lord" included both the invocation of God in prayer and the proclamation of his deeds and promises. Thus from the earliest days, the presence of believers on the earth has been marked not only by their private devotions and prayers but also by their public worship.

At what point in history believers developed an established pattern or ritual of public worship is unknown, but the earliest records of Biblical worship (as well as the idol-worship of the nations) testify to its long-standing practice. Perhaps it developed naturally and inevitably, for "even an individual's solitary worship of God is carried out within certain concrete acts and forms."[1] So also a community develops concrete acts and forms of worship—in other words, a liturgy.

Moreover, the forms that a community develops demonstrate the faith which the community holds. "*Lex orandi, lex credendi*" was the ancient formula: "The rule of prayers [that is, worship]

---

[1] Peter Brunner, *Worship in the Name of Jesus* (St. Louis: Concordia Publishing House, 1968), p. 217.

is the rule of believing." Simply stated, the liturgy is a way that the Christian church confesses and transmits its faith.[2] More than through confessional writings or dogmatic textbooks, doctrine enters and transforms the lives of people as they gather for worship and hear the Word of God proclaimed, sung, and prayed. The *lex orandi, lex credendi* principle also implies that, no matter what the denominational label, if a congregation worships as Baptist or Roman Catholic or Lutheran, the theology of the denomination, contained and presented in its liturgy or worship service, will affect what the members of the congregation believe and confess.

The Lutheran church, on the basis of Scripture, has committed itself to a specific belief and confession about God and about how our relationship with him comes into being and is nurtured. Therefore the Lutheran Confessions assert that the *content* of the worship service, not the details and traditions of the ceremonies, determines and shows the confessional commitment of a congregation or church body. "It is not necessary for the true unity of the Christian church that ceremonies, instituted by men, should be observed uniformly in all places" (AC VII 3). The ceremonies are understood as *adiaphora*, that is, matters neither commanded nor forbidden in the Word of God. Yet, uniform ceremonies "have been introduced solely for the sake of good order and the general welfare,"—keeping in mind, however, "that the community of God in every locality and every age has authority to change such ceremonies according to circumstances, as it be most profitable and edifying to the community of God" (FC Ep. X 3–4).

These insights help prevent useless controversies about the details and traditions of the ceremonies from taking the focus away from the true concern: the Gospel of Jesus Christ as it is presented in Word and Sacraments. The Confessions' guidance on rituals also protect the joyous freedom the congregation enjoys in Christ. Those who would restrict this liberty, whether they command what is not commanded or forbid what is not forbidden, must be resisted.

> If someone presumes to invest with the cloak of compulsion and constraint any act of worship, outside the elements of form instituted by Christ, and accordingly makes legal demands in its behalf, the church is duty bound to reject this demand, demonstrating its freedom in this matter, even though it were oth-

---

[2] *Lutheran Worship Agenda* (St. Louis: Concordia Publishing House, 1984), p. 10.

erwise at liberty to adopt the act in question. But also the reverse is true here! If a ceremony which is a matter of Christian liberty and does not offend against the Gospel is interdicted with the same coercion and constraint, the congregation may feel called upon to give proof of its liberty and, in a given case, retain and practice this ceremony, which it might otherwise also omit.[3]

The Gospel compels neither simplicity nor elaborate ceremony, neither the old nor the new; only a focus on Jesus Christ. The rites, ceremonies, and forms of worship within the Evangelical Lutheran Church, therefore, must conform to the Holy Scriptures and the Lutheran Confessions, which proclaim Jesus Christ. The Lutheran pastor, in exercising his authority in the congregation, must not introduce any practice or ceremony, hymn or prayer, that in any way imparts a contrary message. His integrity and loyalty to his word, given as a solemn promise at his ordination, to "perform the duties of [his] office in accordance with these Confessions," require him to take care that the Scriptural truth, so clearly delineated by the Confessions, be put into practice in every worship service he conducts.[4] As part of that care, he should work with the elders, worship committee, and other worship leaders and planners to insure that the worship life of the congregation truly expresses the Scriptural faith.

The Lutheran Liturgy: Confessional and Ecumenical

The liturgy, or Divine Service of the Evangelical Lutheran Church, provides a model vehicle for a congregation to express and celebrate its faith. The liturgy centers the focus on Jesus Christ and then expands upon and responds to the message of what he has done. The Divine Service (following the preparatory invocation, confession, and absolution) may be divided into two parts: the Service of the Word and the Service of Holy Communion.[5] The *Service of the Word* centers in the proclamation of the Word of God through the Scripture readings and the exposition of the Scripture in the sermon. This proclamation of the Word is surrounded by prayers, psalms, hymns and canticles, and the creed. The *Service of Holy Communion* centers in the proclamation and reception of the Sacrament, again framed by prayers, hymns, and canticles. These items, which form the structure of

---

[3] Brunner, p. 221.

[4] *Lutheran Worship Agenda*, pp. 212, 225.

[5] *Lutheran Worship* (St. Louis: Concordia Publishing House, 1982), pp. 137, 144. Cf. *Lutheran Worship Altar Book* (St. Louis: Concordia Publishing House, 1982), p. 25.

the Lutheran liturgy, are not a set of rote formalities to be properly recited, but living channels of God's Word to his people and of their response to him in prayer, thanksgiving, and praise. Through the repetition of liturgical texts, these words become our own and further assist us in our daily living of the liturgy in much the same manner as our recitation of the Lord's Prayer.

Lutheran Worship, with its initial song of praise, illustrates how a service can retain the riches that have been handed down to us and also can make use of the variety that is possible. The Christian community gathered for worship has always joined in hymns of praise (though in penitential seasons the praise may be muted). For the purpose of praise, early in the Service of the Word, Divine Service I contains a setting of the historic Gloria in Excelsis, while Divine Service II contains not only a different translation and musical setting of the Gloria, but the option of a 20th-century canticle of praise, "Worthy is Christ." Divine Service III, in place of the Gloria, offers a choice of two Reformation hymns of praise. The "Notes on the Liturgy" in the Altar Book provide other seasonal options.[6] Similar options and alternatives are offered for the Kyrie, Offertory, and Nunc Dimittis.

The content of all of these hymns and canticles is Biblical and Christocentric; and the praise and poetry is of a high order. It is not easy to find hymns of equal power and value that could adequately replace these songs or the other liturgical songs which the church has developed over the centuries. Their use, however, cannot be commanded, however high their quality and long their history. The form of the Divine Service is merely the container that brings the Word and Sacrament of God to the congregation. Nevertheless, a Lutheran pastor does well to remember that the songs and canticles of the liturgy have been developed and selected because they do bring to the worshipping congregation the Biblical, Christ-centered message—which the Lutheran church commits itself to proclaim. Over time, a growing faith is nurtured immeasurably through the repetition of these texts.

The liturgy of the Evangelical Lutheran Church is not the sole possession of Lutherans. It is ecumenical in character; portions of it have been used in the church for over 1800 years. It has stood the test of time as an appropriate way to bring the Word and the Sacraments to God's people. The Lutheran Reformers in the 16th century did not break with the past. Although they changed or deleted parts of the Roman Mass in order to bring the service into conformity with the Gospel, they retained the historic canticles

---

[6] *Lutheran Worship Altar Book*, p. 27.

as well as the ancient pattern of the liturgy. As the Augsburg Confession stresses, the Lutherans saw themselves as heirs of the worship practices of the Old Testament and the early church. Unlike the Calvinistic Reformers, they did not seek to ignore the millennium-and-a-half of church history in an attempt to return to a supposed pristine apostolic simplicity. They knew themselves to be richer because of that history, and they made every attempt to preserve whatever was helpful amid the full riches of Christian history and liturgy.

As today's Lutherans reach out with Word and Sacrament to people of different languages, different cultures, and different musical traditions, they need to remember that the content of the Lutheran liturgy, with its structure of *Service of the Word/Service of Holy Communion,* is neither particularly Germanic nor European. Only the musical settings are the products of a distinctively Western tradition, and (as the options within *Lutheran Worship* suggest) musical settings are variable with the tastes and preferences of the individual congregation. The Scripture readings, canticles, prayers, and communion liturgy have not come from nor are they limited to any one culture; they are ecumenical and universal.

The Liturgy: Biblically Based and Christocentric

The liturgy of the Evangelical Lutheran Church is solidly based and rooted in the sacred Scriptures. Much of the service is taken directly from the Scriptures, such as the Scripture lessons, the Introit, the Gradual, the Sanctus, and the Nunc Dimittis. Other portions, such as the collects, the Gloria, "Worthy is Christ," and the Agnus Dei, quote heavily from the Scriptures. The hymns of the service are frequently based on or related to Biblical texts. The sermon, too, is traditionally based on the Gospel for the day or one of the other Scripture readings appointed for the day.

A liturgy thus rooted in the Bible yields two results. First and most important, a worship service that is truly Scriptural will always be *Christocentric.* The words and phrases quoted from Scripture, as well as the exposition of Scripture, have the same purpose as the Scriptures state for themselves: to make the hearer "wise for salvation through faith in Christ Jesus" (2 Tim. 3:15). The liturgical church year leads the worshipping church through the entire story of salvation in Christ Jesus. From the Old Testament days of Advent through the birth of our Lord, his teaching and miracles, his suffering and death, his resurrection, ascension, and sending of the Holy Spirit, to the implications of all of this for daily Christian living—through all this the story of Christ for us is told over and over, year in and year out. Through the observance of the church year and the Sunday liturgy with its appointed Scripture readings, psalms, hymns, and prayers, Jesus Christ remains always the center of the proclamation and worship of the Evangelical Lutheran Church.

As the second result and benefit, a Bible-based liturgy keeps the focus of worship on the *objective* Biblical message. The Lutheran liturgy is a confession of faith that the Gospel message is the proper content of Christian worship. The subjective feelings of the pastor or of the worshiper—apart from this Gospel message—are no essential part of worship. It is not the purpose of worship to excite, uplift, or move the emotions of the worshiper *except* through the message of the Gospel. If there are weak feelings to be uplifted or wounded feelings to be comforted, the liturgy points the worshipping community to the power and the consolation of the Gospel of Jesus Christ. This also applies to the music of the service. The music may "woo" them, but it is the *Word* which will win them.[7] The excitement and comfort of worship must flow from God's objective message if it is to be more than human manipulation.

Such objectivity also guards against the vacillations of worship based upon a pastor's whims and the changeable fashions of the issues of the day. The latest news item or social issue may be the backdrop against which the pastor speaks, or he may highlight current congregational programs or try to touch individual personal concerns. But news, programs, and personal concerns may never be the focus nor essential content of Christian worship. Rather, the Evangelical Lutheran Church is convinced that the objective Gospel of God's grace in Jesus Christ is the true answer to the subjective needs, hurts, fears, and temptations of fallen and redeemed mankind. The historic Lutheran liturgy is designed with that practical need in mind for the Christocentric Gospel.

The Liturgy as Pastoral Care

"Worship is a major, if recently neglected, aspect of pastoral care."[8] The emphasis that has been placed on the pastor's work

---

[7] Working with lay volunteers, the pastor may find it difficult to cultivate this understanding of how music functions in the liturgy. Both *The Pastor and the Church Musician* (Carl Schalk, St. Louis: Concordia, 1980) and *The Theological Character of Music in Worship* (Robin Leaver, St. Louis: Concordia, 1989) provide a starting point for the conversation.

[8] W. H. Willimon, *Worship as Pastoral Care* (Nashville: Abingdon, 1974), p. 47.

in counseling, hospital and shut-in ministrations, and other interpersonal contacts with the parishioner must not overshadow the major work of pastoral care that goes on in the context of worship. Within the liturgy of the Divine Service, the proclamation/explanation of the Word and the administration of the Sacraments apply the Gospel of Jesus to more lives more often than is possible anywhere else. For the pastor to neglect his preparation for worship or give it only routine attention is, at best, shortsighted. The pastor who is conscientious about pastoral care does well to focus first and regularly on the care of the congregation as it gathers for worship.

In the classic work *Pastoral Care in Historical Perspective*, W. A. Clebsch and C. R. Jaeckle distinguish four historic functions of pastoral care: healing, sustaining, guidance, and reconciliation.[9] Obviously, people dealing with a severe personal crisis, sickness, or grief need individual care and a personal application of God's healing, sustaining, guiding, and reconciling Word. However, when God's people come together for worship, they also gather with the need to be healed, sustained, guided, and reconciled. The application of Law and Gospel, Word and Sacrament to their lives is not a secondary spin-off of pastoral care; it *is* pastoral care. As J. A. Jungmann has written, "For centuries, the liturgy, actively celebrated, has been the most important form of pastoral care."[10] In addition, the liturgy's objective, Bible-based, and Christocentric nature serves as a model for the pastor as he ministers to members in their separate needs. The message of reconciliation and forgiveness, life and salvation for the Christians gathered in community applies also to the Christian struggling alone. The weekly format of confession and absolution, Word and application, prayer and Communion, which help order the community worship, may also give form to an individual pastoral visit. Even the very words of public worship and prayer spoken by the congregation on Sunday can be repeated by an individual during the week in a way which reaffirms that the individual, though physically apart from the community, is a part of Christ's one body, the church.

From his visits and conversations with individuals in need, the pastor will learn to appreciate the hurts, fears, and conflicts

---

[9] W. A. Clebsch and C. R. Jaeckle, *Pastoral Care in Historical Perspective* (Englewood Cliffs: Prentice Hall, 1964), pp. 34–66.

[10] J. A. Jungmann, *Pastoral Liturgy* (New York: Herder and Herder, 1962), p. 380.

that all Christians face and will return as a *Seelsorger* to the gathered community with a deeper confidence in the appropriateness and power of the message that he bears. Thus, liturgy is not an alternative or an obstacle to pastoral care, but the very cement that binds together Christians of all times to the source of their care, Jesus Christ.

Hymnody Related to the Proclamation of the Word

While hymnody and sacred song have been a part of Christian worship throughout its history,[11] the Reformation made the hymn an important part of the divine service. In one of his major liturgical writings, the German Mass of 1526,[12] Luther replaced the fixed liturgical texts of the Latin Mass with hymns that dealt with the same theological and Biblical themes. Through the singing of these hymns, the people were able to participate in the service in a way they had never known before: the Gospel was proclaimed and sung on their own lips. No wonder the Evangelical Lutheran Church gained the reputation during the Reformation as the "singing church"! Its hymns spread the message of the Reformation singing the message of the Gospel into the hearts of the people.

In the German Mass, Luther substituted a congregational hymn for the Gradual (the Psalm text that appeared between the reading of the Epistle and the Gospel). A fixed cycle of hymns that related to the Gospel of the week was established, and this cycle of Gradual hymns remained in use for two centuries. The present-day counterpart and descendant of the Reformation-era Gradual hymn is the Hymn of the Day. While the celebration of the Divine Service may include many hymns, all carefully chosen with regard to their function in a particular service, the Hymn of the Day (or "sermon hymn") is the chief hymn of the service. Selected to reflect the Scripture readings for the day, it therefore reflects also the

---

[11] On Maundy Thursday, Jesus and his disciples sang hymns, most likely the appointed Hallel Psalms (Ps. 115–118), on the way from the upper room to Gethsemane (Matt. 26:30).

[12] LW 55:51–90. This form of service was never entirely forgotten; it appeared in many congregations as the Reformation was celebrated yearly. In 1982, the German Mass or hymn service was restored to The Lutheran Church—Missouri Synod as Divine Service III in *Lutheran Worship*.

church year and the season that is being observed. It should be closely related to the sermon, which also is traditionally based on the Scripture readings of the day.[13]

---

[13] In addition to the indices in *Lutheran Worship* (pp. 976ff.), pastors may find assistance in the careful selection of hymns through resources such as *Proclaim: A Guide for Planning Liturgy and Music* (a 12-part series, 1985–1988) and *Creative Worship for the Lutheran Parish* (to be a 12-part series, 1988–), both published by Concordia Publishing House, St. Louis.

2
The Pastor Proclaims the Gospel

This is what is written: The Christ will suffer and rise from the dead on the third day and repentance and forgiveness of sins will be proclaimed in his name to all nations, beginning at Jerusalem. You are witnesses of these things. (Luke 24:47–48)

As witnesses to their resurrected Lord, the apostles did preach the message of forgiveness and repentance, not only in evangelistic outreach to unbelievers (as in Acts 2:14–41; 3:11–26; 17:16–34), but also as the message for the faithful. When God's people came together as an assembly of believers, they followed the pattern of the Old Testament synagogue by placing Scripture reading and its exposition at the center of worship (along with the Christian addition of the Lord's Supper). They listened to the Word of God read and expounded (Acts 2:42; 1 Tim. 4:6–16; 2 Tim. 3:14–4:5; Titus 2:1–3:8). They heard the message of repentance and forgiveness in Jesus' name applied to their lives on the basis of the Old Testament Scriptures and, later, the writings of the Apostles.

Worship, as a human activity, has always been a response to God's activity (see, e.g., Ex. 20:1–11). Our confession of praise and prayer to him always follows upon his Word to us. *Christian* worship, thus, responds to God's ultimate Word to us, his Son. For this reason, from the very earliest days of the church, when Christian people gather for worship they not only sing praises and speak prayers to God; they also listen to his message and hear it applied to their lives for their comfort and renewal (receiving as well the sacramental Word joined to the elements which brings the same message of forgiveness of sins in Jesus Christ). Through the Scripture readings and their exposition God speaks, God is glorified, and the thoughts, hearts, and desires of the congregation are turned to Christ. This work of explanation and application of the Scriptures is a prime task for the undershepherd.[1] Through his proclamation of God's message, his flock hears the voice of *the* Shepherd speaking his Law and his Gospel to their hearts.

In the 1960s and 1970s some church writers suggested that the days of preaching were over; people did not like to be "preached at." Since preaching was no more than one-way communication that demanded an unaccustomed work of receptivity on the part of the listener, it was considered outdated and outmoded.[2] In recent years, however, there has been a rebirth of interest in preaching as an effective means of instructing and grounding God's people in the Word, comforting them in their hurts, and preparing them for their struggles. When the preacher combines his confidence in the Scriptural message with the wisdom and courage to speak that message clearly and directly to the hearts of the listeners, preaching can receive new prominence as both a means of pastoral care and an essential component of Christian worship.

Some have suggested that the key to effective preaching is technical—a matter of the application of the rules for public speaking. There is some validity in this approach. The preacher does undertake intellectual and physical actions in writing and speaking a sermon—actions that can be learned and practiced. Preaching is a craft to be sharpened and honed constantly, and the pastor can improve the art of his preaching in many ways, not least by reading good sermons and books on sermon preparation. He can also listen to good preaching, and for little extra cost view it on videotape. If the congregation has its own video equipment, he can record and critique his own sermons. Given the right conditions and a spirit of cooperation, he may even exchange tapes with his fellow pastors for their mutual evaluation and benefit. Nevertheless, while the art of effective speaking is important and must be cultivated and practiced, good preaching transcends mere technique; it is the proclamation of the Word of God within

---

[1] *Lutheran Worship, Altar Book* (St. Louis: Concordia Publishing House, 1982), p. 30.

[2] Clyde Reid, *The Empty Pulpit* (New York: Harper and Row, 1967). Leander E. Keck, *The Bible in the Pulpit* (Nashville: Abingdon, 1978).

the context of the lives of a specific congregation gathered to hear that Word. The preacher, as a student of Scripture and a believer, must know the message he brings and know how to speak it to the people he addresses.

The Sermon in Relation to the Liturgy

The Scripture readings appointed for the divine service set the theme and tone for the propers of the day, the hymns, and the sermon. The sermon, which enlarges upon the chief thoughts presented in the Sunday lessons, is thus an indispensable part of the liturgy that precedes and follows it. Therefore the pastor, as leader of the congregation's worship, does not have the privilege of preaching about anything that strikes his fancy, such as what *he* thinks about the state of the world, what *he* thinks about events in the church, or even what *he* thinks about God. The sermon is to be an exposition of the Word of God, applying *God's* message to the world, the church, and the individual.

Since the sermon, as a part of the divine service, should be in harmony with the service, the pastor will want to take care not to import any unrelated elements that detract from the theme of the Sunday celebration. Certainly, when an external event—such as a secular holiday, a death in the congregation, a Super Bowl, or a declaration of war—is on the minds of the worshipping congregation, the pastor may well speak to that concern. His task, however, is to point beyond the limits of that event (and the subjective feelings that surround it) to the message of God's Law and Gospel, which is applicable to all manner and conditions of men, all events, all concerns. The Scriptural text for the message is not to be a pretext for focusing attention on a secular event, which will soon pass. For example, even a sermon on Mother's Day ultimately should center on the message of repentance and forgiveness of sins in Jesus Christ, which is the message God has for his people.

The Purpose of the Sermon

As a congregation gathers on a Sunday morning, the people bring a variety of concerns, hurts, and needs. The sorrowful and the impenitent, the oppressed and the unforgiving, the weak and the strong come together to hear a Word that touches them all. They are all sinners who need a Savior. They need to hear the voice of that Savior, calling them to repentance and announcing his forgiveness. The pastor who brings the Savior's message needs to keep his mind on his congregation's ultimate need and his purpose in speaking to that need. The sermon's ultimate purpose, therefore, is not to engage the hearers' minds, entertain their emotions, or persuade their decisions—although a good sermon will be logical, engaging, and persuasive!—but to apply the Word of God to their hearts and lives.

The sermon cannot be simply a logical refutation of error. Tearing down error's positions and running logical circles around them may become a part of a sermon's work, and it may be great fun; but the announcement of salvation in Christ is not a logical construct developed by syllogism from self-evident principles. Good News is *news*. It is to be proclaimed, announced, and applied, not simply figured out.

Nor should the sermon be treated as entertainment in which the preacher holds center stage and impresses the "audience" with his ability to fill their time and tickle their emotions. The preacher has a different vocation. His challenge is to grab the people's attention and keep it focused not on himself but on God's Word and Good News. Like St. Paul, he will labor mightily so that every listener hears the Word of God in a way he can understand (1 Cor. 2:1–5; 9:19–22; Gal. 4:12–16). Preaching Jesus Christ the crucified in a way that imposes no barrier to the listener is work enough to challenge the time and wisdom of the faithful preacher.

The sermon is also not intended as a sales talk to convince people to come to faith. In contrast to the popular Protestant call for a faith decision, the *Gospel* preacher focuses his attention on the Word through which the *Holy Spirit* brings people to faith. The preacher is to proclaim the message, laden with the promises of Christ, so that anyone who by the Spirit's power says, "Amen. That is so," will have the forgiveness, life, and salvation that the sermon promises. As a Gospel message, the sermon is thus the power of God for the salvation to those who believe it.

Know the Word; Preach the Word

Good preaching begins not with sermon study but with *Bible* study. Every day the pastor must begin by reading the Bible for himself in a devotional manner, quite apart from sermon preparation. The faithful pastor, who applies to himself the Word he reads, will find also that the study of Scripture with the technical tools of exegesis will both yield the fruit of growth as a pastor and theologian and provide stimulation to personal meditation and growth as a Christian. Only the pastor who has himself been humbled daily by God's Word and been lifted up and empowered by God's gracious promises is prepared to share God's Word with people who also need to be humbled and lifted up. Daily meditation on God's Word will not happen automatically or by accident, but it will yield rich benefit. When the pastor of God's people undertakes a regular plan of Bible study, he will find himself more and more attracted to it. The pastor will then become a man of prayer—prayer which flows from the Word he reads and meditates upon. Following the example of Martin Luther, the pastor should be able to take any text of Scripture and apply it to himself as an occasion of instruction, of confession, of thanksgiving, and of petition.[3] Johann Bengel's rule applies here:

> *Te totam applica ad textum:*
> *Rem totam applica ad te.*
> Apply yourself totally to the text:
> Apply the text totally to yourself.

As the pastor begins his sermon preparation, he first lets the text speak to him personally. After responding to God prayerfully, on the basis of the text, he then can turn to formal preparation for applying the text to the lives of others.

As the pastor meditates on the Word in sermon study, he will do well to look ahead at the texts which have been selected for the coming Sundays. Whether preaching on a series (e.g., the gospels) or on self-selected texts, the pastor should have an extended view of the themes he will cover over a series of months in order to avoid repetition and/or too narrow a focus. Aware of the texts and topics for the coming weeks and months, the pastor can pick out interrelationships between the texts and build on the distinctive nature of each text. For example, a series of lessons on John 6, the Sermon on the Mount, or the book of Revelation can be an invitation to repetition by an unprepared preacher. Likewise, several lessons on miracles may occur in close succession. Attention to the emphasis of each individual text as distinct from the others will enable the preacher to present not a "miracle sermon" but a sermon on *this* miracle.

Obviously, the pastor will begin his specific preparation for the Sunday sermon very early in the week, ideally on Monday, with a careful reading of the appointed texts. The earnest study of the text begins with the original languages, working with dictionaries, concordances, commentaries, and other aids. Only when the pastor understands the words, sentences, and thought progression of the text in the context of its chapter, book, and all of Scripture will he comprehend the meaning which the text itself speaks (as opposed to any message generated within the pastor's

---

[3] *A Simple Way to Pray,* LW 43:187–212.

subjective feelings). Once he comprehends this meaning, he is ready to outline the thoughts and write the sermon that will apply that particular text to the lives of his people (as well as carry out the theme of the propers for the day). Attention to the very words of the text will permit each text to bring its distinct message to God's people. A sermon on a text that speaks of Jesus as *Redeemer* should differ from one that presents Him as *Christ*, or *King*, or *Good Shepherd*. Here language study will bear its fruit, helping the preacher to see what the text really said in the original, and helping him focus his attention on re-creating that message, that emphasis, under Scripture's one message of repentance and forgiveness in Jesus Christ.

That one message, however, must be properly understood and proclaimed in the light of all that God has said.

> Only he is an orthodox teacher who not only presents all the articles of faith in accordance with Scripture, but also rightly distinguishes from each other the Law and the Gospel. Rightly distinguishing the Law and the Gospel is the most difficult and highest art of Christians in general and of theologians in particular. It is taught only by the Holy Spirit in the school of experience.[4]

The Word which the preacher presents is not an insignificant power. It is the hammer to break the hardened heart and the balm to make the broken spirit rejoice. Only the Holy Spirit can grant the wisdom to know when to hammer and when and how to heal. The Lutheran pastor should draw on the riches and insight available to him in the Lutheran Confessions, the writings of Martin Luther,[5] and C. F. W. Walther's *Law and Gospel*. A continual review of the Law and Gospel principle of the Scripture will remind the pastor of the necessity of preaching the Law in all its severity to the unrepentant heart, and the Gospel with all its sweetness to the heart that has turned in repentant need to Christ. Following the Law/Gospel principle will help the pastor avoid the mistake of turning the Law into a substitute Gospel or making the Gospel into a new Law. Maintaining the Law/Gospel distinction enables the pastor to do his job as an evangelical preacher—letting the Gospel predominate in everything.

---

[4] C.F.W.Walther, *Law and Gospel* (St. Louis: Concordia Publishing House, n.d.), p.1. [Theses 2 and 3]

[5] Franz Pieper commended especially Luther's 1535 commentary on Galatians (LW 26–27) as "the most powerful book ever written on the doctrine of Law and Gospel." *Christian Dogmatics* III, (St. Louis: Concordia Publishing House, 1953), p. 252.

3
The Sacrament of Baptism

The Necessity of Baptism

> Jesus came to them and said, "All authority in heaven and on earth has been given to me. Therefore go and make disciples of all nations, baptizing them in the name of the Father and of the Son and of the Holy Spirit, and teaching them to obey every thing I have commanded you. And surely I will be with you always, to the very end of the age." (Matt. 28:18–20)

In these words just after his resurrection, Jesus directed his church on earth to make disciples by means of two primary and essential activities: baptizing (*baptizontes*) and teaching (*didaskontes*).[1]

All Christian denominations have understood the necessity of teaching, but the Reformed churches have rejected the efficacy of Baptism. They may be of the opinion that, in the view of those who believe in baptism, its efficacy is mechanical and that its power resides in the person or the church, not realizing that the power resides in God, who acts through his Word. As Luther summarized in his Small Catechism, "Baptism is not simple water only, but it is the water comprehended in God's command and connected with God's Word." The water and the Word together comprise the sacrament. Therefore

Our churches teach that Baptism is necessary for salvation, that

---

[1] The use of participles in both cases indicates that there is no temporal priority; Baptism may precede teaching (as it does in the case of the Baptism of infants and young children) or follow (as in the case of adolescents and adults).

the grace of God is offered through Baptism, and that children should be baptized; for being offered to God through Baptism, they are received into his grace.

Our churches condemn the Anabaptists who reject the Baptism of children and declare that children are saved without Baptism. (AC IX, Lat.)

Note the emphasis: *the grace of God* is offered through this sacrament. Baptism is no mere external sign of an outward testimony nor an inward decision to believe and follow Christ. The person being baptized actually receives regeneration, forgiveness of sins, salvation, the benefits of Christ, and a good conscience toward God. Paul refers to Baptism as a burial with Christ in which the faithful are raised with him "through your faith in the power of God, who raised him from the dead" (Col. 2:12; cf. Rom. 6:3f.), and "the washing of rebirth and renewal by the Holy Spirit" (Titus 3:5). Tertullian, in the opening sentence of his treatise *de Baptismo* (from his pre-Montanist period), summarizes the teaching of the apostles: "Happy is our sacrament of water, in that, by washing away the sins of our early blindness, we are set free and admitted into eternal life!" (ANF, III, 669). In summary, Baptism is an act by which the candidate is grafted into the holy Christian church and made a member of the mystical body of Christ.

Having confessed that, some have been concerned about those who are connected to the household of faith but who, either through inadvertence or lack of opportunity, died without being baptized. Is it really necessary? In response, the medieval church suggested that those who thus died somehow benefited from a "desire for Baptism." Later theologians posited the existence of a "limbo" (apart from hell and heaven) of unbaptized infants (*limbus infantum*).

Though there is no scriptural foundation for either of these pious hopes, the conscientious pastor still wants some word to comfort the parents who mourn the death of an unbaptized child or a stillborn child. As a servant of the Word, he cannot say in the name of the Lord anything that the Lord has not revealed; he cannot speak of the unbaptized child as though he or she had in fact been baptized. Yet, it is not the lack of but the disdain for Baptism that results in condemnation. Therefore, the pastor rightly may speak of the mercy of a gracious heavenly Father who knows our need even before we have asked, and may remind the parents that God's activity is by no means predicated upon or limited to Holy Baptism.[2]

---

[2] Cf. 1 Cor. 7:14b. The *Lutheran Worship Agenda* rite for the Burial of the

The Anabaptist reaction against the necessity of Baptism continues today. Some claim that Baptism is not necessary for those who are "born-again," that "outward" baptism is not necessary for those "inwardly baptized by the Spirit." However, since Baptism has been commanded by our Lord for all his disciples, Baptism never may be refused by or withheld from his people. Those who persist in refusing to be baptized need to be confronted with their rebellious attitude towards the Lord's Word. Most of all, they need to be led to feel their need for Baptism, which unites them to the forgiveness of sins that Christ won by his death.

In the same vein, the pastor should ascertain that all who attend the Lord's Supper (including those asking to be confirmed) have been baptized, for in it God joins his people to himself, and in the Eucharist he feeds them. (Likewise, when the pastor receives inquiries from another pastor or congregation about the Baptism of a person, he should respond promptly.)

Necessary for All

The commission which the Lord has given to his church extends to all nations (*panta ta ethne*), the whole multitude of mankind: Jew and Gentile, male and female, adult and child alike. No one is excluded from the promise and invitation of the Gospel. Christ died for all; therefore all are to be baptized into that death.

In the early church the majority of candidates were adults who had heard the Gospel message and had asked to be baptized. In most congregations today, the majority are infant children born to members of the congregation. Whatever the person's age, the nature of Baptism is the same for all: "All of us who were baptized into Christ were baptized into his death" (Rom. 6:3). Thus, those who cannot speak for themselves are baptized upon the request of those responsible for them.

Adolescents and adults are properly baptized after they have been instructed in the chief parts of Christian doctrine and have confessed their faith. Even though they have already received the gift of faith through the Word alone, they also are invited to receive the blessings and promises of Baptism, as did the Ethiopian eunuch (Acts 8:26–39) and Cornelius of Caesarea (Acts 10:1–48). That they have already come to faith does not make the sacrament any less a washing of regeneration for them, nor can they afford to disdain it.

Stillborn (197–201) is a helpful source for thoughts, words, and prayers of comfort, even apart from the burial setting. (See also its predecessor, *Lutheran Agenda*, p. 99–101.)

Instruction Before Baptism

That the Lord's commission comprises two parts, baptizing coupled with teaching, has already been noted. When candidates are of an age to receive instruction in the chief parts of Christian doctrine and confess their faith, this instruction and confession precedes Baptism.

In the case of infants and very young children, teaching will follow Baptism. The responsibility of the parents in this regard is implicit in their parental vocation to bring up their baptized children as Christians. Parents have the primary responsibility for the duties charged to the sponsors in the baptismal rite:

> To remember him/her in your prayers, put him/her in mind of his/her Baptism, and, as much as in you lies, give your counsel and aid . . . that he/she be brought up in the true knowledge and worship of God and be taught [the chief parts of Christian doctrine]; and that, as he/she grows in years, you place in his/ her hands the Holy Scriptures, bring him/her to the services of God's house, and provide for him/her further instruction in the Christian faith, that he/she come to the Sacrament of Christ's Body and Blood, and thus, abiding in his/her baptismal grace and in communion with the Church, he/she may grow up to lead a godly life to the praise and honor of Jesus Christ.[3]

Prior to the rite of Baptism, the minister should take care to remind parents of their responsibilities, instruct the sponsors in their duties, acquaint parents and sponsors with the congregation's educational agencies, and offer his own constant encouragement and assistance.

The Continual Use of Baptism for Daily Living

At one time, many Christians hung their framed baptismal certificate over their bed as a constant reminder, morning and evening, that they had been marked as a child of God (cf. Rev. 14:1). They were thus giving themselves a reminder to help put into practice the words of the Small Catechism,

> The Old Adam in us, together with all sins and evil lusts, should be drowned by daily sorrow and repentance and be put to death, and . . . the new man should come forth daily and rise up, cleansed and righteous, to live forever in God's presence. (SC IV 12)

To put people in mind of their Baptism is a powerful tool for

---

[3] "Holy Baptism," *Lutheran Worship* (Concordia: St. Louis, 1982), p. 200.

a Gospel-centered pastoral ministry. Many people despair of their sins; even faithful worship-attenders may be so habituated in particular sin(s) that escape seems impossible. Thus the Large Catechism reminds,

> When our sins or conscience oppress us, . . . we must retort, "But I am baptized! And if I am baptized, I have the promise that I shall be saved and have eternal life, both in soul and body."
> (LC IV 44)

Baptism and repentance go together. "Repentance, therefore, is nothing else than a return and approach to Baptism, to resume and practice what had earlier been begun but abandoned" (LC IV 79). It is not mere chance that the church's formula of absolution repeats the words of the baptismal formula: we receive forgiveness "in the Name of the Father and of the Son and of the Holy Spirit." As Luther noted elsewhere,

> Understand that this is the significance of Baptism, that through it you die and live again. Therefore, whether by [absolution] or by any other way, you can only return to the power of your Baptism, and do again that which you were baptized to do and which your Baptism signified. Baptism never becomes useless.[4]

What a comforting message the pastor gives when he reminds his people Sunday after Sunday (as well as in special services, especially the Easter Vigil) that justification and the resulting power for sanctification has been sealed to them individually through Baptism! "This is the significance of Baptism, that through it you die and live again," Luther emphasized.[5] Time and again the pastor should be drawn back to the text that captivated Luther (and which guards against co-mingling Law and Gospel):

> All of us who were baptized into Christ Jesus were baptized into his death. We were therefore buried with him through Baptism into death in order that, just as Christ was raised from the dead through the glory of the Father, we too may live a new life. (Rom. 6:3–4)

Luther was so struck by the practical importance of Baptism that in his forms for Morning and Evening Prayer he included all the various items from the baptismal rite (except the water): the Triune invocation, the sign of the cross, and the Apostles' Creed. All personal prayer—at all times and in all places—is meant to remind the believer daily that God has put his name upon us,

---

[4] *The Babylonian Captivity of the Church*, LW 36:69.
[5] Ibid.

that he has taught us the words by which we are to confess him, and that he both tenderly invites us to call upon him as in the Lord's Prayer. Even the divine service begins with an invocation in the divine name into which we have been baptized, "In the name of the Father, and of the Son, and of the Holy Spirit."

Issues Concerning the Proper Administration of Baptism

The Baptismal Formula

No other formula ought to be used in place of the words given by our Lord: "In the Name of the Father, and of the Son, and of the Holy Spirit." Although St. Luke speaks of Baptism as "in the name of Jesus Christ" (Acts 2:38; 8:16; 10:48), this phrase describes the *character* of Christian Baptism as distinct from existing Jewish and Roman rituals and from the baptism of repentance by John the Baptizer. Luke's phrase is not an alternative to the full Trinitarian formula of Matthew 28. Other formulae are to be avoided because Christ has attached his blessing to these words and has given no warrant to alter them. "Nevertheless," Fritz notes in his *Pastoral Theology* (p. 83), "the Baptism of a person who has thus been baptized [with only the words 'in the name of Jesus Christ'] may be considered valid, since, as Brentius says, 'Christ did not make the blessing of Baptism dependent upon certain letters, syllables, or phrases, nor did he tie us down to certain words; for he did not institute a magical performance.'"

The Use of Water

The use of water (not other liquids such as milk, oil, wine, etc.) is required by the word *baptizontes* (Matt. 28:19; John 3:5; Acts 8:36–39; 10:47; Eph. 5:26; 1 Peter 3:21). In the unlikely event that water would not be available and Baptism could not be performed, Christians should take comfort in knowing that faith in Christ saves even without Baptism (provided this important sacrament is not held in contempt). (Note Mark 16:16, Luke 7:30, and John 3:5.)

The Lord's command does not specify the amount of water to be used or the manner of its application. It may be poured or sprinkled, or the candidate may be immersed. The usual practice in the Lutheran Church is that, as the formula is spoken, the water is scooped from the font and poured on the head of the candidate (usually three times, as was the practice of the early church). The water may be warm or cool, still or flowing, the amount small or large—it makes no difference. Baptism is a water of life by virtue of the Word that comprehends it, not because of the water's own nature or activity.

Who Should Administer the Sacrament?

The proper administrant of Holy Baptism is the one who has been entrusted with the public office of Word and Sacrament, Christ's representative and minister to the people.

In an emergency[6] any Christian has the authority. To cite the "Treatise on the Power and Primacy of the Pope,"

> It is like the example which Augustine relates of two Christians in a ship, one of whom baptized the other (a catechumen), and the latter, after his Baptism, absolved the former. (Tractate 67)

Pastors should instruct their people, before the occasion arises, that any child in danger of death should be baptized immediately. *Lutheran Worship* and *The Lutheran Hymnal* provide forms for emergency Baptism for the use of parents and responsible parties or those delegated by them to baptize. Even so, all that is necessary is the water and the spoken Word. (In order to verify that an actual Baptism has taken place, a witness should be present for an emergency Baptism.)

The fact of the Baptism should be immediately reported to the pastor of the congregation who can then acquaint himself fully with the circumstances and determine that the administration was carried out properly. He will then record the Baptism in the congregational register and announce the Baptism to the congregation. *Lutheran Worship Agenda* includes an appropriate order for the Recognition by the Church of Emergency Baptism.

How Early Should Infants Be Baptized?

The people should be instructed to bring their newborn children for Baptism at the earliest possible time. Many places follow the custom that the first time the child leaves the family home is the journey to the baptismal font.

The Use of Sponsors

Although sponsorship is not essential to Baptism and has often been misused, the practice has much to commend it. The writings on Baptism from the early church already speak of spon-

---

[6] The standard Baptism of a child by a theological student, student intern, or Christian Day school teacher is not an emergency. The practice militates against a right understanding of the work and place of the holy ministry and contributes to a spirit of disorder in the congregation.

sors attesting to the sincerity of the adult candidate and offering to support his or her Christian life. In the more recent past, when the mother usually remained at home for a long period of time after giving birth, it was the responsibility of the sponsor to bring the infant candidate to the font. Frequently today, parents and sponsors together present the child.

Christian parents should choose for their child sponsors who are themselves communicant members of a Christian congregation in which the Word of God is purely taught and the sacraments are rightly administered, who will take seriously the responsibilities they are asked to affirm in the church's rite of Holy Baptism. The minister should instruct his people on the qualifications and requirements of proper sponsors and encourage the parents to choose sponsors well in advance of the expected time of delivery.

Christians of good report who do not meet the requirements of sponsors may serve as witnesses to the Baptism. Witnesses do not, however, take upon themselves the responsibilities given to sponsors.

The Value of Baptism in the Sunday Divine Liturgy

The administration of Baptism as part of the Divine Liturgy represents a somewhat recent innovation in the Lutheran church. The practice, however, has much to commend it. Holy Baptism in the presence of the congregation extols Baptism, serves to remind the people of their own Baptism, and underscores Baptism as the sacrament of initiation into the church.

In spite of the reluctance of some parents and sponsors to be "on display" and/or to add time to the service, the request for a private Baptism (e.g., following corporate worship) may reflect a lack of understanding of the nature of Baptism and the church. Therefore, Baptisms ordinarily should be administered as a part of the congregation's chief service (as *Lutheran Worship Agenda* notes).[7]

The pastor should have beforehand all the information needed to prepare the certificate of Baptism and to make the proper entry into the parish register. The certificate should be given to the parents at the time of the Baptism.

In the divine service, Holy Baptism follows the Hymn of Invocation (or a baptismal hymn) and may supplant the usual preparatory rite (Invocation, Confession of Sin, and Absolution or

---

[7] In addition to the regular baptismal rite, *Lutheran Worship Agenda* and *Lutheran Worship Little Agenda* both include a Short Form of Holy Baptism. The longer and fuller form should be regarded as the normal form, and its use should always be encouraged.

Declaration of Grace). Baptism comes first of all in the service, just as it comes first of all in the life of the Christian. By it God's people are gathered to Christ to receive from him and have fellowship around his Word and gifts.

After the blessing which ends the baptismal rite, the service continues with the Introit, Psalm, or Entrance Hymn. After the Collect of the Day, one of the collects for Holy Baptism (*LWA*, p. 366) may be added. When time is limited, the service may pass immediately from the baptismal blessing to the Salutation and Collect of the Day.

Whatever rubrics are followed, the pastor should seek to emphasize the joyous work that God is doing in the Sacrament. Prior to Luther, the church of Rome had identified the blessings as coming through the various rituals (e.g., the sign of the cross, breathing on the candidate, etc.). After Luther, the age of Pietism saw such a a strong pedagogical and didactic style that, in some cases, the somber exhortations detracted from the Sacrament itself and its joy. The confessional revival of the nineteenth century renewed the rite; but misuse once again could cause a confusion between ceremony and grace.

No "Lutheran" Rebaptism

Baptism does not initiate a person into a particular denomination but unites the baptized person with Christ's death and resurrection. It is by nature as unrepeatable as birth. If a baptized Christian were to seek a second Baptism from a belief that a new or fuller blessing would be obtained by it, permitting such a second Baptism would instead undermine the confidence which ought to be placed in the promises God has attached to Baptism. On the other hand, if a person already baptized were inadvertently to be baptized a second time, the second Baptism would add no new gift or blessing, nor would a second Baptism serve as a reaffirmation or ratification.

Questioning the Validity of a Prior Baptism

Those who question whether they have been rightly baptized constitute a special case calling for wisdom and discernment on the part of the pastor. The pastoral goal is to ensure that the believer can be confident of his union with Christ, who has died and risen for him.

The only circumstance in which a possible "second" Baptism could be justified is when the fact of Baptism is in doubt—whether it was done with both water and the Word. As noted above, no Christian should be allowed to doubt that he has been baptized.

If such doubts persist, the person should be baptized for the sake of his conscience and peace of mind.

However, as long as no question of the fact of the Baptism or its proper form are involved, the believer should not concern himself with questions about the minister's faith or life. Nor does Baptism depend on the proper intention of either the minister or the person baptized (or that of his parents and sponsors). Baptism depends rather upon Christ's Word itself, on his institution.

4
The Sacrament of the Altar

In the night in which he was betrayed, our Lord Jesus Christ took bread and the cup, blessed them and gave them to his disciples to eat and to drink, commanding them to "do this" in remembrance of him. This remembrance consists not in our attempts to reenact the supper—doing what he did—but rather in our faithfully receiving what he alone does and gives. We do what he has said to do; we receive what he gives, namely, forgiveness of sins, life, and salvation.

The gathering of the people around the altar to receive the Lord's Supper is the high point of the corporate life of an Evangelical Lutheran congregation. This celebration is the fullness of our Lord's service to his people. In this "salutary gift" he himself provides the means by which his faithful receive the benefit of all his saving person and work.

Matthew, Mark, Luke, and Paul tell us that Christ took bread (*artos*) such as would be used at any meal (Luke 24:30; John 21:13; Acts 27:35; Mark 6:41 *et al*; 8:19 *et al*; John 6:11). By custom, the head of the household broke the bread and, at the thanksgiving prayer which began the meal, gave it to those present. In the Koine Greek, *artos* is the generic name given to bread of whatever kind—white, whole wheat, rye, barley, etc. It would seem, however, that the context of the institution of the Lord's Supper indicates the use of unleavened wheat bread. It is not essential that the bread used in the celebration of the sacrament be unleavened, but it is a custom of long-standing in the Lutheran Church.

In contrast to the generic *bread*, the cup (*poterion*) contains a specific "fruit of the vine": wine (Matt. 26:29; Mark 14: 25; Luke 22:18). Nonalcoholic grape juice, a pasteurized product of the nineteenth century, is not referred to in the institution of Christ, and its use in the sacrament raises a question whether the words of Christ have been followed or not. No other beverage is to be substituted for that which Christ used, for to it alone the Lord has connected his command and promise.[1] The wine may be red, white, or amber. Red wine is not needed to "symbolize" the blood of Christ. The true blood of Christ is in and with the consecrated wine by virtue of his Word, regardless of the color. White or amber wines may be preferred because they are less likely to stain the purificators. Sight-impaired people, however, often indicate a preference for red wine because they can see it better.

The bread need not be broken. Christ broke the bread for the purpose of distribution; he did not make that action necessary for the integrity of the consecration. Large wafers are available for breaking at the altar; but if used, the action should take place during the singing of the Agnus Dei (not at the consecration, lest the people assume it is required).

The heritage of 18th- and 19th-century German Pietism notwithstanding, the Lord's Supper should be offered each Lord's Day to those who hunger for Christ's body and blood and who are prepared to receive it. The fact that some of those present do not wish to receive should not prevent others from receiving. As the Apology (XXIV 1) states, in Evangelical Lutheran congregations the Lord's Supper is celebrated "every Sunday and on other festivals."[2] However, no rules or regulations are to be made concerning frequency. No one is to be compelled to come, nor are policies to be enacted that make it impossible for the faithful to receive the Lord's Supper (SC Preface 21).

The Eucharist[3] Service is to be the chief Sunday service as a matter of course, and the people are to be encouraged to commune. Neither the pastor nor the congregation should approach the noncommuning members of the body with a demand that they

---

[1] For those who cannot tolerate even the smallest amount of consecrated wine, see the counsel given in the CTCR document, *Theology and Practice of the Lord's Supper* (May 1983), p. 16. Whatever the decision, they should be assured by the pastor that in Holy Baptism, as well as in the absolution, they have received all the blessings of Christ's atonement.

[2] See especially Luther's *Admonition Concerning the Sacrament*, LW 38:124–137.

[3] Ibid., pp. 122f. Cf. *Theology and Practice of the Lord's Supper*, (May 1983), CTCR, especially pp. 20ff.; also Resolution 3-08, *Convention Proceedings*, The Lutheran Church—Missouri Synod, 1986.

commune as a condition of inclusion on the roster, lest the unprepared commune unworthily or be driven to despair. Nor should congregations set a minimum standard of annual communion for "members in good standing," lest the sacrament be blasphemed. The Supper of Christ's body and blood is a sacrament of the Gospel, not an ordinance of the Law.

Those invited to commune are baptized Christians who have been instructed in the chief parts of Christian doctrine (Ten Commandments, Creed, Lord's Prayer, Baptism, the Office of the Keys and the Confession, Sacrament of the Altar). Because altar fellowship is the most intimate expression of confessional unity, those who commune at the Lutheran altar are those who are in complete confessional agreement and fellowship with the other communicants. This practice, referred to as *close* communion, is an evangelical expression of the Lutheran church's love for the communicant and for Christ's supper. We do not wish to allow those who are not members of our confessional fellowship to be misled or confused by their participation in the sacrament at our altars. As Fritz points out, "*Abendmahlgemeinschaft ist Glaubensgemeinschaft.*"[4]

Persons who have been removed from the fellowship of the altar may not commune until the suspension has been lifted or the matter has been otherwise resolved, so that no division between the congregations may be caused. (See Unit IV, Ch. 13, regarding the pastoral use of the Lesser Ban and excommunication.) In order that the pastor might carry out his responsibilities in a faithful manner, it should be the congregation's policy that visitors are requested to make their intention to commune known to the pastor before the service.

Worthy Preparation

The necessary preparation for the Holy Supper is that a person believes that Christ, who gave his body and blood for the forgiveness of sins, continues to provide his forgiving body and blood "in, with, and under" the bread and wine in the Holy Supper. As the Small Catechism says, "He is worthy and well prepared who has faith in these words, 'Given and shed for you for the remission of sin.' "

The New Testament passages about the formational church's

---

[4] John H. C. Fritz, *Pastoral Theology* (St. Louis: Concordia, 1932; Concordia Heritage Series, 1977), p. 154.

worship[5] depict the believers gathered with only minimal structure to celebrate the continuing presence of Christ in their midst—to pray, to hear the Word, and to be united with him in the Sacrament of his body. "Where two or three come together in my name, there am I with them" (Matt. 18:20). "This is my body . . . . This is my blood" (Matt. 26:26–28; Mark 14:22, 24; Luke 22:19–20; 1 Cor. 11:24–25). "Is not the cup . . . a participation in the blood of Christ? And is not the bread . . . a participation in the body of Christ? Because there is one loaf, we, who are many, are one body, for we all partake of the one loaf" (1 Cor. 10:16–17).

Where there is joy, there exists the danger that the sinful heart will use that joy as an occasion for a fleshly celebration of self. We, who share that sinful flesh, can understand why some of the Corinthian Christians slipped into a focus on themselves (1 Cor. 11:17ff.)—and why they needed Paul's reminder that the purpose, focus, and power of the Sacrament is Christ alone. It is at this point that Paul gives the exhortation for self-examination, Do you truly understand the implications of what you are about to do: eat and drink the body of the Lord Jesus (verses 23–29)?

Thus, from New Testament times, self-examination (and, related to it, confession of one's sinfulness) became associated with the celebration of the Lord's Supper. This connection is reiterated in the second century *Didache,* which encouraged Christians to confess their sins before partaking in the Sacrament.[6]

Reaffirming both the doctrine and the pastoral concern, the Confessions state,

> We believe, teach, and confess that not only the genuine believers and those who are worthy but also the unworthy and the unbelievers receive the true body and blood of Christ; but if they are not converted and do not repent, they receive them not to life and salvation but to their judgment and condemnation.
>
> For although they reject Christ as a redeemer, they must accept him even contrary to their will as a strict judge. He is just as much present to exercise and manifest his judgment on unrepentant guests as he is to work life and consolation in the hearts of believing and worthy guests (FC Ep VII 16–17).
>
> [Therefore,] confession has not been abolished by the preachers on our side. The custom has been retained among us of not

---

[5] Acts 2:42; 20:7; 1 Cor. 11:33. Cf. also the related concepts in such passages as Eph. 5:29 and, perhaps, Heb. 9:11–10:25.

[6] Luther D. Reed, *The Lutheran Liturgy* (Philadelphia: Muhlenberg Press, 1947, reprinted in the Concordia Heritage Series [St. Louis: Concordia, 1985]), p. 256.

administering the sacrament to those who have not previously been examined and absolved. At the same time the people are carefully instructed concerning the consolation of the Word of absolution so that they may esteem absolution as a great and precious thing (AC XXV 1–2).

The church in its first millennium did not have a formalized confession-absolution rite of the congregation tied to the celebration of the Sacrament of the Altar. Later, in the Middle Ages, the church prescribed a confession based on the pastor's personal prayers spoken at the foot of the altar before the eucharistic service began (which originally were spoken in the sacristy).[7]

Because of the abuses of confession at the time of the Reformation and because of his emphasis on the Gospel-centered nature of the Sacrament of the Altar, Luther's reformation of the Divine Service (his Formula Missae and Deutsche Messe—cf. *Lutheran Worship*, Divine Service III) did not contain a rite of confession-absolution. He was concerned, though, that the people come prepared to the Lord's Table.[8]

> I think it enough for the applicants for communion to be examined or explored once a year. Indeed, a man may be so understanding that he need to be questioned only once in his lifetime or not at all. For, by this practice, we want to guard lest the worthy and unworthy alike rush to the Lord's Supper. . . .
>
> Now concerning private confession before communion, I still think as I have held heretofore, namely, that it neither is necessary nor should be demanded. Nevertheless, it is useful and should not be despised; for the Lord did not even require the Supper itself as necessary or establish it by law, but left it free to everyone when he said, "As often as you do this," etc.[9]

On the other hand, Luther gave careful attention to the proper preparation of communicants apart from the rite of confession-absolution. In his *Instruction for the Visitors of Parish Pastors* (the "Saxon Visitation Articles" of 1528), he wrote that (1) the pastors are to instruct the people to be reverent and penitent, and to desire to improve their lives, that the sacrament may not be dishonored or misused. Those who are guilty of open sins and who show no signs of contrition are not to be admitted. (2) No

---

[7] Ibid., p. 256–7.

[8] For the reformers, however, the use of confession-absolution as preparatory for reception of the Sacrament did not replace its basic use as the pastoral, individual application of the Office of the Keys (John 20:23). See Unit IV, Ch. 2.

[9] *An Order of Mass and Communion for the Church at Wittenberg, 1523*, LW 53:33–34.

one is to come to the sacrament without first seeing the pastor. The pastor is to inquire about his understanding of the sacrament and his need of Christian counsel. Only the penitent who are sorry for their sins are to be admitted. (3) Consequently, pastors are to teach their people (a) to remember the death of Christ which is the price of satisfaction; (b) to receive and take comfort in the sacrament as the effective sign of God's forgiveness; (c) to meditate on the words of the sacrament, "This is my body . . . ," etc., for these words awaken faith; and (d) to receive the sign both to awaken their faith and to instruct them in love, so that hatred and envy are replaced by mutual care and help and every service which God has commanded.[10]

In the decades following the Reformation, as Lutheranism became entrenched as the state church in many lands, some Lutheran leaders reacted against the resulting impersonalization, and they emphasized personal piety—thus paving the way for private confession-absolution to become *the* requirement for attendance at Holy Communion.[11] The Reformed churches in Germany, however, conducted penitential services—which seemed attractive to Lutherans also, especially to those pastors with congregations so large that private confession-absolution for everyone became a burden. Then, in the late 1600s,

> Casper Schade, a pastor in Berlin, provoked a great debate concerning private confession. The Elector of Brandenburg ruled that private confession should be retained for those who desired to use it; however, from that time on, there should be conducted every Saturday, at the time of confession, a confessional service (*ein Buszsermon[sic]*), at the altar, for the better preparation of the communicants; whoever wished to be excused from private confession should be permitted to go to the sacrament without it, provided he had not been convicted of a scandalous life. However, he was to announce his intention of going to the sacrament to the pastor during the previous week.

This confessional service became the general practice throughout Germany, but soon moved into the main liturgy (attached to the *Kyrie*).[12]

Today's methods of using confession-absolution as preparatory for the eucharist continue to vary. Some congregations con-

---

[10] LW 40:292.

[11] Historical information adapted from Fred Kramer, "The Pastor and Holy Communion," *The Pastor at Work* (St. Louis: Concordia Publishing House, 1960), p. 162f., which cites Heinrich Schmidt, *Die Geschichte des Pietismus* (C. H. Beck, 1863), pp. 267f.

[12] Ibid., p. 258.

duct a confessional service before the Divine Liturgy (and some of those offer individual absolution at the altar rail). Some occasionally omit the confession-absolution as a reminder that (1) the rite is optional and not a prerequisite for Communion, and (2) that the Divine Liturgy properly begins with the Introit Psalm. Others follow the practice of asking the communicants to register individually with the pastor, allowing him the opportunity (1) to discern that those intending to commune are able to carry out self-examination, and (2) to offer individual absolution to those making an individual confession.

The procedures for Communion announcement in our generation appear to be minimal. Even where personal registration is required or encouraged, seldom does one find any significant emphasis on catechesis and personal growth. Pastors should make use of every opportunity to teach and provide counsel to their parishioners, make use of the traditional structures provided them, and provide additional opportunities to insure that all communicants will receive the sacrament in a salutary and beneficial manner.

Whatever the congregational practice, the pastor will want to help the members understand the benefits of self-examination and confession: the forgiveness that God in Christ grants through his Word and Sacraments. Many have rebelled against "the pastor being able to forgive sins." The attitude reflects a gross misunderstanding of the Office of the Keys. As Fritz notes in his *Pastoral Theology*, "The Church therefore must insist that it has the power of absolution and, having received this power from God, must use it."[13]

The Usus: Liturgical Considerations

The Holy Scriptures do not provide ceremonial details for the celebration and reception of the Sacrament of the Altar, yet every gathering of a congregation in time and place will involve ritual. The conduct of the divine service is important because the Sacrament should always be celebrated in a manner appropriate to the gifts which Christ gives his people in Word and elements. His Word is to be spoken reverently; his body and blood are to be distributed in a respectful and orderly manner, in accordance with

---

[13] John H. C. Fritz, op. cit., p. 118. As with the consecration of the elements for the Sacrament of the Altar, the Absolution should be pronounced by the pastor. While Christ entrusted the Keys to all Christians, he entrusted their *public* use to his apostles and subsequently to those in the public ministry.

his institution. (For comments on the Divine Service, see Unit III, Ch. 1.)

Luther has left us an inspiring picture of the evangelical congregation gathered to celebrate the Sacrament. He writes,

> For, God be praised, in our churches we can show a Christian a true Christian mass according to the ordinance and institution of Christ, as well as according to the true intention of Christ and the church. There our pastor, bishop, or minister in the pastoral office, rightly and honorably and publicly called, having been previously consecrated, anointed, and born in Baptism as a priest of Christ without regard to the private chrism, goes to the altar. Publicly and plainly he sings what Christ has ordained and instituted in the Lord's Supper. He takes the bread and wine, gives thanks, distributes and gives them to the rest of us who are there and want to receive them on the strength of the words of Christ: "This is my body, this is my blood. Do this," etc. Particularly we who want to receive the sacrament kneel beside, behind, and around him, man, woman, young, old, master, servant, wife, maid, parents, and children, even as God brings us together there, all of us true, holy priests, sanctified by Christ's blood, anointed by the Holy Spirit and consecrated in Baptism. On the basis of this our inborn, hereditary priestly honor and attire we are present, have, as Revelation 5 [:4] pictures it, our golden crowns on our heads, harps and golden censers in our hands; and we let our pastor say what Christ has ordained, not for himself as though it were for his person, but he is the mouth for all of us and we all speak the words with him from the heart and in faith, directed to the Lamb of God who is present for us and among us, and who according to his ordinance nourishes us with his body and blood. This is our mass, and it is the true mass which is not lacking among us.[14]

The minister of the Sacrament of the Altar is the called and ordained servant who has been set apart to oversee, to preach and teach, and to administer the gifts of Christ (AC, Article XIV). In *very* exceptional cases (not for mere convenience), members of offices auxiliary to the office of the public ministry or other qualified men may temporarily be called upon to serve (under proper supervision) in a leadership capacity belonging to the office of the ministry, including the administration of the Sacrament. How-

---

[14] *The Private Mass and the Consecration of Priests, 1533*, LW 38:204f.

ever, performing such functions does not make those who do them holders of the office of the public ministry.[15]

The presiding minister and assisting ministers should be vested appropriately, in vestments that cover their street clothing. Their vestments help remind them and the congregation that the clergy serves not in its own name or by its own authority and worthiness but in Christ's name, in his stead, and under his command. The black Geneva gown so common in late generations came into use in Lutheranism as a service vestment by imperial edict in 1811. Its use was strongly resisted by confessional pastors. Frontier conditions in North America led to its eventual supremacy. Many today consider the surplice and stole or an alb or eucharistic vestments as more appropriate to thankful praise and celebration. The practice in many Scandinavian congregations is for the pastor to wear a chasuble over the alb from the Offertory to the close of the service.

During the Offertory the altar and vessels are prepared for the celebration of the sacrament. If the bread and wine are brought forward at this time, it ought to be done without ostentation; not our gifts to him but the Lord's gift to us of his body and blood stands at the center of our celebration.

The Words of Institution (the *Verba*) are chanted or said reverently over all the elements to be used in the Supper (FC, SD, VII, 75); and only that which will be distributed should be consecrated. It is an old Lutheran practice that the communicants are encouraged to speak the Words of Institution *sub voce* while the presiding minister sings or says them aloud. The *Verba* are the creative words of the Almighty Lord who brings all things to being by the Word of his mouth. The use of his Word in the supper is never simply a recitation of what was said and done in the upper room on the night of his betrayal. By them the Lord who first spoke these words then gives even now what the words say in and under the elements over which they are spoken. They are both Words of Institution and Words of Consecration.

The sign of the cross usually is made over the bread and wine being set apart. If an additional supply is called for during the distribution, it too should be consecrated. Under no circumstances should communicants be given bread and wine over

---

[15] In this matter, of course, there needs to be a concern for the order and unity of practice in the church, lest disunity and confusion in any way detract from the celebration of the Sacrament. See the CTCR document, *The Ministry: Offices, Procedures, and and Nomenclature*, pp. 16, 35–37.

which the Words of Institution have not been spoken.[16]

As Luther makes clear in the Formula Missae and Deutsche Messe, the presiding minister may commune himself first, in the same manner he communes a member of his congregation, with the usual formula: "Take, eat; this is the very body of Christ, given for you . . ." In many congregations, the presiding minister receives the Sacrament from the assisting minister or an elder of the church, each communing the other in turn.

At the distribution, the presiding minister properly ought to distribute the body of Christ. In this important pastoral responsibility, he exercises his episcopal supervision of the communicants. Assisting ministers may distribute the blood of Christ.[17] Communicants may approach the altar in groups or in an orderly line. They may kneel or stand for the reception (whatever helps the communicants to honor the Christ who has set his precious table).

Whatever the manner of distribution, eating and drinking are the two indicated acts; the body and blood are offered to each communicant individually, that they may eat and drink according to the Lord's institution. While not calling into question the Christian churches which practice intinction, Lutherans understand that the word of Christ calls for each communicant to both eat and drink. Accordingly, intinction has not generally been practiced in Lutheran churches.

Communion from the chalice is the historic practice of the evangelical Lutheran church and, while not scripturally mandated, is generally encouraged. The use of individual cups is a 20th century innovation. When there are compelling reasons for the use of individual cups, they should be treated with the same humility and reverence as the chalice and its contents.

After all have communed, the sacramental vessels are again covered or removed.

The Holy Scriptures do not specify the exact moment when the presence of the body and blood of the Lord "in, with, and under" the elements begins and ends. Theological opinions differ on this matter. The classical Lutheran principle "extra usam nulla sacramentum" has been used both to affirm that the body and blood of Christ remain for those to be communed later (e.g., the infirmed), as well as in support of the opposite view that outside of the Communion service itself there is only bread and wine (See also SA, III VI 1). What is clear is that the consecrated bread

---

[16] *Lutheran Worship Altar Book*, Note 28, p. 32.

[17] Ibid., p. 31.

and wine of the supper have been set apart for one purpose, the communion of the people. And therefore the unused elements should be treated with fitting reverence so that the Lord may be honored and that none of his children may be offended or caused to stumble. Therefore, what remains of the consecrated bread and wine, if individual cups are used, may be consumed or stored for future sacramental use. If a large amount of wine is left in the chalice, it may be poured into the *sacrarium/piscina* or poured out on bare earth. It is the responsibility of the presiding or a delegated assisting minister to supervise the disposal of the elements.

Other Settings of the Lord's Supper

Every celebration of the Lord's Supper, whether it takes place in the church sanctuary or at the bedside of the afflicted, is by nature a public, congregational event. As an indication of this public nature of the celebration, the presiding pastor should invite other present and eligible communicants to receive the Sacrament with the pastor and the afflicted. (This might include, e.g., those who accompany the pastor in the visitation and ministry to the sick, or other family members who might be present.)

The Sacrament is normally consecrated in the presence of those who receive it (although some of the earliest church orders provide for the communion of the sick from elements consecrated at the public service). The evangelical Lutheran practice is that the words of Christ's testament should be sung or spoken clearly over the bread and wine in the presence of the communicants that they may receive the Sacrament always with the Lord's words in their ears. In addition, he should use as much of the ordinary and propers of the divine service as is practical under the circumstances.

The pastor may wear at least some of the outward marks of his office and order—Walther suggests as a minimum the *beffchen* (in contemporary terms, a clerical collar) to remind both people and himself that he does not come in his own name or with his own expert word and gifts. By his dress and manner the pastor presents himself as the servant of another. He speaks a word and does a work given him by his Lord.

If the Sacrament is desired at the services of marriage and burial, pastor and people should understand that these services are public and congregational and that the members of the congregation are in all cases invited to attend and participate fully. Indeed, the use of the congregation's place of worship always implies that, whatever the service, it is congregational in nature.

The celebration of the Sacrament of the Altar on such occasions, though discouraged, can only be permitted if the public, congregational nature of the service is acknowledged and all (and only) eligible communicants are invited to participate and receive. On this basis propers for the divine service on the occasion of a marriage and the commemoration of the departed have been provided in *Lutheran Worship*. It would be improper to limit communion participation to the bride and bridegroom or the deceased's immediate family.

Extra-congregational celebrations at synodical and district conventions, seminaries, synodical colleges and high schools, and special gatherings may be held, but it is a synodical practice that they be conducted under the sponsorship of a Lutheran congregation and under the supervision of the host pastor. As the Commission on Theology and Church Relations has pointed out[18], the Scripturally mandated practices are three: an understanding of the reality of the Sacrament; a refusal to commune those who are impenitent; and a supervision in an orderly and evangelical fashion. The document adds as guidelines that extra-congregational and transparochial celebrations of the Sacrament be discussed with the advisory and supervising pastor (including the District President), that a host congregation be secured, and that the congregation's pastor ordinarily be the celebrant.

That the guidelines are not Scripturally mandated can be seen, in part, from the Synod's Biblical understanding of the church that forms the basis for the CTCR's document *The Ministry: Offices, Procedures, and Nomenclature*, September 1981. In it, the Commission affirms that "the church" is not simply individual congregations acting separately, but that they together also may be called "church" and carry out its function of (e.g.) calling a pastor to a non-parish ministry.[19] However, as the document stresses (page 23),

> The New Testament (1 Corinthians) assumes that Holy Communion will be celebrated in a context where the faith and life of the communicants are known. The congregational setting, under normal circumstances, is the locus where the . . . Scripturally mandated Communion practices can be carried out in an evangelical manner and in accord with the doctrines of the church and ministry, and where the mutual responsibility of pastors and members to each other is safeguarded.

---

[18] *Theology and Practice of the Lord's Supper*, May 1983, pp. 23f.

[19] Ibid., pp. 20–21.

UNIT IV
THE PASTOR APPLIES
THE WORD AND SACRAMENT
IN INDIVIDUAL
CIRCUMSTANCES

1
The Calling Pastor

> To perform the functions of a pastor in an evangelical manner;
> to aid, counsel, and guide members of all ages and social con-
> ditions; to visit the sick and the dying; to admonish the indif-
> ferent and the erring . . . .[1]

By virtue of the above words in the call to the pastoral office,
the congregation both invites and expects the pastor to administer
the means of grace not only in the public worship services, meetings, and public gatherings of the congregation, but also in numerous individual, personal, and private circumstances wherever
and whenever need and circumstance dictate.

While the nature of the pastoral call may vary with the circumstances, three basic features should characterize every
visitation:

1. *Role faithfulness*: Regardless of any other roles he may
have—member of a civic organization, participant on a bowling
or softball team, close friend of a specific member—he must always
remember his primary role as pastor. When not functioning as a
pastor, his members may encourage him to "let down his hair."
Yet later, when one of these parishioners seeks professional counsel and aid, previous non-pastoral relationships may lead to a loss
of objectivity and prevent the pastor from carrying out his ministry. Role faithfulness is absolutely essential for both pastor and
parishioners.

---

[1] Quoted from *The Diploma of Vocation* of the Lutheran Church—Missouri
Synod, 1989.

Does this mean operating with a "double standard," a different set of criteria to which pastors must "measure up"? Yes and no. The same Christ is example to all, and the same paradigm of holiness and love is the goal for all. Nor is it really a matter of a "standard" that one must "live up to," but rather a "pattern" that one will "grow into." Nevertheless, in human eyes the answer may have to be "yes." For we must make, as well as we are able, evaluations of human conduct *because*, in God's economy, the conduct of the pastor is paradigmatic of the life of Christ. Also, the consequences of the behavior of these men—whether they succeed or fail—are so far-reaching for the spiritual lives of others. . . . As one who preaches the love of Christ to others, the pastor also portrays that love in his self-sacrifice for other's benefit. As one who urges others to cultivate the fruit of the Spirit in their lives, the pastor shows what "love, joy, peace, patience, kindness, goodness, faithfulness, gentleness, self-control" (Gal. 5:22–23) entail in daily living.[2]

In addition to whatever "pull" the pastor feels to "be himself," he dare not forget the pastoral office's "incarnational aspect" of being God's representative and standing in his stead (cf. e.g., 1 Cor. 4:15f; 1 Thess. 2:13; 5:12).

2. *Purpose and goal*: Whenever a pastor makes any type of pastoral call, he should do so for a specific purpose that grows out of his overall concern for the spiritual life of the parishioner. Establishing and keeping the purpose in mind will help the pastor also manage his schedule effectively.

3. *Preparation*: Adequate preparation consistent with the purpose and goal of the call is necessary.

Personal calls are very time consuming. Therefore the pastor must commit himself to do it systematically and faithfully. Unless he has established a schedule for calling that he follows with rare exception, the pastor should phone in advance to indicate his desire to call. When an established schedule or appointment is set which the pastor is unable to meet, a telephone call is in order.

The General Pastoral Call

Humanly speaking, effective spiritual ministry depends in large measure on building trust levels.[3] Appropriate pastoral call-

---

[2] Grothe, Jonathan F. *Reclaiming Patterns of Pastoral Ministry: Jesus and Paul* (St. Louis: Concordia Publishing House, 1988), pp. 82f.

[3] Because trust relationships are built over long periods of time, the pastor should commit himself also to a reasonable term of service at a given place. Some have suggested that effective ministry begins only after five to seven years in one

ing fosters this mutual confidence and trust. It enables the pastor to keep his finger on the pulse of the congregation. Understanding the hopes, fears, desires, joys, sorrows, and priorities of his parishioners will make the pastor's preaching and teaching more relevant to the support, strength, forgiveness, hope, and love under the Gospel that his people need.

Pastoral Care of the Sick and Hospitalized

The sick and their families often wonder about the relation between sin and sickness: "What did I do that I have to suffer this affliction? Why is the Lord treating me this way?" The question may reflect the age-old tendency towards self-righteousness or may inadvertently imply that God is vengeful and vindictive, directly punishing the sick for specific sins committed. While all sickness/death results from Adam and Eve's original sin, it is not punishment for specific sins. In some instances, a physical cause-and-effect relationship can be substantiated between a specific sin and a consequent disease; e.g., a person who is sexually promiscuous may, as a result of that sin, contract venereal disease. But physical cause-and-effect does not establish divine retribution on the individual level.

The suffering parishioner needs the comfort that God has promised to deal with his people in mercy because of Christ. Because of the predicament that humanity brought upon itself (Gen. 3), God intervened and provided forgiveness for all people through Christ's life, death, and resurrection. The Gospel offers not judgment but comfort and hope in the promises of God, especially this consoling promise that "all things work together for good to those who love God" (Rom. 8:28). The words of 1 Peter 1:3–9, Hebrews 12, and Romans 8 are particularly instructive here.

The pastor can offer only the comfort that God alone gives (2 Cor. 1:4) through his Word. To that end, the pastoral visit includes a meditation (not a sermon) on applicable Scripture, an appropriate prayer with the Lord's Prayer, and the benediction. Depending on circumstances, Holy Communion may also be included.

Keep in mind that prayer is not the Word nor a means of grace. The time available may be short and the attention span limited, but a few well-chosen words of promise from Scripture carry the blessings of God. It goes without saying that the pastor should

---

place (Schuetze, Armand W. and Erwin J. Habeck. *The Shepherd Under Christ* [Milwaukee: Northwestern Publishing House], 1981).

avoid argument and controversy and should remain pleasant, friendly, and open.

As a general guideline, the more serious the illness, the more frequently the patient is to be visited and the shorter the call.[4] As the patient recovers, the calls may become longer and less frequent. Ordinarily a hospital call should last no longer than five to ten minutes, but there are circumstances when common sense will dictate a longer visit.

In many cases, periods of convalescence of varying lengths take place, and pastoral care will extend as long as the need exists, whether in the hospital or at home. The pastor will also remember to extend care to the family of the sick. In fact, at times the family will be the major focus of pastoral care, especially the children who are least able to handle the absence of their father, mother, or sibling.

During extended illnesses, the pastor should include the Lord's Supper as a regular part of his pastoral care. Keep in mind that some members, particularly older members, may associate hospitalization with dying, and consider the Lord's Supper as "last rites." Therefore, the Sacrament should be offered to the hospitalized in as non-threatening circumstances as possible. The pastor might suggest that upon his next visit, one or two days hence, he would be prepared to commune the patient—thus allowing the patient the opportunity to prepare. The spouse, children, and friends who are in communing fellowship with the congregation also may be invited to be present and participate when the pastor makes his call. It is understood that a devotional word from Scripture will be included, that confession and absolution will take place, as well as the consecration and distribution of the elements.

The Presurgical Patient

The presurgical patient requires special attention. Rare is the person who does not experience a degree of anxiety over the prospect of undergoing surgery, regardless of how minor. The pastor will offer spiritual resources that will enable the patient to cope with his fears. The pastor should exercise caution, however, and not presume to know the specific fear. Allow the patient to express his true concerns and worries. Deal with them. Often they grow out of an interpersonal matter with spouse or child, rather than anxiety or worry over the outcome of the surgery.

---

[4] The patient who has been diagnosed as terminally ill is a special case discussed later in Chapter 5 of this Unit.

A pastoral call the evening before the scheduled surgery is usually best since preparation for surgery ordinarily begins three hours before the operation. The pastor should consider meeting the family at the hospital the morning of surgery and staying with them until the patient is in recovery.

Calling on the New Mother

Visits on the obstetrics floor are usually happy occasions. They provide the opportunity for parents and pastor to celebrate the marvelous, creative action of our loving Lord and discuss baptism, its blessings and dynamics.

A few words of caution: The pastor should adhere to the hospital's visiting hours out of consideration for the staff as well as for privacy needs of the maternity ward. When the child is born into a two-parent home, the pastor may wish to schedule his visit to coincide with the father's in order to emphasize a family ministry (shortening the visit, however, to allow the husband and wife time for privacy). In instances when the newborn is not the "perfectly normal, healthy child" for which all have prayed, the pastor will need a keen ear to hear the specific spiritual and emotional pain that this has laid on the parents and minister to this with the assurance of a gracious, loving God in Christ.

The Pastoral Care of the Shut-In

In an aging society the number of homebound or institutionalized also grows. A person may be shut-in for a number of reasons; however, most are aging members of the congregation. If neglected by the church in its ministry, those members will seek spiritual nurture and comfort from other sources. Shut-ins are especially vulnerable to the electronic church. The number of radio and television religious broadcasts has multiplied, and shut-ins have been so enamored of a TV evangelist that some have been led even to "participate" in the Lord's Supper—the "celebration" taking place on the television, the communing in the living room. If nothing else, this phenomenon shows that the spiritual needs of many shut-ins are not being met by in-person ministry.

Since most shut-ins also desire to maintain a significant link with congregational life, sufficient time should be allotted to catch up on congregation news and to let the shut-in express personal feelings and concerns. The pastor can tailor his devotional message to include these ideas in preparation for confession, absolution, and the celebration of the Lord's Supper. If the pastoral call must be limited in time, it should not be done at the expense of the Word and Sacrament ministry.

Pastoral Care of the Mentally Ill and Emotionally Disturbed

An evangelical spirit, a pastoral heart, and sound pastoral judgment are especially necessary when ministering to the mentally ill and the emotionally disturbed.

As in all calls, the pastor will direct the person to the saving promises of God, rooted in the death and resurrection of Jesus Christ, stressing especially the individual application of the forgiveness of sins. Since many mental and emotional problems appear to stem from unresolved guilt, the pastor will determine the appropriateness of a sacramental ministry in each individual situation. (Mental illness and emotional disturbance do not automatically disqualify a person from receiving the Lord's Supper.)

When the pastor learns that a member has been institutionalized, he should determine whether it is appropriate for him to call on his member. If so, he should also inquire about treatment schedules. A telephone call to the institution will save travel time, effort, and possible embarrassment.

Of greater importance, the pastor, as part of the healing team, ought to meet with the doctor to determine an appropriate spiritual approach. The pastor might well cultivate a professional relationship with the physician, for their efforts should support each other.

Pastoral Care of the Imprisoned

In rare instances a member of the congregation is arrested and jailed. Providing pastoral care appropriate to the situation, the pastor can assure the member that he will stand with him in his difficult circumstances, without presuming guilt or innocence. The pastor should not be premature in assuring forgiveness without being reasonably convinced of genuine repentance.

The Pastor, His Family, and Social Calls

The pastor, his wife, or the entire family may be invited by congregation members—by the poor and the wealthy, by the readily lovable or the unappealing—for social gatherings ranging from the informal to the formal. The pastor and his family should always conduct themselves in a manner that will enhance the office of the ministry. The family need not be unbending or humorless in order to be Christ-like. Yet the pastor and his family must be well-schooled in the social graces lest, by their lack of manners and proper etiquette, they become an embarrassment.

While the plethora of etiquette details cannot be spelled out here, the theory behind them can: To show consideration for all and to put others at ease so that the time together can be pleasant and uplifting.

Multiplying Care by and among the Laity

Some congregations view spiritual calls as solely the pastor's responsibility. Yet the Biblical injunctions to visit the sick, comfort the bereaved, and call on the imprisoned are meant for all Christians.[5] Therefore, as an important aspect of his responsibility, the pastor will equip lay members for services for which they have the requisite talents (Eph. 4). He will recruit, train (by leadership and example), and assign members of the congregation to the vital areas of Christian care, applying the doctrine of the universal priesthood for the mutual blessing of the entire congregation.

Priorities and Perspectives

Which type of call takes priority: those on regular members, on prospects, or on delinquents? All calls are vital, yet some are more urgent than others. Time constraints require pastoral judgment as to which call comes first. As a general principle, give priority to those Christians closest to the end of their life—the critically and terminally ill—followed by the aging shut-ins. (The principle does not preclude changing the list of order of importance when events indicate adjustments.)

No matter what the priority, "image" (be an imitator and model of) the Christ who "had compassion." He ministered in one-on-one settings as well as to groups. Jesus not only made himself available, he actively sought the needy. Faithful pastors will do the same, taking seriously the incarnational aspect of the pastoral office. Faithful calling and caring for people is perhaps the most concrete way a pastor can show that he has been touched by the Gospel and, as Christ's undershepherd, compassionately tends those entrusted to his care.

---

[5] Their calls, of course, are not a substitute for his "official visits" as spiritual father of the family. No one can take the place of the called *Seelsorger.*

2
Individual Confession and Absolution

Private (i.e., individual) confession-absolution[1] may be the most important activity in the pastor's role as *Seelsorger*. Just as God provides salvation to individuals (see, e.g., Ps. 51:10; Jer. 31:18; Matt. 18:12–14; John 3:5–6; 1 Cor. 12:3), so private confession-absolution touches the individual. It is nothing other than applying the full Gospel to one hurting soul. The connection between absolution (no matter how applied) and the Office of the Keys is not lost in the Confessions (see, e.g., the Smalcald Articles, Part III, VIII 1). Therefore, the *Augustana* affirms (XI 1), "It is taught among us that private absolution should be retained and not allowed to fall into disuse." And Luther can say, "When I urge you to go to confession, I am simply urging you to be a Christian." (LC V, A Brief Exhortation 32)

The focus of confession-absolution, of course, is not on the enumeration of sins but on the absolution and the God who provides it through his church. The Confessions assure,

> We also keep confession, especially because of absolution, which is the Word of God that the power of the keys proclaims to individuals by divine authority. It would therefore be wicked to remove private absolution from the church. (Ap XII 99–100)

---

[1] Though generally termed "private confession," two points must be kept in mind. First, the term "confession" should be understood to include the absolution that always follows a Christian's confession. Second, the absolution is part of the *public* ministry, even though it may be done in a private, one-on-one setting.

So if there is a heart that feels its sin and desires consolation, it has here a sure refuge when it hears in God's Word that through a man God looses and absolves him from his sins. (LC V, A Brief Exhortation 14)

At the same time the people are carefully instructed . . . so that they may esteem absolution as a great and precious thing. It is not the voice or word of the man who speaks it, but it is the Word of God, who forgives sin, for it is spoken in God's stead and by God's command. . . . We also teach that God requires us to believe this absolution as much as if we heard God's voice from heaven, that we should joyfully comfort ourselves with absolution, and that we should know that through such faith we obtain forgiveness of sins. (AC XXV 2–4)

We advise: If you are poor and miserable, then go and make use of the healing medicine. He who feels his misery and need will develop such a desire for confession that he will run toward it with joy. (LC V, A Brief Exhortation 26–27)

While some sections of the Confessions (e.g., the *Augustana*) focus specifically on private confession-absolution between the pastor and lay individual, the Book of Concord does not limit this gift from God to that setting. In the Large Catechism, for example, written in 1529, Luther speaks of three kinds of confession;[2] privately to God; to a neighbor sinned against; and privately ("secretly") to a third party—the first two required and the third "left to everyone to use whenever he needs it."[3] However, Luther adds concerning private confession-absolution,

If you are a Christian, you should be glad to run more than a hundred miles for [private] confession, not under compulsion but rather coming and compelling us [the pastors] to offer it. For here the compulsion must be inverted; we must come under the command and you must come into freedom. We compel no man, but allow ourselves to be compelled, just as we are compelled to preach and administer the sacraments.

---

[2] LC V, A Brief Exhortation. The Small Catechism, written at the same time, differentiates only between confession before God and before the "confessor"(SC V), a distinction Luther had previously made in 1520 in *The Babylonian Captivity of the Church*, LW 36:85f.

[3] Luther had previously made this three-fold distinction in 1526 in *The Sacrament of the Body and Blood of Christ—Against the Fanatics* LW 36:354–361. The reader is urged to review these pages in their entirety along with the pertinent sections in the Confessions.

The Place of Confession-Absolution in Pastoral Counseling

Walter J. Koehler points out in his *Counseling and Confession*,[4]

> Today few people come to a pastor with the intention of making a formal confession. Instead they come to discuss problems, to seek direction and help, and to consider God's will for their lives. . . . It is one of the conclusions of this study that the pastoral counseling process could serve as an excellent preparation for the act of individual confession of sins.

> To a certain extent, the proclamation of the forgiveness of sins (the key ingredient in all of the public ministry, including private confession-absolution) excludes the activities usually associated with "counseling"—identifying problems, setting goals, etc. However, private confession-absolution and counseling together might be pictured as a physician dealing with some itchy, spreadable skin disease. To be sure, the doctor sees his primary goal as curing the disease; but at the same time he needs to treat its outward manifestations lest, by scratching, the disease spreads and becomes harder to cure. Similarly, the pastor understands that he will use the Office of the Keys (1) to treat the real disease of humanity's sin, as well as (2) to support the individual in overcoming sin's expression in the disruption of human relationships.[5]

Some Practical Suggestions for the Use of Confession-Absolution in the Counseling Setting

Uncover the Sin Involved. In some cases, this will be difficult. For example, a person may come with a sense of guilt over that which is no sin—e.g., a single adult wanting to move out of the parent's home in order to establish psychological individuality. If, in this example, the single adult needs the reassurance of God's grace, the pastor ought not withhold it. However, the sin of hostility that might exist between that person and the parents should not be confused with the adult need for psychological separation/individuality. Thus, going full circle, absolution might be used to free this single adult of a false guilt so that counseling techniques can help him or her understand and deal with both the psychological need and uncover the sin of hostility which is dealt with in absolution.

---

[4] Concordia: St. Louis, 1982, p. 58.

[5] For more on this discussion, see the beginning paragraphs of Unit IV, Ch. 3.

Some penitents will come for absolution fully aware of their sin. If so, the pastor should not burden consciences by unduly asking for details and explanations—which might, however, suggest to the penitent that the sin is either too slight or excusable.

On the other hand, formal absolution is neither required nor appropriate for every counseling situation. In some cases, the counselee may be seeking help in dealing with an issue in which sin, *per se*, is not involved. In other cases, the counselee may not be ready or able to confess any culpability. And some counselees will come for help in applying the grace of God which they already know is most assuredly theirs. Only as the pastor listens to the person's heart will he determine the need for private confession-absolution.

Formalize and Pronounce the Absolution. Lest the counselee misunderstand the pastor's absolution to be conditional upon some human factor (such as a full enumeration of sins, an intention to do certain acts to be reconciled with the person who has been hurt, etc.), and lest the counselee confuse the absolution with some general sage suggestion, the pastor will do well to establish a method that clearly presents the word of absolution for what it truly is. At the very least, he might use the same words the person is accustomed to hear during the Divine Liturgy,

> Upon this your confession, I, as a called and ordained servant of the Word, announce the grace of God to [all of] you, and in the stead and by the command of my Lord Jesus Christ I forgive you [all] your sin[s] in the name of the Father and of the ✠ Son and of the Holy Spirit.[6]

The rite for Individual Confession and Absolution (*Lutheran Worship*, p. 310–11) ably meets this recommendation to formalize the absolution, although (depending on circumstances) the penitent may perceive its use as too formal. In that case, the pastor might simply hear the confession, pronounce the absolution, offer a prayer on behalf of the penitent, lead the Lord's Prayer, and pronounce the benediction.

In addition, body posture and location can help emphasize the absolution as proclamation. For example, the pastor might place his hand on the penitent's bowed head and, at the name of Christ, make the sign of the cross on his forehead (in remembrance of that same sign at baptism). If the counseling session is taking place within the sacristy/church office, pastor and counselee might move to the altar rail or next to the baptismal font for the confession and absolution. Depending upon anticipated local

---

[6] Divine Service I, *Lutheran Worship* (Concordia: St. Louis, 1982), p. 137.

response, the pastor might even don a stole to further symbolize that in pronouncing absolution he is functioning as Christ's representative in the public ministry.

Confidentiality: To the extent that speaking the absolution is being the voice of God, so hearing the confession is being the ears of God. To the confessional prayer of Psalm 51, to "wash away all my iniquity and cleanse me from my sin . . . [to] create in me a clean heart," the absolution responds with Ps. 103:12, "As far as the east is from the west, so far has he [God] removed our transgressions from us." Therefore, under no circumstances should a pastor reveal anything told him in confession by a penitent. Normally, the so-called confessional seal will be recognized and respected by civil authorities, but even if it were not, the pastor must stand by the promises which he has solemnly made before the altar and the congregation in his ordination and installation (i.e., not to divulge the sins confessed to him, *Lutheran Worship Agenda*, pp.212, 225). The pastor who uses the specifics heard in the confessional (even if from a previous parish) as "sermon fodder" drives his flock away from this most blessed opportunity for personalized justification.

The pastor may be confronted with the rare dilemma of hearing the confession of a sin that is also a grievous crime (e.g., criminal physical abuse of a child or murder). Such a penitent should be encouraged to report himself to the civil authorities, assured that the Lord goes with him and confident that the Holy Spirit who has worked repentance in his heart will give him the strength to (1) make peace with his neighbor, (2) make restitution to those whom he has wronged, and (3) submit to the authorities, even to the punishment of the state God has instituted for him. The pastor can offer to accompany the penitent on this most difficult journey, thereby both strengthening his pastoral relationship and maintaining the confidentiality of the confessional. If all efforts to persuade the person to confess to the authorities prove useless, the pastor may question whether the confession he heard was a true confession to God.[7] In the event that a pastor feels he must report the information to the civil authorities, he should inform the penitent of his intention to do so, thereby avoiding the charge of "betrayal of trust." The pastor cannot allow himself to become a party to the crime by abetting it through silence and,

---

[7] Cf. AC XII 6, Ap XII 131–132, 169–170. Absolution, of course, is not dependent upon subsequent works of faith, and the amended, new life in Christ, is never perfect. However, faith cannot coexist with the intention to sin or a deliberate persistence in sin (FC Ep III 11; IV 11, 19; Ap IV 142–144).

thus, belie the church as the people of God. No simple answer can be given for the "how" of resolving this dilemma; it is part of the heartache that stands alongside the joys of being a *Seelsorger*.

Encouraging Individual Confession-Absolution in the Congregation

Given the reality of religious life in North America, few congregations and and laypeople have ever experienced the joyful freedom and relief of the personalized justification offered in private confession—and, therefore, may be hesitant to try it.

One procedure some pastors have found helpful is a mid-week service during Lent (or Advent) that includes a confessional litany followed by individual absolution at the altar rail, the pastor speaking each person's name. While certainly not as intense as absolution following private confession, laity who have experienced this limited personal absolution report a heightened awareness of the impact of God's grace.

Even though not requested as such, the pastor may look for and use confession made during counseling as an occasion for vocalized absolution. The pronouncement may seem "out of character" to the penitent, but that feeling allows the pastor to explain his role as *pastoral* counselor under the Office of the Keys.

In addition, the pastor might well set aside an evening a week (or time on a Saturday) for "visiting the pastor in his office"—a time that normally would prevent no one from making an appointment. Announcing this as (among other things) "a time to discuss how God's grace and love touch the difficulties of life" will help the laity anticipate something more than casual conversation.

A retreat (e.g., for the church council, couples club, or youth) provides an excellent opportunity to carry out the practice of private confession-absolution. Following adequate preparation by the pastor at the retreat, an hour or two may be set aside for private self-examination, during which time the pastor is available for private confession-absolution. Even if only one person uses the opportunity, its on-going availability and benefit will be established.

Just as important as making private confession-absolution available to the laity is the pastor's own private confession and reception of absolution. Granted, neither is commanded in Scripture; but the pastor can hardly extol the benefits of that which he himself has not even tried. Nor will he be adequately helpful in overcoming his parishioners' hesitancies if he hasn't discovered and dealt with his own. The pastor who makes private confession and receives private absolution soon rejoices with Luther:

If I knew that God were in a certain place and would absolve me I would not go to some other place, but would receive absolution in that place as often as I could.[8]

---

[8] *The Sacrament—Against the Fanatics*, LW 36:359.

3
The Pastor as Counselor

The members of a congregation look to their pastor to nurture their Christian faith and life as well as to help them with particular problems. Even though most pastors are not primarily counselors by training or calling, they often serve in that capacity. Individual pastoral counseling, while drawing upon and benefiting from extensive research and practice in the broad field of counseling, is intended to facilitate the application of God's Law and Gospel for those who turn to the pastor for help in problem-solving and amending their lives. In addition to all the resources of the Christian faith (see, e.g., Ch. 2 on confesson-absolution), the pastor also uses counseling techniques compatible with Scripture.

The Theological Understanding for Individual Counseling

The objective of pastoral counseling is the same as for everything the pastor does: To offer peace from sin, forgiven through Christ, which works to bring about a substantial and radical change of mind and life.

Human beings, because of sin, are at birth spiritually bankrupt, mere husks of humanity. In order for any human to live out even some of the potential that God intended (sanctification), he must become aware of his sorry state; trust that Jesus Christ has covered the sinfulness of all people and has offered, through faith, the potential for wholeness; and feel that the Holy Spirit brings about this change in the individual's entire being.

This indispensable basis for pastoral counseling is summarized by St. Paul in 2 Cor. 5:17–20.

> If anyone is in Christ, he is a new creation; the old has gone, the new has come! All this is from God, who reconciled us to himself through Christ and gave us the ministry of reconciliation: that God was reconciling the world to himself in Christ, not counting men's sins against them. And he has committed to us the message of reconciliation. . . . We implore you on Christ's behalf: Be reconciled to God.

It is on the basis of this reconciling work of God in Christ that St. Paul makes his appeal in Rom. 12:1–2.

> Therefore, I urge you, my brothers, in view of God's mercy, to offer your bodies as living sacrifices, holy and pleasing to God— this is your spiritual act of worship. Do not conform any longer to the pattern of this world, but be transformed by the renewing of your mind. Then you will be able to test and approve what God's will is—his good, pleasing and perfect will.

These words of St. Paul clearly show that pastoral counseling is the imparting of the mercies of God. And this has as its ultimate effect the renewal of mind for the transformation of thoughts, feelings, and behavior—toward obedience to the will of God and for personal fulfillment and happiness.

For that purpose, the pastor uses confession, absolution, and prayer in counseling; and for the person properly prepared he encourages participation in the congregation's celebration of the Lord's Supper.

Some Specifics of the Pastoral Counseling Process

The task of pastoral counseling begins with the counselor *and* counselee identifying problems, both the obvious and the underlying issues—especially that of one's sinful nature and the problems it causes (Rom. 7:15–23). Following that, they must agree on and set goals for changes in personal behavior, identify hindrances to reaching the goals, and determine what is to be done to overcome the obstacles and achieve the objectives. When the counselor is a pastor, he has the special ministry and privilege to communicate the Gospel as God's own means for accomplishing all this (Rom. 7:24—8:16).

Ordinarily pastoral counseling should be short-term (a period of six to eight sessions) at a mutually-agreed-upon schedule. Such an agreement between the two parties should be reviewed and modified from time to time by the agreement of both. When it seems advisable, a pastor may suggest referral to a specialist. However, when referral takes place, the pastor continues to relate to the counselee exclusively as a spiritual advisor and, depending upon circumstances, sometimes in cooperation with the primary therapist.

The pastoral counselor's success in speaking the truth in love requires listening caringly and carefully before talking so that the counselee is able to hear the Word as accurately and nondefensively as possible and not resist the Holy Spirit working through the Word in a forthright discussion. To do so, the pastor must avoid becoming defensive (just as he also helps the counselee to be nondefensive).

As much as possible the counseling pastor adopts a nondirective-directive approach. He begins with people where they are and *leads* them to analyze their problems and discover the help that God has for them. For an outstanding Biblical model of this kind of counseling, read Jesus' conversation with the Samaritan woman at Jacob's well (John 4:1–26).

Principles of Diagnosis

Most parish pastors are not mental health professionals and have no clinical training for diagnosing mental disorders. However, pastors need to be specialists in diagnosing spiritual problems for which they are expected to have special competence and responsibility. A pastoral counselor must not be content to think only in medical or psychological terms. His primary role is to understand people's concerns theologically and to supply theological resources for their needs.

Paul W. Pruyser, in his book *The Minister as Diagnostician*[1] (in the chapter "Guidelines for Pastoral Diagnoses") suggests exploring a number of themes with the counselee:

- The holy
- Faith
- Grace
- Repentance [which, the Lutheran pastor knows, grows out of sin and guilt]
- Providence
- Relationships
- Vocation

For these issues, Pruyser offers the following questions:

---

[1]Paul W. Pruyser, *The Minister as Diagnostician* (Westminister Press: Philadelphia, 1976). Many secular professionals in the field of mental health use *Diagnostic and Statistical Manual of Mental Disorders* (Third Edition-Revised) (Washington, D.C.: American Psychiatric Association, 1987).

- What is sacred to the counselee?
- Does the counselee trust God and his Word?
- Does the counselee feel a need for grace from God and gratitude for the good things he receives from God?
- Does the counselee feel sorrow for sin, accept responsibility for his behavior, and seek God's forgiveness and behavior-amending grace?
- Does the counselee trust God to care for him in life and death?
- Does the counselee feel alienated from others or involved with others?
- Does the counselee have a sense of mission and a willingness to take part in the purposes of God?

Characteristics of Caring and Helping Relationships

The way a pastoral counselor relates to his counselee is of the utmost importance. Note well the three primary characteristics of a caring and helping relationship:

- positive regard for the counselee,
- authenticity, and
- empathy.

Positive regard blends warmth, caring, acceptance, and respect for a person. As he expresses the love of God, the pastor accepts, values, and respects people—without necessarily agreeing with everything they think, say, and do.

Authenticity means that the pastor is genuine and truthful (Gal. 4:16), that he avoids role playing and defensiveness, and that his words and behavior match his inner feelings.

Empathy is the ability to perceive, in some measure or another, the person's experience and to communicate that understanding back to the individual. The pastor listens as the counselee speaks; and even though he cannot identify with or approve the person's experience, he begins to grasp what the person feels. He cares about what the counselee has experienced and responds by showing that he understands what the counselee has said.

The Cycle of Abuse

Physical and sexual abuse, destructive both to individuals and to their families, is no one's right. Yet, some perpetrators, with confused and erring conscience, use Prov. 23:13–14 or Eph. 5:22 to justify their abusive patterns, ignoring Matt. 18:6; Eph. 5:25, and the Fifth Commandment.

This abusive cycle of human behavior within the family structure is well known to psychotherapists, law enforcement agencies, and victim-assistance organizations. Since members of the Christian community are not immune to this sinful behavior pattern, the pastor needs to know how the cycle works and what resources (in addition to Law and Gospel) are available for both the abusers and the family victims. He needs to keep in mind that he, like the family and community, may be so surprised at the presence of abuse that he denies the reality of the problem and, as the family often does, allows the demoralizing abuse to continue. The pastor needs to remember also that his responsibility is not to cure the problem or change the family, but to apply Law and Gospel so that the Holy Spirit might work in all those involved.

How the Cycle Works

Some victims come to believe that they deserve the abuse and/or do not deserve a relationship with the abuser unless they are suffering—thus encouraging the abuser and completing the abusive cycle. Within this cycle, both abuser and victim often become "locked in" to destructive behavior. Even if they wish to stop the harmful behavior, they may not have the internal resources to do so.

As with any breakdown in human relationships, the problem is sin—but that *general* statement isn't enough to help the pastor or the family caught in the cycle of abuse to apply the Law properly. In this situation, sin has so enmeshed itself into the weave of life and so twisted the fabric that life seems to those caught in abuse to be no longer wearable. While the pastor will never abdicate his role as *Seelsorger*, those caught in abuse need human psychiatric help to unravel their lives so that they no longer prevent the Law from accusing the true problems and so that the Gospel is no longer prevented from having its full sway.

Caught up in this codependent cycle, both abuser and victim need to rebuild their internal resources (physical and psychological as well as spiritual) and revise their family patterns in order to stop the cycle. The pastor, applying Law and Gospel, will be of significant help (especially in the light of Rom. 8:22–25). But no matter how skilled, the pastor on his own usually will not be able to break the cyclical pattern.

The Pastor's Legal Responsibility

The "sanctity of the confessional" notwithstanding, federal and state laws require the pastor to report cases of abuse to the local law enforcement authorities. Unwillingness to report abuse makes a pastor subject to arrest. He should accept this, however, as a benefit. The protection of law enforcement relieves the pastor from attempting to rescue the victim or trying to break the cycle by himself. Thus, the pastor is able to carry out his proper role of conveying the means of grace to all parties involved.

Understanding the Victims

Looking beyond individual personalities and styles of response, victims display some common patterns. All have been traumatized. All lack control over what has happened to their bodies and their minds. Because they have been unable to stop the unpleasant experience, they feel totally helpless and may adapt to repeated abuse.

The abused may include not only wives but also husbands, children, and the elderly as well. Regarding the latter, the pastor may be one of the few who notices that a shut-in is being abused and, therefore, the only one who can report the abuse to the authorities.

The victims need protection to stop the abuse. Promises by the perpetrator to "never do it again" may be sincere but meaningless. The perpetrator usually needs to be prosecuted before the abuse will stop. Therefore, a victim's power base increases tremendously upon learning that the judicial system will punish the abuser and provide protection for the victim.

To break the pattern, the victim may have to be separated from the abuser. Many communities have shelters for abused women. Some have "abuse hotlines." Every community has an agency designated to protect children from abuse or neglect, and they provide placements for them. Some abused children are placed with nonabusing relatives, some in foster care, and still others in children's guardian homes. Most communities also now have means of protecting the elderly from abuse.

Victims frequently need long-term therapy to recover from the trauma of abuse. They will need to retell their story many times to regain control of themselves. They will need to relearn the value of their lives in God's eyes and in their own (Eph. 1:4; John 10:27–28).

Ministering to the Abuser

Because of the addictive nature of the abuse, perpetrators often deny the abuse and pretend everything is all right. When they do admit abuse, they will often shift the responsibility for it to the victim or to another family member.

When the Law exposes abuse, the perpetrator must accept total responsibility for his actions. When that happens, the perpetrator often feels a deep sense of remorse—and a total helplessness that could lead to depression or even suicide. In addition to the Law, God's forgiveness and the pastor's support are fervently needed. The pastor needs to listen and be compassionate as he leads the offender to rely on God's forgiveness in Christ, strength, and hope (cf. especially Rom. 8:1–11; Phil. 4:13 and 1 Cor. 10:13). However, the pastor should assume that the psychological problems continue to exist and and will usually lead to further abuse unless outside help is obtained.

That additional help normally must be court-ordered. Even so, abusers will usually drop out of the program (unless there is pressure to continue) because effective treatment is uncomfortable. Some are better candidates for recovery than others; and some perpetrators need to be separated permanently from their potential victims.

The pastor, of course, will coordinate his treatment of the spiritual problem with the counseling work of professionals who are working with the offender and the family. Many checks and balances need to be in place so that the abusive behavior does not resurface.

Ministering to the Family

Members of the family usually must become involved to some degree in the counseling and recovery process even though they may resist, believing that they are not part of the problem. In fact, every member of the family system is affected. Particularly when the victim and the perpetrator continue to live together in the same house, the new system of safeguards and precautions needs to be strong enough to protect the victim. "Law" to curb is still needed because sin is still present—and always will be (even in the most peaceful household).

The pastor can help the abused family to stop denying that the family has a problem and help them face the deeply rooted shame that is often present. Nonabusing family members may have a range of feelings which they need to express—guilt, jealousy, anger, and rejection. The pastor can help the family members express their feelings—which must be done before the family is able to hear God's forgiveness, understanding, and acceptance that the pastor offers. And he can help the family members find their part in the solution.

To summarize: The pastor's role is

1. To report abuse to the local law enforcement agency, because the sin of abuse is a crime.

2. To listen to the thoughts and feelings of family members caught in the abusive cycle, and to apply the Law and the Gospel to the specific situation.

3. To help break the abusive cycle by working cooperatively with both local law enforcement agencies and local counseling

centers, seeing the application of Law also in its theological light (the first use of the Law, as a curb), adding the spiritual dimension of forgiveness and the power of the Spirit to change lives.

The Pastor and Possible Litigation

Years ago, suing the pastor for malpractice was virtually unthinkable and unknown. Until now, such litigation (except for criminal and moral charges) has been more of a nuisance than a matter of substance. However, cases of litigation evidently will increase and require more attention.

The pastor can take steps to prevent incidents that could trigger litigation, especially events involving church discipline and counseling.

Church discipline procedures and the Biblical basis for them should be carefully explained as a part of premembership instruction. As a condition of church membership, the person should understand and be able to explain how the procedure is implemented in the congregation—and agree to it.

In counseling, the pastor needs to maintain his proper role of extending pastoral care. As people come to him with their problems, he will put them into a pastoral care context, reminding them that he is not a specialized counselor and that he counsels by applying Scriptural principles, using Law and Gospel as appropriate. The pastor should promptly refer cases beyond his competence to "professionals" and stick to his own "profession" of Law and Gospel.

In scheduled counseling sessions, the pastor ought to serve only those who are members of his congregation. If he tries to help a walk-in, it is especially important for the person to understand that the pastor is not a professional counselor but a pastor who uses the Bible as his primary resource. His counseling proceeds from a theological framework rather than clinical psychology, sociology, or professional counseling techniques.

Regardless of whom he advises, the pastor should first of all point out Biblical principles that apply (using specific Scripture passages). Following that, he may suggest God-pleasing alternatives and possible solutions, but should avoid recommendations for specific action. The counselee must decide what is right, what is best under the circumstances, and what he or she will do, since the counselee must live with the consequences of the decision.

The pastor needs to exercise special discretion when counseling women—and not merely out of fear of litigation. Some women seeking help cannot avoid becoming emotional within a proper empathic relationship provided by the pastor. Some abuse the relationship and develop a dependence on the pastor; and a few become romantically attached to him.

Nor is the pastor himself beyond temptation from what Luther described as "the combustible tinder of the sinful flesh." The pastor is vulnerable too; he needs to be aware of it at all times and consciously avoid temptation. Therefore, he should exercise care as to where he meets with the counselee. A simple general rule is to place the counselee between the pastor and the exit door to the room, and to maintain some physical distance. In some situations, he will want a third party to be present in order to avoid any appearance of impropriety (and possible slander).

Concluding Remarks

Although the pastor has a limited amount of time for counseling and usually is not trained for long-term care as a psychotherapist, the pastor can provide unique help for people as a short-term spiritual counselor. He often has the advantage of a long-term pastoral relationship with his counselee and, as a result, has entree to the counselee's home and family.

The pastor should set about counseling with a deep conviction that he has much to offer. He has essential resources for helping persons with personal problems that humanistic counselors do not have and that even other Christian counselors may not be able to use as effectively. These resources are the Law and the Gospel, God's Word that enables people to have an abundant and eternal life in Jesus Christ through the working of the Holy Spirit.

Even when he decides that referral (preferably to Christian therapists) is appropriate, he has a valid ministry that supports and undergirds the counseling that others might provide. Whatever the professional counselor might do, the Christian still needs the support and follow-up of competent pastoral care.

4
The Ministry of Word and Sacrament with the Aging

The Aging of the Church

America increasingly belongs to the old. The average retiree can expect to enjoy another 15 or 20 years of relatively good health. In a rapidly increasing sense, the aging are the church's future.[1]

The church has always had elderly members. In days past, when extended families filled our pews, the elderly were not singled out as a group with unique problems. The church rightly continues to oppose the simplistic assumption that all persons of a certain age or older are categorically considered a problem.[2] Rather, whatever people's age, they continue to be individuals who carry the characteristics of personality and practices that have always been a part of their lives.

Conversely, older adults often take legitimate pride in the wisdom that comes from having "done their part" in child rearing, in having contributed to society through the work force, in having led the local congregation in dealing with the death of the previous generation, in facing their own physical limitations and ultimately, their transfer into eternity. In addition many activities of life have taken on a different meaning—moving to a new home,

---

[1] Tim Stafford "The Graying of the Church," *Christianity Today*, Vol. 31, No. 16 (November 6, 1987), p. 17.

[2] Martin Marty, "Cultural Antecedents to Contemporary American Attitudes Toward Aging," *Ministry with the Aging*, William M. Clements, ed. (San Francisco: Harper & Row, 1981), p. 57.

a vacation "away from it all," visiting relatives, a trip to the doctor, shopping, going out at night, or a good time.

With this in mind, the pastor does well to remember three assumptions for ministry with the aging:

1. Older adults are individuals who share, with people of all ages, the same basic needs, desires, aspirations, and hopes.

2. Older adults have a right to expect and receive pastoral care (in all that this entails) from their pastor and church.[3]

3. Older saints offer great resources for a congregation because of their experience, time, and commitment.

The plaintive cry of the psalmist, "Do not cast me away when I am old; do not forsake me when my strength is gone" (Ps. 71:9), finds response in the words of Isaiah, "Even to your old age and gray hairs I am he, I am he who will sustain you. I have made you, and I will carry you; I will sustain you and I will rescue you" (Is. 46:4).

Unfortunately, in our youth-oriented society where the highest and greatest good is to be and to stay young, aging is considered to be an unwelcome intrusion, and the aged to be unwelcome reminders of our own mortality.[4] Even studies of clergy attitudes towards ministry with the aging demonstrate an amazing insensitivity to the elderly in the congregation.[5] Yet human worth is measured in the worth God has assigned and placed upon us by his creating, providential care and his redeeming love in Christ Jesus. Old members, no matter what their age, are part of the whole church. As such, they are to be included in the ongoing life of the parish—both as recipients of ministry as well as being prepared to help and serve others.

That ministry, of course, takes into account various research data. For example, life satisfaction correlates intimately with spiritual well-being. Also, when compared with older people in general, those who are church members, who read their Bible and who attend church frequently or listen to religious broadcasts, are

---

[3] Lyle Schaller, *Parish Planning* (Nashville: Abingdon Press, 1971), p. 9.

[4] Beth B. Hess, "America's Aged: Who, What, When, and Where?" *Growing Old in America*, Beth B. Hess, ed. (New Brunswick: Transaction Book, 1980), p. 16.

[5] Daniel O. Moberg, "Needs Felt by Clergy for Ministries to the Aging," *Gerontologist*, Vol. 15, No. 2 (April 1975), p. 169. Cf. Walter Moeller, "Social Gerontology," *Post-Easter Convocation* (Concordia Theological Seminary, Springfield, Illinois, now Fort Wayne, Indiana, 1976), p. 10. Cf. also an unpublished study by Phyllis M. Ladrigan, "Education in Aging for the Clergy: Incidence and Importance and in the Future" (Nazareth College of Rochester, New York).

more likely to be well-adjusted in their old age.[6] Many have a zest for life that is celebrated in thankfulness and praise. On the other hand, particular spiritual concerns confront the elderly: loneliness, boredom and lack of purpose, anxiety, fear, and guilt. (Many express a sense of "moral guilt" and/or guilt as "human failure.") Not every aged person carries all or any of these burdens; but the very frequency of their occurrence suggests that the promises of a gracious God must touch the hearts and lives of the elderly so that they may find refuge, strength and hope in the Rock who alone is their hope: Jesus Christ.

Administering Pastoral Care

The pastor's priority in administering care to the elderly is that of addressing their needs with a holistic approach (1 John 3:17). In addition to the assumptions previously listed, the undershepherd should keep in mind the following principles:

Integration: Strive to keep older adults integrated in all aspects of the church's life and ministry. This runs counter to the general societal expectation that the aged should "disengage" in order to let youth take over.

Adaptation: Adapt or develop facilities and services that will meet both the needs and capabilities of older adults, individually as well as a group.

Comprehensiveness: Full pastoral care encompasses the spiritual, emotional, social, and physical needs of all persons in the congregation.

Some Practical Considerations

Regarding Worship

With increased longevity, mobility and good health, older adults should be allowed to anticipate their continued, normal worship with the gathered people of God. This may not be as easy for the congregation as it appears. The church may have to make structural and environmental modifications to provide easy access, adequate lighting, and proper acoustics. For those who are partially mobile, other accommodations may have to be made— for example, Communion services at special times (morning or early afternoon), transportation, assistance with entering and ex-

---

[6] Robert C. Atchley, *The Social Forces in Later Life* (Belmont, California: Wadsworth Publishing Co., Inc., 1977), p. 287.

iting the sanctuary, and specially designed worship services to accommodate unique physical needs.

Regarding Christian Education

Contrary to popular perceptions, the older adult not only can but does learn. Indeed, greater control of one's time and broader interests in this period have the potential of making it the most instructive era of a person's life. And—good news for the church— older people are more likely to study religion than other subjects when they decide to become students.[7] Because of the varying physical circumstances of older adults, congregations need to develop creative approaches for Christian education. Bible study may need to be rescheduled at convenient times and in accessible places—perhaps outside the church property in neighborhood groups led by capable, trained lay leaders under the supervision of the pastor. Individualized Bible study might supplement the pastor's sacramental ministry. The same might apply to ministering to and with residents of convalescent centers and homes for the aged. (Given the fragmentation of many families, such regularly scheduled events often become the highlight of those otherwise dispossessed.)

In addition to the study of God's Word *per se*, the Christian community can help people apply the Word to one of life's most consequential transitions: retirement. In spite of much talk, society has not clearly defined what it is—other than suggesting that retirement and "old age" is devoid of social meaning because the retired person is no longer "producing."[8] Christians, however, can view retirement in a vastly different way. Preretirement preparation programs can help and enable older adults, under the Word, to enrich and make more meaningful the days and years which the Lord affords, to be able to rejoice in his blessings, and to serve joyfully in his church. (Many Christian preretirement programs are readily available.[9])

Helping Older Adults to Serve

Older adults, especially those who are bored and who lack purpose in life, eagerly welcome the opportunity to thank and praise God through meaningful service to others. Once again the

---

[7] Ibid., p. 289.

[8] Margaret Clark and Barbara Anderson, *Culture and Aging* (Springfield, Illinois: Charles C. Thomas, Publisher, 1970), pp. 8f.

[9] At this printing, two pre-retirement programs are suggested for consideration: The Aid Association for Lutherans' SMART program, and that of the American Association of Retired Persons.

pastor and congregational leaders need be creative. By and large, older adults are healthier, more mobile, have more time, more resources, and a wealth of experience and skills than ever before. If not used, these will atrophy—to the detriment of the individual and the church. The ways in which these capabilities are used, however, must go beyond the token and perfunctory and be commensurate with the spiritual maturity, skills and experience of the individual. Tokenism here is ageism at its worst, and the church is poorer for it.

Again, study preretirement materials for suggested ways to identify and make use of the many benefits older adults can bring to the church's ministry.

Regarding Temporal/Bodily Well-Being

The needs and comforts of the body also belong under pastoral care. Not that the pastor shifts his primary concern from the eternal to the temporal. Rather, in accordance with strong scriptural exhortation, the pastor and congregation do care for one another's physical needs. More often than not, this requires not the expenditure of funds but the investment of personal concern. Specific activities might include a daily check on the general well-being of an elderly person (especially when living alone), a warm meal, a friendly visit, a gift of food, an article of clothing, the delivery of medicine, some information on how to manage a report form, or help with a legal problem.[10] Other ways include transportation and errand services, and enlisting volunteers from the congregation to do minor home repairs and yard work. These services grow especially important when family, friends or neighbors are not available or in positions to help. To do less would fail to honor and esteem the aging as God calls us to do (Ex. 20:12; Eph. 6:4; Lev. 19:32).

Shut-Ins

Shut-ins, no less than other members, have the right to expect the pastor, as God's appointed servant in the congregation, to be faithful and regular in the administration of a Word and Sacrament ministry to them. At the same time, the pastor must exercise care lest the emotional needs of disinherited shut-ins overshadow his pastoral ministry to the whole congregation. Nor should the pastor see this ministry as solely his responsibility. Every member of the body of Christ has the privilege of calling on the sick, on

---

[10] Arthur H. Becker, *Ministry with Older Persons* (Minneapolis: Augsburg, 1986), p. 178.

the elderly, and on the shut-in. The pastor himself, of course, carries out the sacramental ministry. But he can and should recruit and train capable laypersons who, by the grace of God, enrich the church's total ministry of the Word and of Christian care.[11]

Generally, the term *shut-ins* includes the institutionalized, because many of their needs are similar. However, the latter have many unique needs—the very needs that brought about their institutionalization. The pastor often can determine and meet the resultant spiritual needs after a session with the appropriate health-giver. In addition to the personal needs of any one individual, the pastor should consider the general effects of being institutionalized: boredom, loss of privacy, the feeling of helpless dependency, possible embarrassment over the loss of total body control, the feeling that no one truly cares about them, and the frequent despondency that looks for the peace of death.

In addition to ministering to the individual member in an institution, the pastor seeks out evangelism opportunities to serve the residents of the convalescent center or home for the aging as a community, many of whom are the forgotten of our society. For example, worship services on a regular basis are appreciated both by the residents as well as by the administrator, the nursing staff, and the activity directors of these facilities. Here the pastor will find a ready audience for the comforting message of forgiveness, salvation, and the abundance of life through Christ Jesus, the crucified and risen One.

Again, the pastor can extend the caring ministry of the church through the participation of trained laity. This opportunity has become vastly more practical through the use of audio and video cassettes, camcorders, and VCRs. The constantly reducing costs of the hardware have opened more doors than our forebears ever thought possible. These, of course, should be only a supplement to personal pastoral care and to brotherly love and care.

Advocacy

Who should speak for the elderly? Who answers the questions of guardianship, of patients' rights, of life-support systems, of dignity, of the need for institutionalization? Sometimes a voice can be found within the aging person's own family, but not always. God has not omitted these issues as concerns for those of the household of faith.

---

[11] Arthur H. Becker, *The Compassionate Visitor* (Minneapolis: Augsburg, 1984). Cf. also an unpublished D.Min. dissertation by Norbert H. Mueller, "A Lay Ministry to the Aging Shut-In Using Devotional Materials to Foster Spiritual Growth."

The specific involvement of the pastor and the individual answers depend so completely on the specific situation that the best advice for sound pastoral ministry is, "Seek out the advice of the brethren"—both the brethren in the public ministry as well as those in the congregation entrusted with the oversight of the ministry (the elders, deacons, or whatever title they may have).

In addition to individuals, who should speak for the elderly as a group? The pastor can assume leadership in sensitizing the congregation and equipping the members to more active participation in caring concern. He may also be the main advocate in promoting necessary societal changes in the community. In this matter (which need not involve unionistic worship), the pastor might very well align himself with other community leaders to lobby on behalf of the elderly, to correct injustices, to engage in the positive pursuit of justice, and in the prevention of injustice.[12]

Summary

Aging is not merely a lockstep march toward death. It is primarily a remarkable opportunity under God to grow and mature in the faith as we serve our Lord, our church, and our community in new, meaningful ways. The joyful life of the Christian has many enemies, not the least of which is the last great enemy: death. But God has defeated all our enemies and has given us life in the name of Jesus Christ. He enables us to live this life to the fullest as he creates, nurtures, and sustains our faith by the precious means of grace. For the faithful who are aging—which includes us all— this is the hallmark of the pastoral ministry.

---

[12] Becker, *Ministry with Older Persons*, p. 196.

5
Applying Word and Sacrament to the Dying and Bereaved

Few North Americans today are growing up with death as a frequent and normal part of life. In the past the home provided a support structure for dealing with the rhythm of life as births, sickness, and death happened right in the home. The church and the pastor were part of this—so intimately that the pastor often was considered part of the family.

Society has changed. The multi-generation household, i.e., the extended family, for the most part, no longer exists. Births take place outside the home; sicknesses are treated outside the home; newly marrieds move away from parents and siblings; death is hidden in a hospital or rest home. Few people have any experience to teach them how to deal with dying and/or any grieving for the dead.

With increasingly longer life expectancy and lower infant and child mortality rates, our youth-oriented society encourages us to live with the erroneous conception that "we are always going to be here."

We have hidden the aging and have ignored the dying. For the most part, we have become a populace uncomfortable with its own mortality. This is as true for pastors as it is of people in general.

As the pastor begins to come to grips with ministering to the terminally ill, he may find it necessary to come to terms with his own mortality, with his own process of dying (which began at conception and birth). The pastor, as God's representative, needs to live in that awareness, utilizing every moment of life as a precious opportunity that anticipates our glorious translation into eternity. He needs to apply the means of grace in terms of Law and Gospel to himself as well as his flock in order to strengthen faith and renew hope.

Some have suggested that the pastor cultivate the necessary sensitivity by contemplating how he would feel if he were diagnosed as terminally ill. The exercise is inadequate. No one in fact has any more guarantee of tomorrow than anyone else. The pastor as well as the terminally ill must have the house in order, "for tomorrow we die." As a result, every Christian is dying but living each engifted day to its fullest, experiencing God's goodness as he prepares to be with God in heaven (Rev. 7:9–17).

Pastoral Care of the Dying

Increased longevity, sometimes by extraordinary means, has led to a new discipline of caring for the dying, one that takes into consideration the emotional, mental, and spiritual dimensions of life. This became necessary because, generally speaking, societal attitudes towards the dying have been negative, often resulting in social ostracism and isolation.[1] Long-term friendships are cut off in the face of terminal illness, the nonaffected person often cutting himself off from ever visiting or communicating with the person who is ill.

One discipline has divided the process of mourning into *anticipatory grief* and *grieving in bereavement*. The former is "that grief work aimed at loosening the bonds of attachment to the dying, making loss less painful when it occurs."[2] The latter is that grief work which deals with the loss when it occurs.

The division has helped caregivers understand the interaction between the one diagnosed as terminally ill and the spouse/loved one. Both experience *anticipatory grief*; however, it causes real problems when the two do not occur at the same time. For example, the terminally ill person may have already come to grips with the inevitable while the spouse refuses to accept the diagnosis. When, in this situation, the pastor discusses with the pa-

---

[1] For a further discussion and explication of this phenomenon, cf. Susan Sontag, *Illness as Metaphor* (New York: Farrar, Straus, and Girous, 1978), which describes and discusses the effect that different types of illness have on interpersonal relations.

[2] Michael R. Leming and George E. Dickinson, *Understanding Dying, Death, and Bereavement* (New York: Holt, Rinehart, & Winston, 1985), p. 99.

tient the assurance of the resurrection, the spouse may well become angry with the pastor, denying the reality and pinning hope on a medical expert, on untried cures, even on the power of prayer and special intervention by God.

As implied earlier, anticipatory grief by healthy friends or spouse can be carried to such an extreme that they cut themselves off entirely from the one dying. In their effort to "make loss less painful when it occurs," they unintentionally add to the grief of the terminally ill. If nothing else, the pastor can encourage such timid friends to practice the "ministry of presence"—to at least "carry each other's burdens" (Gal. 6:2) by keeping watch (as Jesus asked the disciples, Mark 14:34).

Five Stages of Grief

Controversial as it may be, the stage model popularized by Elisabeth Kuebler-Ross (denial, anger, bargaining, depression, acceptance) has been used with success.[3] This scheme can assist a pastor to shape and apply pastoral care as the patient (and his friends and loved ones) work through the terminal diagnosis of the doctors. Realizing that this stage model is *descriptive*, not prescriptive, the pastor will tailor his pastoral intervention to the situation at the time of his call. (Certain conditions may indicate a ministry of presence rather than profound words. There is an "incarnational" aspect of the pastoral office which manifests itself in the mind of the laity. To many, the pastor's care represents and manifests God's own concern for the individual. By his presence, the pastor may absorb the anger, lend strength to the weak, give guidance to the helpless, and protection to the vulnerable.)

In Kuebler-Ross' stages of bargaining and depression, the patient goes through many manifestations of guilt. Some is legitimate—e.g., as the patient considers his life under God's law. Some is simply assumed—e.g., as the patient assumes that his diagnosis is punishment for a particular sin. Or the patient may feel guilt for putting his family through so much heartache. Society attaches an ugly stigma to catastrophic illness.

Whatever the cause of the guilt, the patient demands pastoral attention and the assurance that God in Christ Jesus is not vengeful or vindictive. Rather, God always deals with his people in mercy and in accord with his forgiving, saving, redeeming, and life-giving will for all his children in Christ. In this connection, the pastor might emphasize God's grace in Baptism. Just as certainly as the

---

[3] Elisabeth Kuebler-Ross, *Death and Dying* (New York: MacMillan, 1969), *passim*.

patient was washed in the water and the Word, so certain is God's promise that no one can snatch us from his hand.

When using the stage model, note that a person's resignation or giving up on life is part of *depression*, not acceptance. During the latter, the person comes to terms with the reality of the present situation, yet determines to live each day as a gift from the Lord to be lived as fully and as productively as possible.

During each stage, the pastor surely tries to prepare the patient for death by providing the certainty of God's grace, life, and salvation through the crucified and risen Christ. To that end, the pastoral visits should be frequent, the devotions rich in the saving message of the Gospel, and the means of grace, the Lord's Supper, regularly offered.

The pastor should remember also those people who are affected by the illness and probable death of their loved one, including any children within the household. Though often forgotten in the grieving process, they, too, will be working through the same stages and suffer similar emotional responses. The pastor will help the entire family to interpret what is going on in such a way that their faith is strengthened and their hope increased. (Bear in mind, though, that little children think in very concrete imagery. Therefore, much terminology and symbolism will not be understood.)[4]

One additional caution when using the model of stages: No time limit can be arbitrarily set as to when the patient or loved one should have worked through and come to accept the reality of death. Indeed, some individuals never accept the imposed diagnosis. No two people react in precisely the same manner when confronted with the possibility of terminal illness. Although the stage model may be of help to the pastor in shaping the form of his pastoral care, he must remember that some people progress through the stages; some manifest only one or a few of the stages; and some may begin at one stage, skip others, and move back and forth between two or more of the stages. In addition, some people sink so deeply into one stage that pastoral ministry may be inordinately difficult. For example, a person can become so depressed that he or she begins fantasizing. (Also, some medicines induce hallucinations.)

Every illness is a reminder of our ultimate mortality. Therefore the pastor uses not only the occasion of terminal illness but also

---

[4] Two books from Concordia Publishing House, St. Louis, have proved helpful in working with children: *If I Should Die, If I Should Live* (Joanne Marxhausen, 1975), and *What Happened When Grandma Died?* (Peggy Barker, 1984).

any illness as a way of preparing all his people for the time of their death, holding before them the ultimate victory over death which believers have by faith and their incorporation into Jesus Christ by their Baptism.

The Hospice Movement

The pastor and the church are not the only ones concerned about emotional and spiritual care for the terminally ill and their families. Within recent decades, the hospice movement has spread from its center of rebirth at St. Christopher's Hospice in London, England, to the United States, with numerous centers established throughout the country (usually associated with a medical facility). Under the principle "caring not curing," hospices use a multidisciplined approach of doctors, nurses, therapists, social workers, chaplains, and volunteers to address these needs—as well as the physical needs of the dying patient and his family. As just one of its significant and comforting features, the hospice program promises that someone from the team is no more than a telephone call away, on call around the clock on an "as needed" basis. They also promise that the terminal patient will not die alone. Stressing pain control and positive outlook, the people serving in the program attempt to assist the patient in maximizing opportunities so as to live as normally as possible during the time remaining of his earthly pilgrimage.[5] In the best interests of the patient, the pastor will certainly want to work with the team.

Choosing Eternity/Euthanasia

The discussion of euthanasia, "beautiful death," has become increasingly acceptable in our society. The suffering and pain usually associated with debilitating and terminal sickness have made death an attractive option for many.

> Properly speaking, euthanasia entails direct intervention, the killing of human beings, with or without their knowledge or consent. It may be briefly defined as the administration of a lethal dose to the patient or the deliberate refusal to use even ordinary means of sustaining life.[6]

The Commission on Theology and Church Relations of The Lutheran Church—Missouri Synod, in its report "Euthanasia

---

[5] Sandol Stoddard, *The Hospice Movement* (Briarcliff Manor, New York: Stein and Day Publishers, 1980) discusses the philosophical constructs undergirding the hospice movement, using case studies drawn from three settings.

[6] *Report on Euthanasia with Guiding Principles (1979)*, The Commission on Theology and Church Relations (The Lutheran Church—Missouri Synod), p. 9.

with Guiding Principles," provides helpful instruction:

> 1) Euthanasia, in its proper sense, is a synonym for mercy kill-ing, which involves suicide and/or murder. It is, therefore, con-trary to God's law. 2) As Creator, God alone knows with certainty whether a disease or an injury is incurable. 3) Each person, no matter how infirm and socially useless he or she may appear to be, deserves to be accepted as a being created in the image of God. 4) When the God-given powers of the body to sustain its life can no longer function and doctors in their professional judgment conclude that there is no real hope for recovery even with life-support instruments, a Christian may in good con-science "let nature takes its course."[7]

With regard to this last point, the Christian will prayerfully try to come to a God-pleasing decision. Thus, the above document suggests that the following people be involved in the determina-tion whether to cease aggresive life-prolonging procedures:

> a) the patient (if capable of discussing the facts) to help in de-termining the general reaction of bodily strength and suffering and in making a decision that is legally and morally acceptable; b) the doctor to help determine whether support systems are still helpful and whether there is any hope of recovery; c) the nearest of kin to gain concurrence in decisions reached; d) the pastor to give spiritual guidance and counsel in reference to treatment and care and to provide spiritual assistance and com-fort and support.[8]

As the first point above acknowledges, the patient may at times be unable to participate in the decision-making process. This has led to the recent phenomenon of the person writing a *Living Will.* Such a document expresses the individual's wishes concerning the type and extent of medical care to be administered, should the person become terminally ill and the death process irreversible. A number of states have officially recognized the va-lidity and, in that sense, the legality of the Living Will. For a sam-ple, see the end of this chapter.

(As part of or alongside a Living Will, more and more people are donating their organs after death to be used to benefit the living. This practice may well be encouraged by the pastor.)

Ministering to the terminally ill patient strongly tests the pas-tor's compassion, pastoral skills, the quality of his own faith in the goodness and mercy of God, and the degree to which he has become comfortable with his own mortality. The pastor has only

---

[7] Ibid., pp. 28–29.
[8] Ibid.

one acceptable remedy for death: life—life made possible by our justification by grace through faith in the atoning work of Jesus Christ, life assured by the resurrection of Jesus Christ with whom our hope for eternal bliss is inseparably bound (1 Peter 1:3–5).

Pastoral Care of the Bereaved

At the Point of Death

One author defines mourning as "a complex set of emotions by which we adapt to the disorientation of major change in our lives."[9] While this definition may sound too clinical, it acknowledges that people grieve over any significant loss (such as losing a part of the body, a job, or even a spouse through divorce). The more significant the loss (i.e., the more major the change), the greater the dissorientation—and the greater the demand for pastoral care.

Death, of course, represents the most extreme of "major changes." A voice has been stilled—the presence of a loved one gone. The *disorientation* may come across as numbness, with the bereaved in some state of shock. Sometimes it will show itself in uncontrollable sobbing, disbelief, perhaps even anger. It is okay to grieve, but not as those (1 Thess. 4:13) "who have no hope" (*hope* understood as an objective thing "stored up for you in heaven" Col. 1:5).

Whatever grief's manifestation, the pastor represents the presence of God, who alone provides any true orientation and stability to life. This focus on Christ might well be incorporated in a Scripture reading and prayer, concluding with the Lord's Prayer and benediction.

If the pastor is with the family at the time of death, he should make sure that the person or persons most directly affected not be left alone to shift for themselves. A caring social network in the congregation (explained later in this chapter) needs to be put into operation.

At times the pastor will be called on to inform the family of the death, particularly if it was sudden and/or accidental. In such instances, the pastor will guide the conversation tactfully so that the person is led gradually to an awareness of the seriousness of the situation and might draw the conclusion that the loved one has died. (At times the news will have to be verbalized as such.)

---

[9] From a taped lecture by Dr. Glen Davidson at Concordia Theological Seminary, Fort Wayne, Indiana, October 5, 1982. Cf. his book *Understanding Mourning* (Minneapolis: Augsburg, 1984), p. 6.

In such instances, the "incarnational aspect" of the pastoral office takes on special importance. As God's representative, you are there in God's stead. Therefore, keep in mind that people may say things that are not meant, but that arise temporarily out of feelings of frustration and sudden loss. Resist being judgmental concerning what is said or done. Let the first wave of shock work itself out. And be prepared to smooth the process of grieving by explaining grief reactions to family members.

As the initial reaction subsides, look for an appropriate moment to collect together in a brief prayer the thoughts, feelings, and hurts precipitated by the occasion. Hold these up before the throne of God's grace, asking for strength, help, and deliverance that he alone can give to the bereaved.

Before leaving, be sure the bereaved will not be left alone. If necessary, the pastor himself will take the person home and remain with him or her until family or a responsible neighbor or church member arrives to provide the needed care.

On-Going Pastoral Care

The pastor must be sensitive to the length of the person's bereavement. Adapting to the major change (death) may take up to 24 months on the average and reach a climax from 12 to 20 months after the death has occurred.[10] Not that a person ever completely stops grieving; he or she will again function at or near the capacity prior to the death and bereavement.

To some extent, the length of time may depend on how "socially acceptable" the death was. Some are considered useful; some a waste. Some are regarded with compassion; some with an attitude that imputes guilt to the survivors (e.g., a death due to sudden infant death syndrome).[11]

Faith, of course, helps a person through the process; but not even the strongest trust in Christ can remove the necessity for grief. And unless it is handled constructively, the results can be disastrous. For example, bereavement places a person under extreme stress, disturbs the immunological system, and makes the person particularly vulnerable to illness, two and one-half times normal at risk to heart attack, and three to three and one-half times to certain kinds of cancer.[12]

In addition, society as a whole is reluctant to "give permission" to grieve, preferring instead to politely ostracize those who

---

[10] Davidson, *passim.*

[11] Lemming and Dickinson, op. cit., *passim.*

[12] Davidson, pp. 21–22.

mourn. Aware of that attitude, some people suppress their emotions to such an extent that they cannot respond appropriately in a social setting. Others, in the extreme, move into alcoholism, drug abuse, or sexual dysfunction.[13] At the very least, society in general fails to realize the integral and possibly debilitating effects of loneliness.[14]

Every pastor faces the temptation to assume that, once the "full-time" service given to the family between the death and the funeral is over, the pressing need for his presence has also come to an end. Because of the lengthy and lonely process of grieving, the pastor needs to continue to program for visits with the bereaved. The schedule could well include a call within a week of the committal; at least monthly for six months; then at regular intervals for the next two years, paying particular attention to birthdays, anniversaries, and holidays—times in which family relationships assume great importance.

This caring ministry should not be carried out exclusively by the pastor. The congregation exists to help provide a "nurturing social network."[15] Part of the pastoral task is to recruit and train sensitive and caring people, enabling them to help bereaved members do the necessary "grief work." People need such a network. If not provided by the congregation, other willing groups are available. Without disparaging the contributions these groups make, the members of the Christian congregation have been specifically called by our Lord to care for each other and to carry one another's burdens. Pastor and people together must communicate caring concern for the bereaved, so fulfilling the will of our Lord.

Appendix

LIVING WILL

(Sample Only)

Instructions for my care in the event of terminal illness.

My faith affirms that life is a gift of God and that physical death is a part of life, the completed stage of a person's development. My faith assures me that even in death there is hope in the sustaining grace and love of God. Because of my belief, I wish this statement to stand as the testament of my wishes.

---

[13] Ibid., p. 22.

[14] C. S. Lewis, "Of Grief Observed," *Death: Current Perspectives* Third Edition, Edwin S. Shneidman, ed. (Palo Alto: Mayfield Publishing Company, 1984), pp. 394-398.

[15] Ibid., p. 24.

I, _____, request that I be fully informed as my death approaches. If possible, I wish to participate in decisions regarding my medical treatment and the procedures that may be used to prolong my life. If there is no reasonable expectation of my recovery from physical or mental disability, I direct my physician and all medical personnel not to prolong my life by artificial or mechanical means. I direct that I receive pain and symptom control. However, this is not a request that direct intervention be taken to shorten my life.

This decision is made after consideration and reflection. I direct that all legal means be taken to support my choice. In the carrying out of all my will as stated, I release all physicians and other health personnel, all institutions and their employees, and all members of my family from legal culpability and responsibility.

Signed: _____   Date: _____

Witnessed By: _____   _____

Sign and date before two witnesses. This is to insure that you've signed of your own free will and not under any pressure. If you have a doctor, give him or her a copy for your medical file and discuss it to make sure he or she is in agreement. Give copies to those most likely to be concerned if the time comes when you can no longer take part in decisions for your own future. Discuss your intentions with them and enter their names on the original copy of the Living Will. Keep the original nearby, easily and readily available. Look it over once a year, redate it, and initial a new date to make clear that your wishes are unchanged.[16]

---

[16] This form is available from the American Protestant Hospital Association, 1701 E. Woodfield Rd., Schaumburg, IL 60195. Somewhat different forms are avaliable from the Catholic Hospital Association, St. Louis, MO 63104; and from Concern for Dying, 250 West 57th Street, New York, NY 10019.

6
Pastoral Care and the Christian Funeral

Death is the ultimate rite of passage associated with human existence—and, even apart from Christianity, the human heart needs to solemnize the event in ritual appropriate to the event and reflecting human dignity and worth.

Scripture, of course, prescribes nothing concerning a funeral. Still, the church has sought to place the disposition of the earthly remains of a believer into a Christian context that bears witness to the faith and hope it confesses. Remembering that the funeral climaxes the antecedent and subsequent responses surrounding a death, the pastor will work with the bereaved so that their private and public lives witness to their hope in Christ.

In addition to the pastoral calls discussed in the previous chapter, the pastor should always discuss with the family the details of the funeral and committal services. The family (or previously, the decedent) often will have specific requests. They usually may be honored unless spiritually inappropriate.

One additional call should be considered integral: at the funeral home or wherever the viewing takes place. Normally, this occurs toward the end of the visitation hours, after which the pastor may lead the bereaved in a brief meditation. Keep in mind that the visitation is a grueling experience for the family and that, therefore, the devotion should be brief yet uplifting.

Local Customs

Within a few days of a pastor's installation, he should meet first with the congregational elders and then with a frequently-used funeral director to discuss local customs—what they are, why they are followed (if possible to determine), and which (if any) direct people away from the centrality of Christ.

If not prepared, the new pastor will learn very quickly the importance of local tradition. Especially during rites of passage, people feel "complete" when custom is followed and cheated/hurt when not.

These customs range from the procession and recession of the casket, family, and pastor to where the pastor should stand during the committal. During the words, "Dust to dust," some want sand or dirt placed on the casket, some want flower petals, and some would be shocked if anything except the sign of the cross were made over the casket. While this latter is but one example, it should remind the new pastor of the necessity to discuss every detail in advance with the elders and local funeral director.

The Funeral Service

Normally held in the church sanctuary, the funeral is a worship service that marks the translation of a saint of God. Therefore, the components of worship are to be utilized: the Word read and proclaimed, praises sung, and prayers spoken. These help preserve theocentricity and prevent the funeral from becoming centered in the remains encased in the casket. (In a funeral home, the "praises sung" may have to be by a soloist, but many mortuaries have an organ available for hymn singing.)

The sermon should clearly present "the reason of the hope that is in us." Our gracious God has given a remarkable message to proclaim, a message that alone can give consolation and hope to the bereaved. The believer as well as the unbeliever who may be present need to hear both Law and Gospel. Together with all the saints of God, the believer can stand boldly in the day of judgment because the righteousness of Jesus Christ has been reckoned to him, and he is reconciled to God. It is his by faith. Jesus' promise, "Because I live you also will live" (John 14:19), points to the resurrection from the dead. As Paul assures, "Your life is now hidden with Christ in God. When Christ, who is your life, appears, then you also will appear with him in glory" (Col. 3:3–4). In baptism, the believer is united to the risen Christ and will live in the presence of God through all eternity. This is the hope that belongs to all the people of God in Christ Jesus—to the deceased and to the bereaved who believe. Personal reference to God's working in and faithfulness to the departed are in order; they are examples to those still part of the church militant.

Ordinarily the committal takes place directly following the funeral service. Local customs and traditions may be retained, provided (as above) that they are consistent with the Christian faith and meaningful to the people. The ceremony itself should be brief and not an occasion for prolonged "wailing over a loved one who will lie in the cold, dark ground."

Post-committal social gatherings are common throughout the country. A church group and/or friends and neighbors bring in food for the bereaved family and friends. The wise pastor will make a meaningful appearance also at this gathering in which, again, simply by his presence, he assures the family of his concern and sympathy. He also will not be surprised at what might appear as a somewhat lighthearted atmosphere. The family has completed an ordeal with heavy heart. Now that this rite of passage is over, the emotions need a change of pace—a "re-creation," if you will— before returning to the hard work of rebuilding lives. In addition, the occasion of the death may also be the occasion for a long-overdue family reunion, and the relatives need the time for strengthening their relationships before returning to their several homes. If nothing else, the socializing itself serves as a reminder that, in the hope of the resurrection, God's people can move ahead.

Memorial Contributions or Flowers?

The question should not be either/or but how much is enough. The absence of all flowers—symbols of the resurrection and eternal life—is not appropriate. Yet, more and more families are designating worthy agencies to receive memorial contributions in lieu of flowers. This practice deserves the pastor's encouragement and support as he points people to the needs of the living.

Potential abuse arises when the family desires to erect a memorial (often within the sanctuary) to ensure that the deceased will be remembered for generations to come. The abuse is compounded when the family designates the memorial funds for a specific object that the congregation may not need or want. Some of this can be avoided if the church has established an approved list of items for memorial monies. If such a list does not exist, the pastor might suggest that the family wait before making a decision.

Open or Closed Casket?

Some authorities point out that a casket which is open at least some time for the bereaved to view the corpse has therapeutic value, that the process helps the bereaved to accept the finality of the death and feel a sense of "closure."

Theologically, the question belongs to adiaphora. There are times, however, when an open casket may hinder the bereaved from finding comfort in the Savior. For example, local tradition may dictate that the casket be reopened after a service and the family view the corpse one last time—thus redirecting the bereaved's focus from Christ as proclaimed in the Word to the body of the deceased prone before them.

Local tradition to the contrary, the pastor will remember that he is to help people understand and use rituals that will focus their attention on Christ. In that faith, a mediating position can be espoused toward traditions that otherwise would be discouraged.

Funeral Palls

Many Protestant Christians have revived the use of a pall over the casket during the service. This liturgical cloth, usually decorated with a Christian symbol of the resurrection or eternal life, has much to commend it. In addition to drawing the worshipper's attention to Christ, it helps ease the social pressure to have an expensive coffin so as not to look cheap.

Cremation

Not too long ago, the church viewed cremation negatively. Because the general public associated the practice with heathen religions and/or an attempt to disprove the possibility of the resurrection, Christians were reluctant to consider it.

In itself, the practice has no theological significance and may be used in good conscience. In fact, because of space limitations in some areas (e.g., West Berlin, England), and because of health considerations, cremation is increasing in favor. Cost, too, is a legitimate consideration; although the family considering it for this reason should be reminded that cost is saved only when there is no public viewing and, thus, no need for embalming and use of the visitation room.

Memorial Service

Because of our mobile society, the nature of some fatal illnesses, and occasionally because of cremation, a growing number of families have turned to memorial services separated in time (and sometimes distance) from the committal. In such situations, private graveside services are usually held for only the immediate family. At a later, convenient time, a memorial service is held for the extended family and friends. This service differs little from an ordinary funeral service; however, because of the intervention of time, the bereaved may be more willing to have the service focus on the joy of the resurrection rather than their own grieving.

An Annual Service of Commemoration of the Blessed Dead

This service has a long and hallowed tradition of observance on All Saints Day (November 1) or the nearest Sunday to it. Some congregations use the New Year's Eve service to commemorate those who died during the year drawing to a close. Whatever the date, the observance gives opportunity to the pastor and his people to be reminded of their own mortality, to the brevity of life, the certainty of death, and above all to the victory and eternal destiny of life everlasting that belongs assuredly to those who are in Christ by faith as a gift of God's grace.

Officiating in Special Circumstances

Funerals for Nonmembers

The previous discussion assumes that the deceased was a member of the congregation. However, frequently the pastor will be requested to officiate for a nonmember—someone to whom he ministered in the hospital or a relative of a member. Since the only comfort for the bereaved that God offers is intricately and inseparably tied to the death and resurrection of Jesus Christ, the pastor must have reasonable assurance that the person died in saving faith. If the pastor or reliable witnesses have such first-hand knowledge, the pastor may in good conscience consent.

In balance to the above, the pastor keeps in mind that he represents the church and the theological position upon which his denomination is grounded and which it professes. By offici-ating at a funeral, the pastor in essence attests to the fact that the deceased nonmember died in the faith espoused by the pas-tor's denomination. Indiscriminately conducting funeral services contributes to the universalism popular in present-day society. However, since funerals benefit the living, not the dead, the pastor will seek the counsel of his congregational elders in any unusual circumstances.

With the above in mind, if the Lutheran pastor does officiate at the funeral of a nonmember, the service ordinarily is not held in the church sanctuary; this privilege is reserved for members of the congregation.

Funerals for Victims of Suicide

Before consenting to officiate at the funeral of a suicide victim, the pastor will want to make a full inquiry—not so much for a reason to avoid the question of officiating as to find a reason (even if weak) to accept the opportunity. Especially important in such situations is the state of mind of the deceased and whether the deceased was aware of what he/she was doing. Other important factors that need to be evaluated by the pastor along with the congregation's elders are the following:

1. As in the previous discussion, the service benefits the living and is part of the congregation's witness. Death is especially difficult for the bereaved of the suicide of a loved one. Usually the family feels a tremendous burden of guilt that an excessively judgmental pastor only exacerbates by refusing to officiate.

2. No one can determine with certainty the faith (or lack of it) in another person. People have been heard to say even at the funeral of a church member, "If the pastor only knew . . . ." On the other hand, when the deceased's ongoing life and the circumstances of his death manifest an absence of faith in Christ, the pastor cannot conduct a *Christian* burial service which offers the comfort of the hope of salvation for the one who has died.

3. What and how much will the pastor say in his sermon? Would the pastor have to explain away or excuse his participation in the funeral? How clearly can he point to the incarnate Lord who invites all to cast their burdens upon him?

4. Is the family asking/insisting that the service be conducted in the sanctuary, with everything that implies?

The pastor, with the congregational elders, will need a mutually-drafted general policy, based on sound theological principles, to govern the funeral for a victim of suicide—a policy that still will have to be applied to each situation.

As the pastor wrestles with any difficult case, he will find it especially helpful to consult with fellow pastors.

Funerals with Unionistic/Syncretistic Involvement

When asked to participate in funeral services with clergy of another denomination not in church fellowship with The Lutheran Church—Missouri Synod, the pastor will faithfully honor and uphold the fellowship practices of the Scriptures and Confessions and decline. Joint participation with clergy not in fellowship conveys an ambiguous message that results in confusion. In fact, such confusion more than likely led to the invitation itself.

Funerals for Lodge Members

Care must be taken to differentiate between funerals for *Christians who are lodge members* and funerals that include *participatory leadership by lodge representatives*. The latter is to be strenuously avoided. If the pastor even suspects that such might be the case, explain the situation to the family. Remind them that even a "surprise" presence by lodge representatives at the graveside announces on behalf of the deceased that the universalism espoused by the lodge was the actual faith of the deceased. Were that true, the family should respect the pastor's insistence of non-involvement.

Christians who are lodge members present a different question to the faithful pastor. While the strongest faith lays hold of the perfection of Jesus Christ, the weakest faith lays hold to that same perfection. Even the spark of faith is saving faith. In every case, the pastor points to the faithfulness of God to the covenant made in Holy Baptism. He is not as quick to let go of us as we are of him (2 Peter 3:9).

Funerals Involving Military Rites

The military rites involved with a funeral do not relate to the deceased's faith but to his commitment and loyalty to his country. If such participation is expected, find out from the funeral director the specifics of the involvement and how to accommodate to this special honor for the deceased.

Summary

The bittersweet death of a Christian causes pain as well as gives an opportunity to assuage that hurt with the comforting Gospel of the resurrection. Despite tear-filled eyes and sorrowing spirits, the bereaved find rest in the arms of Jesus. While some clergy find "success" in numbers, the *Seelsorger* will be deeply appreciated and long remembered as the one who brought the balm of the Gospel.

7
Pastoral Care
for Chemical Dependents
and Co-Dependents

Generally speaking, drugs have been a blessing to humanity. Consider life without vaccines, aspirin, or penicillin (or their substitutes for those allergic to the originals). Yet because of their very ability to change body chemistry, drugs have always been subject to misuse.

Physicians and the government seek to monitor the use of prescription drugs that have mind-altering properties. But some people abuse any drug—prescription or not, legal or not. Because of the chemical effect on the mind (usually pleasurable), many people become psychologically and/or physically dependent upon these drugs and lose control over their use, which causes progressively more serious problems for both the dependent persons and their families as co-dependents.

Some have estimated that at least 10 million Americans are chemically dependent on alcohol. If so, then at least another 50 million family members are suffering the results.[1] Millions more

---

[1] Jean Kinney and Gwen Leaton, *Loosening the Grip: A Handbook of Alcohol Information* (St. Louis: Times Mirror/Mosby College Publishing, 1987), p. 22. Statistics show that in America 17.5 million persons, age 18 and over, are problem drinkers—that is, persons who may not have lost control over their use of alcohol but who are having problems with alcohol use. In addition, it is estimated that

are pathologically dependent on other drugs—and thus additional millions are included in the number of sufferers.

In a typical Lutheran congregation, at least 30 percent of the members may be adversely affected by drug dependency. Because people recognize the church's care for all, victims of chemical dependency frequently turn to the pastor for help. Therefore, the pastor must understand the problem and be ready to provide the needed pastoral care.

The Cause of Chemical Dependency

Research increasingly points to the probability that chemical dependency results not only out of a dependency-encouraging environment but also from an inherited predisposition toward chemical dependency (which may be akin to the chemical imbalance that causes clinical depression in some people). Strong evidence indicates that this inherited predisposition is especially the case among alcoholics.

Spiritual factors also are often a part of the cause of chemical dependency. Some persons seek and believe they have found a way to overcome their sense of alienation from God and other people, a way to rise above their personal feelings of insignificance and insecurity. Howard J. Clinebell, Jr., in *Understanding and Counseling the Alcoholic*, states that "alcohol provides a pseudosatisfaction for the alcoholic's religious needs." He adds, "The alcoholic thus seeks to satisfy his religious needs by nonreligious means."[2] In reality, whatever dependent persons experience, it results from anesthetized minds. But for a time they seem convinced that they have found the solution to unmet personal needs. So as long as they derive benefits from drug use, they believe they cannot obtain the benefits elsewhere.

Chemical Dependency from a Christian Perspective

The Bible talks about only one chemical abuse, that of alcohol.[3] While wine is a good gift of God (e.g., Ps. 104:14–15), the Bible also warns against its abuse as part of "the acts of the sinful

---

one out of five youth in the 14- to 17-year age range have a serious drinking problem. This would total 2.8 million teenagers, and approximately 81.6 million family members who are affected by alcohol problems. Ibid., p. 48.

[2] Howard J. Clinebell, Jr. *Understanding and Counseling the Alcoholic* (Nashville: Abingdon Press, 1968), p. 73.

[3] Some connect drugs and potions to the "witchcraft" and "magic arts" (*pharmakeia*) of Gal. 5:20 and Rev. 9:21.

nature [that] are obvious" (Gal. 5:19–21). Alcoholism and other chemical dependencies, like every other human disorder and illness, have their roots in the human condition of original sin. Likewise, the willful abuse of alcohol (and, by extension, all chemicals) is a sin.

While both original and actual sins are judged by God, the pastor needs to keep in mind that (1) *he* cannot judge when a person has slipped from willful sin into uncontrollable behavior; and (2) that all sins are forgiven in the atoning death of Christ Jesus. Faith, no matter how weak, is still saving faith. Therefore, in promoting recovery, the pastor will lead the dependent person to repentance so that he may receive the forgiveness of sins and the life-renewing power that God makes available to penitents through faith in Christ Jesus.

Because the dependent's abuse of chemicals involves loss of control, the view can be defended that this is a sin of weakness rather than a deliberate sin that destroys faith. Yet, chemical dependency can be dangerous to faith. In using drugs to "save his life," the abuser increasingly looks to them as his god. He runs the very real risk of thrusting God's saving presence out of his life. Jesus' words apply, "For whoever wants to save his life will lose it, but whoever loses his life for me will find it" (Matt. 16:25).

Dependency-Creating Chemicals

The mind-altering drugs that people use[4] are basically classified as follows.

- Depressants to the central nervous system:
  alcohol, barbiturates, methaqualone, minor tranquilizers, and pain-relieving narcotics such as opium, morphine, codeine, and heroin.
- Stimulants to the central nervous system:
  cocaine, amphetamines, caffeine, and nicotine.
- Hallucinogens:
  LSD, mescaline, peyote, psilocybin, and phencyclidine.

Most of the above chemicals have the ability to produce physical as well as psychological dependency—and sometimes a disposition for dependency on other such drugs (termed "cross-dependence"). A combination of many of these substances, especially a mixture of alcohol and other drugs, multiplies the effects of each on the central nervous system and is particularly danger-

---

[4] Some chemicals, such as marijuana and inhalants, produce the effects of more than one category.

ous. And while withdrawal from drugs can be painful, withdrawal from the combination of alcohol and barbiturates is life-threatening.

Understanding and Ministering to Chemical Dependents

The Nature Of Chemical Dependency

Drug dependency is more than abusing chemicals; it is their continued and uncontrollable use with resultant problems in one or more aspects of a person's life. The chemically dependent person cannot consistently predict when he will begin using the drug, how extensively he will use it, or if he will stop. In fact, chemical dependency is a progressive and ultimately fatal condition for which there is no known cure. However, treatment can lead to abstinence and recovery.

In order to participate in the treatment process, the pastor should understand how chemical dependency progresses. Various professional care units have developed charts to profile the downward progression of the illness through its stages and demonstrate how chemical dependency is destructive to every aspect of a person's life. The pastor should approach the local treatment center for whatever is used locally.

A chemically dependent person, by the very nature of the illness, has difficulty recognizing the condition. Though sometimes feeling guilt and shame, the dependent person generally uses self-protecting defense mechanisms: *denial, rationalization*, and *projection*.

The dependent person *denies* the problem with chemicals, and thus fails to see the relationship between drug use and other apparent problems in one's life.

In turn, the dependent *rationalizes*, claiming no greater use of alcohol or other drugs than other people and insisting that any other personal problems are of little significance.

Finally, the dependent *projects* the cause (and blame) for personal drug use and its problems on others.

The dependent person instinctively seeks to protect personal use of chemicals, viewing drug use as essential to well-being.

Only when the pain of compulsive drug use becomes greater than the pleasure derived from it will the dependent person be open to help. At that moment, one's personal lack of will power to bring about recovery becomes obvious, conceding personal powerlessness over the use of psycho-active chemicals and that life has become unmanageable. Finally, at this critical point, the dependent person is willing to hear from the pastor (and/or any caring person) that God's help and the assistance of many other caring and competent people are the only remaining means to gain freedom from chemical bondage. Without such help, dependent persons can only despair, continue to use drugs, commit suicide, or go insane.

Pastoral Care for Dependent Persons

Chemically dependent persons who come to the pastor are usually fearful, guilt-ridden, and self-condemning. Generally, they are experiencing physical as well as emotional and spiritual pain, but they probably have come only because of the coercion of others. Therefore, to be able to convey God's acceptance (not approval), the pastor should listen in order to understand the counselees' personal view of their problem and in order to be empathetic to their emotions.

The pastor should help the chemically dependent person
- Understand, recognize, and accept the illness;
- Lower defenses and hear what God wants the counselee to hear: Law and Gospel; and
- Obtain professional treatment.

Therefore, the pastor does not use the Law judgmentally, but uses it to help the counselee understand why life is chaotic—that, while ultimately the problem stems from original sin that all of us have inherited, *personal* drug dependency is destroying the counselee's relationship with God and life with others. Although the person's drug abuse may be uncontrollable, the dependent still has the ability, the will, to choose change. Refusal to attempt to do so runs counter to God's will and is under God's judgment.

Then, so that the counselee does not despair, the pastor offers hope by speaking the Gospel of God's forgiving love and help in Jesus Christ with all its reconciling, comforting, and life-changing power.

Since chemical dependency is a loss-of-control illness affecting the person physically, mentally, emotionally, and socially as well as spiritually, the pastor should encourage the counselee to obtain suitable multi-disciplinary treatment beginning with chemical dependency treatment centers readily available in most areas. The centers provide inpatient and outpatient treatment for dependents as well as their families. The fellowships of Alcoholics Anonymous, Narcotics Anonymous, and Cocaine Anonymous also offer recovery resources. For some, participation in a self-help group will be an adequate treatment of choice.

Whether persons choose medical treatment programs or only participate in a support group, the pastor must provide ongoing pastoral care and the fellowship of the Christian community. It is imperative for the pastor to assist participants in a Christian understanding and use of the *Twelve Step Program of Recovery*[5] advocated in treatment centers and self-help groups. The program will help change the intrapersonal dynamic as well as help produce drug abstinence as a way of life.

Understanding and Ministering to Co-Dependents

The Nature of Co-Dependency

The term *co-dependency* is used for family members and others emotionally close to chemically dependent persons. Like the dependent person, they too suffer (and have their own identifiable illness). Co-dependents are confused, angry, guilty, and afraid. Like dependent persons, they too practice denial, rationalization, and projection. For these family members, life is chaotic. They struggle to bring order out of the chaos. They too attempt new behaviors that usually do not help recovery (though the methods often keep the family functioning in some minimal way). Frequently the family behaves in ways that allow the dependent person to continue justifying the abuse of drugs.

Children of abusers, if untreated, continue to be co-dependents even after they leave home. As they grow, they continue to show particular problems. They may demonstrate an inability to trust and/or to establish intimate relationships, a strong need to control others, a denial of feelings, an exaggerated sense of responsibility, and impulsive behavior. They may experience a sense of low self-esteem, depression, isolation, and difficulty in maintaining satisfying relationships.

Pastoral Care for Co-Dependents

Many chemical dependents and co-dependents turn to the pastor for help. Usually co-dependents come first, often presenting problems other than chemical dependency. As in every counseling setting, the pastor is to speak the truth in love (without sacrificing/confusing truth or love) and is to support his words with his caring pastoral presence. He will strive to speak the Law and Gospel in ways that enable people to hear God's Word non-defensively and thus allow the Holy Spirit to work.

In providing pastoral care, the informed pastor assists family

---

[5] The *12-Step Program of Recovery*, intended for wide acceptance in a pluralistic society, needs to be undergirded with Christian understandings when, for example, it speaks of God as "The Higher Power" and of "God as we understand Him."

members in identifying and discontinuing hostile and protecting behaviors that encourage drug use. He guides them in practicing a "tough love" that unselfishly allows the dependent person to experience the pain of drug use and its attendant behavior. Likewise, the pastor encourages family members to live apart from the loved one's destructive behavior—and yet to do so without withdrawing their "tough love" care and helpful availability.

The goal of the pastor is to help both dependents and co-dependents become involved fully in the recovery process that has already begun by getting in touch with him.

Support groups are available for co-dependents as well as for dependents. Among them are Al-Anon and Alateen for the family and friends of alcoholics, and Families Anonymous and Nar-Anon for those close to persons dependent on other drugs. Al-Anon has special groups for adult children of alcoholics.

The pastor can be especially helpful by informing family members about *intervention* and by encouraging them to consult with a specialist who will explain and facilitate this process. Intervention begins when people close to the dependent person, as a group, confront him with specific information about his drug abuse and hurtful behavior (i.e., to apply the Law to this situation). The goal is to increase the level of emotional pain so that the dependent will ask for treatment. Competent intervention facilitators may be found in local treatment centers, as well in area offices of the National Council on Alcoholism.

Conclusion

Professionals in the field speak of chemical dependency as a spiritual illness that also affects a person physically, mentally, emotionally, and socially. Treatment centers and self-help groups recognize and emphasize that spiritual resources are necessary for the recovery of dependents and co-dependents. Their counsel that recovery results from surrendering one's will and life to a higher power underscores the need for competent pastoral care in recovery from the sin-illness of chemical dependency. After all, the full recovery that God intends can be found only in a right relationship with God through faith in Jesus Christ. The Lord Jesus Christ alone provides the essential resources for *full* recovery. Of himself he said, "I have come that they may have life, and have it to the full" (John 10:10b).

8
God's People
with Special Needs

What excitement the disciples must have felt (Matt. 4:23–24)! They saw before their own eyes the fulfillment of the prophecy of Isaiah:

> Then will the eyes of the blind be opened and the ears of the deaf unstopped. Then will the lame leap like a deer, and the mute tongue shout for joy (35:3–6).

Yet the disciples must have acknowledged the reality that other texts imply: Jesus healed only one of the many people at the Pool of Bethesda (John 5:2–8); only some Israelites afflicted with leprosy were sent home clean.

In the role of servant under Christ, the church keeps in mind and heart both the commission to "make disciples of all nations, baptizing them . . . and teaching them" (Matt. 28:19–20) as well as, following Pentecost, the model of a healing ministry: "By faith in the name of Jesus, this man whom you see and know was made strong. It is Jesus' name and the faith that comes through him that has given this complete healing to him" (Acts 3:16).

The two are not unrelated. People with special needs[1] com-

---

[1] This term includes people with various physical and emotional disabilities, e.g., epilepsy, blindness, schizophrenia, etc. Those who bear those infirmities have indicated to the American culture quite strongly that they do not appreciate the older term *handicapped* (which describes a person's *attitude* toward his disa-

prise a vast proportion of "all peoples/nations."[2] Because those special needs affect the entire person, they must be addressed as part of sharing the Gospel. But the large numbers do not justify every approach to pull them onto the rolls. An emphasis on mere statistical growth denigrates the church as the body of Christ and the pastor as Christ's undershepherd. The true model of the servant church grows out of God's own promises in such passages as Is. 35:3–6 and Hosea 6:6 and their fulfillment as spoken by His Son, " 'I desire mercy, not sacrifice.' For I have not come to call the righteous, but sinners" (Matt. 9:13).

The pastor who seeks to carry out a Gospel-centered ministry to all people—including those with special needs—will experience a number of tensions.

- How can I correctly present the miracles of Jesus to those in need of such miracles?
- How do I apply God's message of hope to specific individuals with specific special needs?
- How can this congregation be sensitized to develop programs and facilities that will include *all* people?
- How large a part does the fear of embarrassment/doing something inappropriate play in ignoring those with special needs—and how can I help my parishioners overcome that fear?
- How shall I overcome my own fear of promising more than I/the congregation will deliver?
- Is this mentally disabled person capable of understanding sin and grace and, therefore, of receiving Holy Communion?[3]

---

bility). The term *disabled* also is acceptable.

This separate chapter is devoted to special ministries, but the division is artificial—yet beneficial insofar as it enables the pastor to reach each person uniquely; for each of us is, in fact, unique.

[2] Two million hearing-impaired people live in the U.S.; one out of every 1,800 babies is born with cystic fibrosis; each week 200 additional young people are diagnosed with multiple sclerosis; six-and-a-half million persons are mentally disabled.

[3] Under most circumstances, the mentally disabled may be confirmed and receive the Sacrament. The ability/inability to memorize, e.g., the Six Chief Parts corresponds poorly to one's level of faith.

The process of Christian education leading up to the confirmation of the mentally disabled will need to be personalized, should focus on an understanding of personal responsibility for sin and the total grace of God, and should be personalized with the help of the family.

Further information may be obtained from Christian institutions such as Bethesda Lutheran Home, Watertown, Wis., and Good Shepherd Lutheran Home of the West, Terra Bella, Calif.

The above list should not cause inaction but rather give direction to the pastor's ministry. Success and hope abound. Every faithful pastor of a few years can recount the affirmation of the sick-made-well who have said, "Pastor, I know that the doctors and medicine did the work, but it wouldn't have happened without God making it work. Thanks for standing by me." Or, "God bless you, Pastor, for teaching [my retarded son] about Jesus. I had given up hope. But when he took Communion this morning for the first time, I wept with joy." Or (via a translator), "I didn't think the church or God cared much about us deaf people. But now that you found a signer to stick with me at church, I finally understand why my parents back home go all the time."

This chapter, therefore, focuses on the pastoral ministry to those with special needs. No excuses are acceptable for by-passing those with special needs. Christ's miracles of healing demonstrate that most clearly. He never turned anyone away; instead he sought them out. He loved them, had compassion on them, and helped them. A Christ-centered pastor and congregation will do no less.

The Inclusive Congregation

Imagine a congregation at worship that invites and offers facilities, staffing, and a Christ-like welcome for the retarded, those in wheel chairs, patients with AIDS, and those with prolonged mental illness intermingled with so-called "normal" people. To the world—and even to some in the church—such a congregation might appear as a gathering of losers, of untouchables. Such groups gathered on hillsides and in doorways to hear Jesus[4]— groups of the healthy and the sick, the beautiful and the ugly, the poor and the rich, the loved and the unloved.[5] Jesus' own words offer encouragement for us to assemble similar groups: "I tell you the truth, whatever you did for one of the least of these brothers of mine, you did for me" (Matt. 25:40). His words require no extensive interpretation.

The pastor does not question *whether* he and the congregation will minister to people with special needs, but *how*. The tensions (as previously mentioned) exist but are not insurmountable. The congregation itself may increase the tension by looking at the cost. The community may add its disapproval when "the unsightly" become more visible. None of these, however, temper Jesus' invitation,

---

[4] Mark 1:32–34, the disinherited; 2:15–17, Christ's own purpose and mission.

[5] Matt. 11:28; Mark 5:1–20; Luke 22:50–51.

> Come to me, all you who are weary and burdened, and I will give you rest. Take my yoke upon you and learn from me, for I am gentle and humble in heart, and you will find rest for your souls (Matt. 11:28–29).

Inclusiveness Begins with a Christ-like Attitude

Sad but true, far too frequently people with special needs are avoided—willingly, unwillingly, unknowingly. In some cases they almost qualify as nonpersons. People affected with AIDS probably present an extreme example, but a clear example they are. In fact, they may well qualify as the "lepers" of our day, people who should remain at a safe distance and cry out, "Unclean!"

This attitude of alienation, guilt, and fear on the part of the average person toward the disabled is rather common, even among pastors. One woman, trying to encourage her church to work with the disabled, wrote tragically,

> I found out that handicapped people petrify our members. I found out that a wonderful lady who was handicapped in a wheel chair and had muscle spasms intermittently was shunned by our members and stared at by others. She was not welcomed. She was wheeled in and out at the end of the service with very little warmth.[6]

The pastor's first task, then, is to change the attitude and understanding of God's people. But that task begins with the pastor himself and how he perceives those with special needs as fellow humans of equal worth and dignity in the eyes of Christ.

An Attitude of Seeing the Value in Others

The point bears repeating: people with special needs have value, not because they represent statistical growth but because our Lord values them just as he values all people—perhaps more so (based on the Isaiah passage cited above that Jesus quoted concerning himself). Listen to his vision that he shared with the apostle John:

> There before me was a great multitude . . . . They were wearing white robes . . . . "These are they who have come out of the great tribulation; they have washed their robes and made them white in the blood of the Lamb. . . . Never again will they hunger; never again will they thirst. The sun will not beat upon them, nor any scorching heat. For the Lamb at the center of the throne will be their shepherd; he will lead them to springs of living water. And God will wipe away every tear from their eyes (Rev. 7:9–17).

---

[6] Source unknown.

No matter what our physical condition, God values and loves each one of us so much that "He gave his one and only Son, that whoever believes in him shall not perish but have eternal life" (John 3:16).

An Attitude of Seeing the Contribution of the Disabled

Pastors as well as laity can profit from the contributions that the disabled bring to the congregation—profits far more valuable than those counted in the collection plate.

Many of the disabled are equipped to contribute their time and talents the same as other members. A blind man can tune a piano as well as a sighted person. An epileptic can care for the church library quite capably. A deaf person can serve on the altar guild along side someone mildly disabled mentally. The congregation benefits as every member exercises good stewardship of time and talents (Eph. 4:16).

Yet, even when some disability does deny the individual the opportunity to serve, that person does more than occupy space in a pew. His or her presence in worship stands as a sign of God's mission in a fallen world, a sign of God's grace and redemption. He or she is an eschatological reminder that, at the end of time all will be made right. He or she carries an affliction *for the sake of other people*, affording them the opportunity and challenge to serve. There are no wasted lives in Christ's kingdom; there are no losers, only winners under the cross.[7]

An Attitude of Being Flexible

Those congregations with a Christ-like attitude understand that, since no two people are alike, no single method will serve the special needs of every disabled person. The key is flexibility. One deaf child might need individualized confirmation instruction; another might be able to join the regular class.

As part of the flexibility, do not be afraid of mistakes. Overconcern for the disabled can lead to an embarrassing patronage that exacerbates the problem. On the other hand, the disabled will laugh *with* you as you together search for workable approaches. Genuine love, persistence, an inquiring mind, and a healthy sense of humor will bring success. Reach out in the love of Christ for human hearts, and the formula will never fail.

An Attitude of Overcoming Fear

It is an ugly truism that even "normal" Christians can be afraid of the disabled. An older deaf-blind person, a Downs-syn-

---

[7] Matt. 2:16–18.

drome teenager, an autistic child—every disabled person has the ability to make others feel very uncomfortable. At times, even church members may prefer that the disabled be taken care of "in some other place than here; their presence is distracting."

Some institutions and agencies (including the church sponsored) do provide the necessary Christian community. However, the nation can provide institutional care for only a small percent of any population segment—for the mentally disabled, only three percent. The body of Christ cannot ignore the other 97 percent any more than it can forget about the 3 percent served in institutions.

The fear (and even anger) that the average church member may feel could well be a surface emotion that masks other feelings. These may include fear of not knowing socially appropriate verbal and body-language responses to the disabled; fear of being asked (directly or by implication) to commit additional time and/or energy to caring for someone in need; fear of being laughed at by others because of openly displayed care; or fear of confronting one's own emotions concerning being disabled. (The converse of these fears may afflict the disabled as well.)

During his personal visits, the pastor will help his members work through those fears, to understand and verbalize what is behind them, and to increase confidence in Christ's love because "perfect love drives out fear" (1 John 4:18).

An Attitude of Overcoming Judgment

In the past, many Christians erroneously held the suspicion that a sickness or disability was somehow a chastisement from God and could be overcome if they bargained with God. The rise in AIDS has rejuvenated and calcified that conviction on a national basis.

That understanding simply is not true. To be sure, when a person gets caught in a fire, he gets burned. But "getting burned" in no way defines "getting caught in a fire" as sin; nor is "getting burned" a punishment. In the same way, AIDS has not defined homosexuality as a sin; God did that long before. Nor is AIDS a *direct* punishment from God for some specific sin. The same must be emphasized for parents of a child who dies of sudden infant death syndrome or who contracts cystic fibrosis. The miracle of the blind man in John 9 shouts Christ's reply to such a thought— as does the child who has contracted AIDS from a blood transfusion.

The pastor can and must proclaim that sicknesses and disabilities witness to the fact that we live in a fallen world, not Eden, and that, therefore, God sent His Son to redeem both people and the world (Rom. 8:18–22).

An Attitude of Overcoming Condescension

Briefly, an attitude of condescension can negate any effort of pastoral ministry. No ministry *with* people can occur when the pastor or laity believes that "they can't do anything, those poor people; we'll just take care of them." While a few (*very few*) people are totally dependent on others, most disabled people know that, with some accommodation to their special needs, they can contribute as much or more than most to the overall ministry of the congregation. In fact, their special needs often *increase* their sensitivity toward others. A condescending attitude robs both the disabled as well as the rest of the church from the blessings that the disabled person can contribute.

An Inclusive Church Plans for the Cost

Every ministry of the congregation requires an investment of energy, time, and money. Ministering with and to those with special needs is no exception. However, no matter what the property committee or treasurer may think, the greatest cost is energy and time.

The Human Investment

Before anything else, the needs must be determined. Someone has to complete the detail work of identifying the disabled by name, address, phone, and the special needs they have. Although this list may begin with the membership, it must reach beyond into the community. (By itself, the list is incomplete until the disabled have been visited personally and their needs discussed.)

A second list will contain the human resources within the congregation—people who can provide transportation, capable teachers who can be further trained if necessary, signers for the deaf, persons to make spiritual calls at home or in an institution, and sensitive individuals to be partners with the disabled to handle any personal needs while at church. This list also is incomplete until the needs of the disabled are met.

The Financial Investment

What factors help or hinder the full participation of all people? Once again, consult first with the disabled themselves to determine their special needs. Contact private and governmental agencies for information and assistance for an inundation of information. Then the congregation will be able to evaluate what must be done. The list might include

- Moving the pews so that at least one aisle provides access for wheelchairs;
- Adjusting the lighting and acoustics;
- Rearranging educational rooms;
- Purchasing educational and worship materials such as braille hymnals and Sunday school courses for the mentally disabled;
- Providing a usable entrance to the church and access to the nave; or
- Remodeling bathrooms.

The dollar-and-cents figure ought not hinder the church's work. Just as a congregation would not think of opening its doors without a place for "normal" people to sit, so it should view the needs of all people. Such costs are part of the congregation's standard operating budget.

An Inclusive Church Uses Every Resource

The congregation first will want to work closely with church-sponsored agencies such as those listed in *The Lutheran Annual*. Secular agencies will respond likewise. While they cannot supply the spiritual ministry necessary, they can assist, e.g., in the purchase of church-owned wheelchairs for on-site use and in recommending building design changes.

In addition, secular organizations such as Alcoholics Anonymous provide a human and healing ministry that the church ought not ignore. Indeed, some Lutheran congregations have allowed and even encouraged AA chapters to use their facilities. While Lutherans do not support the organization's deistic view of God, the alcoholic need not confess that view in order to be a member. Since the church does not offer a matching organization or service, the pastor ought to consider how he and the congregation might support its work.

The same holds true for many nonreligious organizations. While they may be used as tools for an extended view of the church's own ministry, they also offer the opportunity for the church to support *civic righteousness*. Such groups might be invited to use the church's facilities; and the pastor might even be encouraged by his congregation to take an active part in their work. Doing good works is not conditional upon the recipient's faith or lack of it.[8]

Conclusion

Ministering with and to disabled people has always been carried out by God's people. God Himself commanded through Moses, "Do not curse the deaf or put a stumbling block in front of the blind, but fear your God. I am the Lord" (Lev. 19:14). One also recalls the hospitals, leprosariums, medical missions, schools for the deaf and other institutions established by the church and dedicated Christians.

These are mentioned, not to induce guilt as motivation, but to illustrate the joy God's people have when they see before their own eyes the fulfillment of Isaiah's prophecy in Jesus:

Then will the eyes of the blind be opened and the ears of the deaf unstopped. Then will the lame leap like a deer, and the mute tongue shout for joy (35:3–6).

---

[8] Matt. 25:35; also 5:14–16.

9
Cults and New Religions

The cults, the so-called "new religions," are a special category of concern for the Christian.[1] Although many of these revive ancient heresies or pagan religions, they are enjoying new acceptance and success throughout the world. They may be divided into subcategories such as

- Western expressions of Hinduism/Buddhism;
- Synthesis of Christianity and eastern religions;
- Isolationist and "end-time" groups;
- Revivals of pantheism and nature worship;
- Occult new interpretations of Christianity;
- Satanist and witchcraft enclaves; and
- Substitutes for religion such as secular humanists, consciousness-raisers, organized atheists, and self-deifying "new agers."

The new religions are a force to be reckoned with, for even

---

[1] Information on the various kinds of organizations that are of concern to the evangelical Christian may be found in a series of books published by Concordia Publishing House (1977 to 1988):

How to Respond to. . .
- *the New Age Movement* (Philip H. Lochhaas)
- *the Cults* (Hubert F. Beck)
- *Transcendental Meditation* (Keith A. Gerberding)
- *the New "Christian" Religions* (Philip H. Lochhaas)
- *the Eastern Religions* (Philip H. Lochhaas)
- *the Occult* (David W. Hoover)
- *Satanism* (Bruce G. Frederickson)
- *the Science Religions* (Frederick R. Harm)

the most conservative estimates set the number at well over 3,000 separate organizations. They are often difficult to describe or analyze, for new ones appear quite suddenly, while others disappear, divide, merge, or assume new names. Some have exhibited remarkable staying power and are well on their way toward becoming institutionalized religions or new denominations.

Why these new religions have risen to prominence so quickly, especially among the young people, is a matter of conjecture. Certainly many youth have felt a disillusionment with society, a loneliness born of the popular philosophy that the individual must create his own happiness, a disappointment that science and technology have failed to solve mankind's most pressing problems, the lack of generally-accepted and dependable moral standards, a bleak future of no frontiers and few opportunities, a betrayal of ideals by popular heroes and heroines, and the discovery of corruption in trusted institutions (including those churches that have forsaken the supernatural and have turned to human potential instead).

To the disillusioned, the new religions offer warmth, acceptance, and simple human friendship. Each member participates fully in everything, thereby finding a personal identity. In place of free choice based on eroded morals, members are provided a strong moral/ethical standard (although, among some groups, applied only to certain chosen virtues). Amazingly, few followers ever mention that the group's doctrine (rather than life-style) attracted them.

Usually a new religion is headed by one leader, a strong father-figure who may be regarded as a master, a messiah, a discoverer of new truths, or even as a deity. He may use familiar Christian words but assign new meanings to them. Sin and salvation may be defined simply in terms of obedience or disobedience to his commands. He is generally very dogmatic about his "revelations" and rigidly moral about the particular virtues he has selected. Paranoid about someone displacing him as leader, he feels compelled to provide solutions, no matter how simplistic, to every problem the world faces. He sometimes maintains absolute control by demanding that his followers surrender all their possessions, relinquish all decisions, and allow surveillance over all their movements.

The profile of the average convert to the new religions is
- Age 18 to 26;
- Educated;
- Serious about life and the future;
- From a comparatively stable home;
- Having some religious background; and

● Facing a change in life.

That last item, facing a change in life, often provides the key to why people join. The recruiter engages a person at just the moment when he or she, for the first time, is faced with an adult decision: graduation from high school or college, a move to a new city, a divorce or death in the family, a breakup with a lifelong friend, the sudden realization of one's own limitations—anything that will make the person vulnerable to someone who steps in and offers at least some stability for life.

The Role of the Church

The rise of the new religions presents an unusual challenge to the church of Jesus Christ. Unlike other organizations, the new religions generally do not tolerate dual membership. Rather, often with hostility, they require the convert to forsake all other religious allegiances, and they remove the convert from familiar surroundings and prior spiritual influences. More often than not, the Christian congregation and its pastor will never reach such individuals (though the church's effort will continue). Pastoral care, then, must focus first on prevention, and second on counseling the families and loved ones of those who have become involved with one of the new religions.

Prevention Education

Prevention begins with faithful and clear proclamation of God's Law and Gospel. No other tool exists—and none is needed, for Law and Gospel carry the power of God's Holy Spirit. Yet, these must be proclaimed with an awareness of the needs of people in contemporary society for an eternal, unchanging standard of right and wrong, for assurance of forgiveness and acceptance in Jesus Christ, for the opportunity to put faith into action through Christian love and service, and for personal recognition, identity, friendship, and support within the group—as well as a fatherly leader.

Prevention includes providing adequate staff and budget to help the church's youth be "the church of *today*" in Christian witness and service. Of particular importance is support for youth during change. Prevention also includes education about the new religious groups that are active in the community in which the congregation is located, their tenets and their methods of recruitment. Special programs should be arranged for the church's youth, for few of the new religions can recruit successfully where their targets have been forewarned.

Counseling the Families

A special kind of ministry is needed for the families of those who have become entangled in one of the new religions. Their loss is felt sometimes as keenly as a death in the family. Assure the family that God is not dead; pray with them and for them. Help them avoid all self-condemnation and self-pity, for the majority of those who affiliate with the new religions come from homes where the parents did many things "right" (humanly speaking). Urge the family to deepen its own spiritual life and involvement in the church, for their own sakes and to the glory of God. Impress upon them the importance of continuing to communicate love to their family member, remembering that true love does not depend upon reciprocation, even as Jesus loved us and died for us "while we were still sinners" (Rom. 5:8).

Above all, assure the family that no Word of God spoken to their loved one in the past, no training in church and Sunday school, no Christian example has ever been wasted, and no prayer in Jesus' name has ever gone unheard. Point the family to John 10:27–29 and the unimpeachable character of the God who made this promise.

Urge the family members to draw their friends and acquaintances into their circle of concern by requesting their prayers and spiritual support. (In addition, check if your community has a parental support group that offers understanding and guidance— spiritual and/or legal.)

Serving Those Who Return

Pastors also have a special ministry to those who have left a new religion, as converts frequently do after two or three years. Clearly, what may be true of one new religion is not necessarily true of another; but striking similarities appear in the accounts given by thousands who have re-entered society after several years in one of them.

- They agree that rejoining society can be much harder than leaving it.
- They experience the "fishbowl effect," the feeling that they are being watched out of curiosity or distrust.
- Facing choices and decisions once again creates culture shock.
- Sometimes they suffer physical problems and dysfunction due to diet or untreated illnesses and other chronic conditions and exhaustion from an endless round of recruiting and fund-raising.
- They encounter emotional problems and guilt over having permitted themselves to have been misled.

- They suffer "floating" or "flashbacks" into a trancelike state where they cannot be reached through their senses.
- They rightly fear the possibility of harassment by members of the groups they left.
- They are not easily reintegrated into the former church, for they feel that they have been betrayed by "religion" and are now distrustful of all spiritual offerings.

At this point, the conscientious pastor will recognize his own limitations and his need to refer the "prodigal" to a trained Christian counselor who has encountered these phenomena before. (Some areas have provided "halfway houses" for those having difficulties in readjusting to normal society.)

And remember that the families of the former cult member often need as much or more counselling than the former member.

10
Christian Admonition and Discipline

Christian Admonition

The body of Christ is to be a caring community reflecting Christ, its head. Touched by the love of God in Christ, Christians accept the privilege and responsibility of nurturing and supporting the spiritual and bodily needs of one another. The Savior clearly said, "My command is this: Love each other as I have loved you" (John 15:12). John reminds us: "This is love: not that we loved God, but that he loved us and sent his Son as an atoning sacrifice for our sins. Dear friends, since God so loved us, we also ought to love one another" (1 John 4:10–11). And, because the power of the devil, the world, and our sinful flesh combine to lead the weak astray—and even the strong from time to time—Paul reminds the Galatian Christians, "Brothers, if someone is caught in a sin, you who are spiritual should restore him gently. But watch yourself, or you also may be tempted. Carry each other's burdens, and in this way you will fulfill the law of Christ" (Gal. 6:1–2).

There was no limit to what the Savior would do and the patience he exhibited in reclaiming the lost and the erring. The trilogy of parables recorded in Luke 15 articulates God's perseverance in seeking the erring and God's yearning to forgive and to restore the lost to the household of God.

Nor will the pastor spare any effort to help the congregation reclaim the erring or lost member, letting "the Word of Christ dwell in you richly as you teach and admonish one another with all wisdom" (Col. 3:16). The task is not self-righteous, but a genuine interest and concern for a fellow member who breaks with the worshiping community, who repudiates the nurture of the means of grace, or who succumbs to the temptations that assault all of us. The goal is for all to be kept safe in our Savior's flock.

Yet even Christians often ignore those who need spiritual help, as though it is none of their concern. Occasional expressions of concern, therefore, have a hollow ring—as, for example, when a member has been absent from worship for a number of years and the caller from the church then says, "I am here because we care about you." Such sporadic attempts seem to indicate that, no matter what relationship people have with the Lord, they will be saved anyway.

Although the pastor has the primary responsibility to provide leadership, *all* congregation members are accountable to God for their fellow believers. To withhold spiritual care from others is an offence against God, the creator and savior of us all.

As an example to the flock, the pastor should demonstrate a caring affection for all the members of the congregation. He should lead by giving them opportunities to carry out the same caring concern for each other. (Those opportunities, however, do not include letting the pastor's office serve as a repository for gossip and innuendo. If a member comes bearing tales of others, that member should be counseled to carry out personally the responsibility of admonition.)

Church Discipline: A Ministry of Reconciliation

Properly used, the church discipline process is positive and helpful, an opportunity to teach others to apply the Law and the Gospel rightly,[1] and a way for the Gospel to motivate people to put their faith into practice (Eph. 2:10; Gal. 5:24–26; Rom. 8:1–17).

Matthew 18 should never be used as a quick way to get rid of a delinquent. Church discipline is a ministry of reconciliation (2 Cor. 5:19). The objective is to reconcile the person with God, with the congregation in general, and with individual members

---

[1] For example, in Matt. 19:16–24, Jesus applies the Law. In Acts 16:25–34, Paul applies the Gospel.

Pastors (and elders) should again and again study C. F. W. Walther's *The Proper Distinction Between Law and Gospel* (St. Louis: Concordia, 14th printing, 1986; copyright 1929, 1986).

Additional reading should be given to *Church Discipline in the Christian Congregation* (November 1985), The Commission on Theology and Church Relations (The Lutheran Church—Missouri Synod).

(including the pastor). Pastors exercise great influence in the parish when they, as peacemakers (Matt. 5:9), apply the principles of Christ (Matt. 7:1–5; 18:1–15) and St. Paul (2 Cor. 5:11–6:2; Gal. 6:1–5), and when they train their members how to bring about reconciliation.

Implementation of the reconciliation process involves more than just going through Matthew 18 mechanically, step by step.[2] Paul's writings offer good practical advice. The person who attempts to prevent a brother or sister from falling from grace must be spiritually oriented (Gal. 6:1–5), fully attuned to what is meant by life in the Spirit (Gal. 5:13–25), and must be aware that, at the same time, Scripture applies to both parties: "There is now no condemnation for those who are in Christ Jesus" (Rom. 8:1).[3] This assumes that the erring member is a child of God until proved otherwise (Matt. 13:24–30).

To achieve this reconciliation, three factors must be clear:

Attitude: The mind of Christ and an awareness of his presence is fundamental to church discipline. Christ himself said:

> Whatever you bind on earth will be bound in heaven, and whatever you loose on earth will be loosed in heaven. Again, I tell you that if two of you on earth agree about anything you ask for, it will be done for you by my Father in heaven. For where two or three come together in my name, there am I with them (Matt. 18:18–20; cf. John 20:21–23).

The passage requires us to take seriously what it means that Jesus is present in the church. Since Christ is present, the church will strive to exhibit the same qualities of patience, perseverance, love, forgiveness, and compassion that Christ showed. The church must act out of a passionate concern for the eternal welfare of the erring person.

Purpose: The ultimate purpose throughout church disciplinary proceedings is, through repentance and absolution, to restore the person into full fellowship with the church. Therefore, the church cannot place a limit on the time for each step of Matthew 18. The church has a sacred obligation to do everything possible to bring the person back into a vital, saving relationship with the Lord Jesus Christ. A person who becomes a member of

---

[2] Both John H. C. Fritz (*Pastoral Theology* [St. Louis: Concordia, 1932, 1945, Heritage Edition 1977], pp. 232–256) and George H. Gerberding (*The Lutheran Pastor* [Minneapolis: Augsburg Publishing House, 1902], pp. 260–270) give excellent procedures for carrying out Matthew 18.

[3] The pastor needs to be well versed in what is taught in Rom. 7:7–8:17 as he proceeds with the reconciliation process.

a Christian congregation in effect *requests* such caring concern; and the congregation, in receiving a member, promises to provide it.

Means: The Word, rightly divided as Law and Gospel, provides the sole means to summon the erring to repentance and to offer assurance of forgiveness. Appeals to expediency, self-advantage, or various expressions of loyalty fail to take seriously the spiritual peril in which the person is involved and run counter to the ultimate purpose of reclaiming the lost.

The Lesser Ban

As the first official act of applying the Law to the unrepentant, a pastor may exercise his responsibility for the spiritual welfare of a person by withholding the Lord's Supper. This is called the "lesser ban." The pastor may invoke this when a person manifests an impenitent spirit by bearing a grudge, refusing to forgive, or living in unrepentant sin— i.e., binding one's self by sin, refusing the grace of God. The pastor deals with the person on a personal basis while the problem has not been resolved, praying that, thereby, subsequent steps toward excommunication will not be necessary. "There has been neither absolution on the one hand nor excommunication on the other."[4]

Excommunication

Cause and Definition

According to Matthew 18, when a person remains adamantly impenitent, the church has no choice but to take the steps toward declaring that person "a pagan and a tax collector" (verse 17). Excommunication means that a person has cut him- or herself off from the grace of God and has been *declared* outside a saving relationship with Jesus Christ. The person who dies in that impenitent state would be eternally lost.

Actually, sin itself does not require excommunication or separation from the Christian church. Everyone sins daily and needs the forgiveness that God freely gives because of Christ. Rather, failure to recognize our sinfulness and being *persistently* impenitent severs us from God and prevents forgiveness and restoration from taking place—whether or not the church pursues church discipline.

Consequences

Excommunication declares that the impenitent person is outside the pale of the church (yet may still worship with it). The

---

[4] *Church Discipline in the Christian Congregation*, p. 21.

excommunicated person may no longer receive the Sacrament of the Altar nor be a sponsor at a baptism. All rights and privileges of membership in the congregation are forfeited, and the person is moved from the membership list to the list of prospects to be sought for Christ. Anyone who dies in this unrepentant state is not to be accorded a Christian burial.

The person who withdraws from the congregation before excommunication takes place obviously cannot be excommunicated. However, this by no means relieves the congregation of the responsibility to admonish the person about persistent impenitence or to point out its eternal consequences.

Because a Christian congregation excommunicates in the name of the entire Christian church, the action ideally should be upheld throughout the Christian church on earth, regardless of a congregation's affiliation. (This shows how important it is that excommunication be for a valid reason).

Separation vs. Excommunication

At times, separation from the congregation rather than excommunication is in order. For example, differences over a non-fundamental doctrine (i.e., a doctrine that is not essential to saving faith) may disrupt the confessional harmony that unites the members of the congregation. If continued instruction in true doctrine does not prove convincing, the dissenting person should be urged to become a member of a tradition more in harmony with his or her confessional stance.

Pastoral Responsibility toward Excommunication

The pastor should not accept the role of policeman, enforcer, prosecutor, judge, or jury. The verdict of excommunication must be rendered by the congregation. A unanimous ballot does not appear to be a Biblical requirement, though it may check impetuous action.[5] And, if any person cannot affirm the action, that person may need to be counseled in understanding Scripture.

The pastor's responsibility, when the excommunication process reaches the final stages, involves three procedures:

1. The pastor must make sure that everything has been done in accord with Scripture.

2. The pastor should do all he can to bring the person to repentance and avoid excommunication.

---

[5] Unanimity does not seem to be a Biblical requirement. When the evidence of sin and impenitence are indisputable, the congregation is not bound to that traditional rubric. Ibid., p. 22.

3. On behalf of the congregation, the pastor announces the excommunication and, should the person repent and be received back into the fellowship of the congregation, he announces the reinstatement.

C. F. W. Walther, in his thesis on ministry "The Voice of Our Church on the Question Concerning the Church and the Ministry," says,

> It is certain that the office of the keys in a more narrow sense, namely, the power publicly to loose and bind, is also entrusted to the incumbents of the ministry of the Word. . . . Here he [the pastor] deals not merely with a clear doctrine of the divine Word but with a judgment of a person's spiritual condition [*Seelenzustand*]. And this judgment is of such a nature that it closes heaven to the person in question and forbids him brotherly fellowship with Christians, and vice versa. Therefore, although the public enforcement of excommunication belongs to and must remain with the incumbents of the ministry of the Word, according to the Lord's command and sacred institution, nevertheless, it must be carried out according to the Lord's express command and order only after the whole congregation (that is, the minister and hearer) has considered and made the final judicial decision on the matter. . . . For this reason even Paul did not desire to excommunicate the incestuous person at Corinth without the congregation, but he wrote them that, though he himself regarded the sinner as deserving excommunication, the congregation itself ("when you are gathered together") should put away from among themselves that wicked person (1 Cor. 5:4, 13).[6]

Conclusion

The practice of Christian admonition and church discipline is a difficult and sensitive responsibility; it also measures how seriously Christians take their total concern for one another. Christian discipline will be largely unpracticed, abused, or ignored as long as a Christian congregation (and/or a pastor as the leader in exercising the Office of the Keys, John 20) fails to make serious attempts to develop a genuinely Christian, caring community. When members assume responsibility for the spiritual welfare of each other, Matthew 18 will help them to demonstrate that concern.

---

[6] C. F. W. Walther, "The Voice of Our Church on the Question of Church and Ministry," *Walther and the Church*. William Dallmann, W. H. T. Dau, and Theodore Engelder, ed. (St. Louis: Concordia, 1938), p. 83.

UNIT V
THE PASTOR CARES
FOR THE FAMILY

1
"Male and Female He Created Them"

Male-Female Sexuality

God, who fashioned male and female with a free will in order to worship the Creator, chose not to work a special act of creation for each person. According to Gen. 1:28, God's first command to Adam and Eve is to bear children, to share in his ongoing creative activity. This command is not given in isolation; bearing children is not a duty performed for a jealous taskmaster. Instead, God created them male and female, with a sexual drive and with a loneliness evident already when a "suitable helper" for Adam could not be found among the animals (Gen. 2:20). Together, the sexual drive and the need for intimate fellowship would drive people from father and mother (Gen. 2:24) to establish a family in which the next generation would be nurtured, in human love, to worship God. As Luther wrote,

> It is of the highest importance to him [God] that persons be brought up to serve the world, promote knowledge of God, godly living, and all virtues, and fight against wickedness and the devil. (LC I 208)

> [Married people] can do no better work and do nothing more valuable either for God, for Christendom, for all the world, for themselves, and for their children than to bring up their children well. . . . In fact, heaven itself could not be made nearer or

achieved more easily than by doing this work.[1]

Thus, God created male/female for the sake of marriage and the family rather than marriage as one among many expressions of sexuality. The confessions affirm this:

God created man[kind] for procreation (Gen. 1:28). (AC XXIII 5)

Gen. 1:28 teaches that [humans] were created to be fruitful and that one sex should have a proper desire for the other. (Ap XXIII 7)

[God] established it [marriage] as the first of all institutions, and he created man and woman differently (as is evident) not for lewdness but to be true to each other, be fruitful, beget children, and support and bring them up to the glory of God. (LC I 207)

The God who made us male and female wants people to embrace their sexuality with a zest for living. He created their capacity for romantic attachments and emotions. Male and female are not like dissimilar musical instruments; they are more like a violin and a bow, each essential to the other, the two "equalling" one. As the CTCR describes it,

Having created the woman, God brings her to the man, and he in turn responds with those words which we have read rather too solemnly: "At last!" At last, here is one who is "bone of my bone and flesh of my flesh." This is an expression of "joyous astonishment." . . . The predicament of man's loneliness—his "aloneness"—has been discerned and overcome by God's creative Word. A relation has been established in which one may come to know oneself and the other in a fellowship of love.[2]

While this is God's plan for humanity in general, it cannot be applied stringently to any one individual.

There are some (although few) exceptions whom God has especially exempted—some who are unsuited for married life and others whom he has released by a high supernatural gift so that they can maintain chastity outside of marriage. (LC I 211)

Nor must *all* fellowship be male-female. People need human association; they need to be completely open with someone and trust that their self-revelation won't be used against them; they need to be accepted as complete persons.

---

[1] *A Sermon on the Estate of Marriage* (preached Jan. 16, 1519), LW 44:12.

[2] *Human Sexuality: A Theological Perspective* (September 1981), The Commission on Theology and Church Relations (The Lutheran Church—Missouri Synod) as prepared by its Social Concerns Committee, pp. 6–8, 14.

Yet God's underlying purpose for implanting the need for human companionship in general remains: To impel a man and a woman to pledge fidelity to each other as they come together in the unique act of ultimate human fellowship—sexual intercourse—and thus participate in God's process of creating more people who worship him.

After the Fall: In God's Grace

In the beginning God created male and female. He created variety in sexuality—physiological and psychological differences to be understood and respected. He created *families*, not random individuals. And God saw that it was very good.

The ideal was quickly shattered. Both male and female disobeyed the word of the Lord (Gen. 3). The goodness within was gone. Due to sin, sex would no longer be what it was meant to be. People's relationships—including relationships as male and female—were changed by a corrupted human nature whose trademark was self-centeredness, seen expressed in the fear and shame of Adam and Eve. Upon all families the awful curse of sin had fallen.

The Fall, however, neither ended nor began human sexuality. The Christian view of maleness and femaleness is defined (in part) by the doctrine of creation.

> In the article of creation Scripture testifies not only that God created human nature before the Fall, but also that after the Fall human nature is God's creature and handiwork (Deut. 32:6; Isa. 45:11; 54:9; 64:8; Acts 17:25, 26; Rev. 4:11; FC SD I 34)

Christians, furthermore, talk about their maleness and femaleness (and relationships) in the context of God's gracious forgiveness of sins in Christ Jesus. Sexual sins are neither more nor less damning than any other category of sin (even though they, more than other sins, often deeply trouble the Christian). Pastoral ministry gives to repentant hearts the gracious message of the Gospel, even as Jesus gave it to the prostitute who wet his feet with her tears and whom he declared forgiven (Luke 7:36–50). The prodigal son also "came to his senses" and was accepted by his forgiving father (Luke 15:11–32). So also in Christ the relationship of the husband, wife, and children (and all others in the household) is transformed.

Christians also understand their sexuality as part of life in the Holy Spirit. Human sexuality takes on a new look, a new freshness, when a person becomes a new creation in Christ. That which was good is good again—a new creation, again and again, daily.

The God who created sexual desire has given the full benediction of his Spirit upon that desire. Therefore, St. Paul exhorts, "Since we live by the Spirit, let us keep in step with [i.e., follow] the Spirit" (Gal. 5:25).

Transmitting this Christ-centered framework for sexuality to the next generation is one of the most important yet most difficult challenges facing the people of God. The church as organization (including the pastor) has access to only minimal time in the lives of children. Even parents may feel outrun when comparing their "quality time" to the effective time of the media and advertising with their children. Rather than despair, adult Christians, with the pastor as leader and teacher, need to plan their best efforts in this matter that defines self-identity. Specifically, the body of believers must provide (beginning with early childhood) the Law and Gospel teaching to strengthen sanctified lives in home and family, which God has set as the basic unit of human society.

The "common wisdom" of the society around us assumes that sexual expression is equal to sexual intercourse; it encourages pubescent children to explore and experiment with their "grown-up" sexuality; it tells teens that a choice made with their brief wisdom is a wise choice *for them.* In reality, this mad rush for sexual experimentation has resulted in more traumas than the glamour magazines ever envisioned.

First and worst, people are learning to separate sex from love and its commitments. It can be done—but those who promote it and those who believe it often ignore the human tragedy that results. The act of sexual intercourse is so personal, interpersonal, and obsessive that the individual craves an enduring commitment from the lover.[3] After experiencing x-number of partners without lasting commitment, intercourse may finally become an end in itself—with the possible result that an individual may become incapable of receiving or giving the commitment necessary for an enduring marriage.

Second, and almost as tragic, some who totally give of themselves expect that their partner has done the same—only to learn later (after a pregnancy or a lover's spat) that not only commitment but true friendship and companionship as well never did exist. Again, the individual eventually may learn to expect no commitment, not even in marriage—and not to commit him- or herself to anyone.

Third, the one-flesh unity described in Genesis is questioned and made impossible by casual sex. In addition to God's norm,

---

[3] Ibid., pp. 16f.

faithfulness and self-giving describe what people *want* to happen in marriage. But those who sleep around have learned to assume that "I" exist for "me"; no one else is going to care for me; no one else is going to "take me as I am, warts and all"; no one else is going to stand by me "in sickness and in health."

In addition to being disobedient to God's command and false in its assumptions, a qualitative difference separates marriage and sleeping together. The marriage commitment should be a public, voluntary, and deliberate declaration that the couple will face life together for as long as their lives last. Only as people resolve to remain in the relationship and to work out their difficulties together can the trust be established that will promote the mutual confidence necessary for handling internal and external pressures.

Against this backdrop, the argument concerning whose responsibility sex education should be—parents, church, school—leads nowhere, for sex education is but one part of transmitting the whole culture, with its values, to the next generation. Parents, of course, have the primary responsibility for the entire process of rearing their children, teaching about sex as well as about science and math. In some areas (math or driver's education, for example) it may not be important that the teaching carry a specifically Christian content; the general society's agreed-upon practice may suffice. But because moral values are central to any discussion of sexuality, parents will want to join with other Christians in educating their children to appreciate God's gift and guidance. The specific programs of adult Christians working together is not of first concern—such cooperation might be the production of Christian sex education materials for use in the home; it might be the parochial school; it might be workshops for parents. Before making these decisions, other factors need to be considered.

1. What is the context of the congregation and/or the parents? What information and expectations about sexuality is the general society transmitting to all—adults and children alike? What is the local community background?

2. What is the milieu of the children? What information about the children can the church learn from the local schools, hang-outs, etc.?

3. What needs do the children (as well as the parents) express? Do not expect these to be the same.

4. In what way(s) will the lay leaders in the congregation be involved in goal-setting and in reaching those goals? Which board(s) will be involved—Christian Ed.; Youth Ministry; a special Family Council? Which of the various educational arms of the congregation—if any—should participate?

5. Who are the best resource people available? Must they be members of the congregation, or might health professionals be asked to participate?

Once these issues are resolved, the pastor and congregation are ready to plan any specifics regarding the materials[4] and the processes (which might include workshops and/or classes for parents on what it means to be male and female). The church also has a wonderful opportunity to provide a healthy atmosphere for singles of all ages to be together—educational programs, retreats, service activities, and recreation. The church has available many resources to support the congregation's ministry to youth and singles. Most of all, beyond any programs provided, the body of believers can demonstrate a Christian spirit and attitude toward sexuality that permeates all activities and will be carried into associations not organized by the congregation.

In matters of human sexuality, Christian people stand as "lights in the midst of a perverse generation." Only by investing time, energy, and dollars in the Christian education of the next generation can the church continue to be a light—not only a priceless light to pass on to the children of the church, but also a light to shine out to the generation around.

---

[4] Synod's Board for Parish Services has long made available through Concordia Publishing House a distinguished, graded sex education series supported with video-cassette presentations. The Christian parent or pastor will appreciate Concordia's excellent spiritual framework for understanding sexuality.

2
The Pastor Cares
for the Married

The Estate of Marriage

United Under God

As it pertains to the life of this world, marriage has social (civil) import. But in origin, it is not a human arrangement. God has instituted it for the being and well-being of this life.

God called male and female into existence and created them in his image (Gen. 1:26f.). In their being and in their relationship with each other they are to reflect something of God. They do not exist for themselves nor for their own fulfillment. Rather, they are to care for God's creation and have been blessed to be able to bring forth their own kind (1:28). This dual responsibility is granted with the view that it will be used in accord with God's good and gracious will. The male/female relation in Genesis 1 is presented as a harmony with no apparent divisions of labor or separated responsibilities. In the image of God, both are one in purpose, one in obligation.

Genesis 2 highlights another dimension. God made a "helper suitable," whom Adam describes as "bone of my bones and flesh of my flesh." Moses thereby points out the physical and emotional closeness of male and female that parallels "the image of God" relationship between male/female and God. Male and female mutually commit themselves to be united as one, working together for the common purpose of establishing a home (2:24) that will bring glory to God and provide an atmosphere where God's purposes may be gladly carried out.

Scripture describes marriage as a lifelong union of one man and one woman, entered into by mutual consent (e.g., Gen. 24:57–58). Essential to the relationship is the commitment the two make to forsake all others and remain faithful to each other in sickness and in health,[1] a commitment to resolve or manage under God any problems.

The union of husband and wife extends to the most intimate sharing in sexual intercourse. In this act, which Scripture calls "knowing," man and woman unite with one another in a most intimate union of giving and receiving. The knowledge of that fellowship—like the knowledge of the fellowship in which God knows those who are His—can never be fully communicated apart from the experience of the union itself. In this union, the partners also learn to know themselves even as they know the other. However, because of sin, many people develop a distorted view of sexuality—which eventually destroys the very thing most want: a relationship of love with someone who cares and with whom the individual can grow and become a more healthy self.

The pastor as educator must continually keep before his people the beauty of the divine purpose of creating the male/female duality.[2] Marriage in the Biblical presentation has to do with God, with growth, with change, with development; and for post-Fall people, with being two people alive together in Christ, with sanctified life in the Spirit. Scripture pictures marriage as two people discovering in the forgiveness of sins a spiritual oneness in Christ as well as a sexual union. Within this context, the reconciling presence of God in Christ is conjointly acknowledged and joyfully celebrated. Therefore sexual intercourse outside of marriage is contrary to God's will and is sinful.

Humanly speaking, happy and permanent marriages can be developed apart from Christ. Similarly, Christian couples are not guaranteed this success/happiness; the "devil, the world and our flesh" can gain the upper hand because Christians are *simul justus et pecator*. Yet, equipped with certain "gifts" of the Lord (in-

---

[1] Luther comments in his 1519 sermon on marriage, "Marriage is a covenant of fidelity. The whole basis and essence of marriage is that each gives himself or herself to the other, and they promise to remain faithful to each other and not give themselves to any other" (LW 44:10f).

[2] Luther commented, "When I began writing on the estate of marriage, I was afraid that . . . I would be kept busier with this one topic than with my entire cause apart from it. If there were nothing else to suggest that the estate of marriage is a godly estate this fact alone should be enough to convince you, namely, that the prince of this world—the devil—sets himself against it in so many ways to resist it with hand and foot and all his strength; indeed, that fornication is not diminishing but on the increase" (LW 45:385).

cluding reliance on divine forgiveness, striving for unity, and cultivating a sense of meaning, hope, faith, and Christian love), the Christian prays that he or she will live a sanctified life under the Spirit. Only then can a couple put aside the old, self-centered being that destroys relations, and daily bring on the new, which permits reconciliation and peace. That will strengthen a good marriage rather than heal a sick one.

Order Within the Family

Although many have used "the order of creation"[3] and Eph. 5:22–33 to support male superiority, the concept of the male as the family dictator cannot be pressed into Ephesians (any more than Prov. 31:10–31 supports the feminist movement). To the particulars of family life Paul applies the preceding section, which enjoins Christians in general to live a life of love (5:2) that includes a reciprocal yielding in love in the Spirit (v. 21). The following verses (22–33) appeal to responsible people who have been freed from the destructive issues of their previous non-Christian home life, to people who understand Biblical responsibility and mutual interdependence.

Paul begins this section by pointing out that the woman's submission is that of a *wife* to her husband (not just any woman to any man). Turning to the husband, Paul avoids the word "submit"; but the love for which he calls demands a radical putting self aside in order to benefit the wife. Contrary to the prevailing custom, the husband is to "give himself up" for his wife "as Christ loved the church." The husband is not to "lord it over" his wife; Jesus Christ is Lord over both—the source, standard and motivation of both their stations under God. The husband's headship has been qualified in and by Christ, by the way Jesus meets and treats sinners in order to save them: in love (5:1) and the Spirit (v. 18).

Drawing from the fact, mode, intention and achievement of Christ's love, a husband learns what is the essence of love. In Christ the husband displays a love that is given from above, a love that transforms the doubt, fear, and distrust of the woman to a response of loving subordination. It is love reaching out, gaining trust and drawing love back from the beloved. Here is the joy that belongs to those who are able to do good, to spend themselves, to effect changes from which not only the chosen partner but also a wider public can profit. Such love is good not only for the beloved

---

[3] In contrast, Luther commented in his 1535 lecture on Genesis, "The wife was made subject to the man by the Law which was given after sin" (LW 1:137f).

but also for the lover. It is so because it resembles the love of Christ for his church and the joy of the church in its servanthood.

Likewise, Peter reminds Christian husbands to treat their wives as "heirs with you of the gracious gift of life" (1 Peter 3:7). He reminds both of their status before God. Together, they both depend totally on God, the Creator and Redeemer. Equally sinners; equally saved. That the woman differs from the man, that they will have to decide what functions each will carry out during different stages of marriage, that at times one must give in to the other—all goes without saying. But Christian love means giving people opportunities, not subservient limitations. Both husband and wife have a divinely created dignity.

The words of St. Paul to free people in God apply to all relationships, whether within marriage or otherwise:

> Therefore, as God's chosen people, holy and dearly loved, clothe yourselves with compassion, kindness, humility, gentleness and patience. Bear with each other and forgive whatever grievances you may have against one another. Forgive as the Lord forgave you. And over all these virtues put on love, which binds them all together in perfect unity. Let the peace of Christ rule in your hearts, since as members of one body you were called to peace. And be thankful. (Col. 3:12–15)

Strengthening the Christian Family

An Intentional Ministry

Having established the family as the basic unit of society, God obliges parents to provide for their children's bodies (1 Tim. 5:8) as well as their spiritual needs (Eph. 6:1–4; Ps. 78:1–8; Prov. 6:20–22; 22:6; Deut. 6:1–9). Although in this generation one might more appropriately speak of Christians in a family than Christian families, church and pastor will do whatever they can to foster faith within the families of the church.[4] This obviously touches formal Christian education—plus much more.

Congregations need to be intentional about their ministry to families. Worship services can be designed with families in mind. In addition to age- and role-specific programs and groups such as mens clubs, LWML, youth groups, etc., events such as family nights and couples retreats encourage meaningful sharing for all ages and help families to learn and grow together in experience, speech and prayer.

---

[4] The term *family* is used herein to include single parents and couples without children in the home as well as two parents with children at home.

The church also needs to be conscious of the life cycles within families and that each stage has its own needs and behaviors. Thus, different family programs will aim at, e.g., parents with teens, empty-nest parents, retired persons, and the like. Those who work with couples say that marital crises arise about every five years (tied somewhat to the changing stages), and that the intensity of the crises vary according to the couples' expectations, personal satisfaction, ability to communicate, psychological and spiritual maturity, and successes at handling previous difficulties.

The pastor will want to have available a variety of resources—retreats, workshop concepts, marriage enrichment programs, etc.[5] Every pastor quickly learns the benefits of strengthening the family as compared to treating those that have deteriorated.

The Single Parent

The church's ministry to single parents needs to be appropriate to their individual circumstances—widowed, divorced, or never married. Each carries its own burdens. No single parent has an easy job. God established two parents for mutual support and relief. When the second parent is no longer present (for any reason), the one remaining needs all the spiritual and emotional support possible from fellow Christians.

While the *Seelsorger's* responsibility is to apply Law and Gospel, the art of doing so is not simple. Some single parents feel no need for the Law; others have applied the Law so severely to themselves that an additional dose would totally crush them. Similarly, the freeing and enabling Gospel needs to be applied in a way appropriate and specific to the needs of the particular single parent. Widows/widowers still may be dealing with their grief or may feel threatened by day-by-day demands. Divorced parents, in addition to the preceding, struggle under their relationships with the "ex"—visitation arrangements, residual emotional stress, etc. Single-parents-never-married live under a stigma which hampers them from living out forgiveness. Whatever the situation, the pastor needs to help the individual focus on and trust the objective fact of justification and the empowering presence of the Holy Spirit, and then to work with the individual to put that faith into practice by the power of the Spirit.

---

[5] In addition to the excellent resources available through the Synod's Family Life Department, the pastor should be familiar with other programs promoted within Christianity (realizing that new ones are constantly being developed). Some of these will be helpful; some less so—the criterion being whether the program directly and indirectly encourages sanctification as a result of justification.

While the primary arena for the above is a one-on-one ministry of the Word between pastor and parishioner, hurting Christians need others in the body of Christ to support and encourage their growth in sanctification. And because new single parents tend to feel isolated and excluded within a short period of time, the church that does not quickly reach out to these people may well lose them.

Single-parent support groups within the church, circuit, or district can provide a meaningful connection to the church as a whole. Although one, general, single-parent group can certainly assist all three types, many prefer the benefits of separate groups in which each feels somewhat more understood. (Baby-sitting services to enable single parents to attend such groups present a clear sign that the church cares for everyone.)

In addition to providing a coordinated ministry to single parents, the pastor will want to reach out also to their children. These children in particular need to hear that every type of family (Gk: *patria, oikos*) is an imperfect, sin-infected type of the "whole family in heaven and on earth [which] derives its name" from God the father/*pater* (Eph. 3:14–15). The church also can help the children in their sanctification by providing the role-model of the missing parent. Church sponsored activities such as youth groups and men/women offering special trips and experiences can help these children have a more rounded experience of life.

Single, Non-Parent Adults

This growing number of people rightly feels left out when the church emphasizes a family ministry that concentrates on adults with children. In order to minister to their needs, the congregation can intentionally plan parallel events for singles—Bible studies, social gatherings, participation in the congregation's offices and boards, worship leadership, etc. It can also plan for their participation in "family" events by assisting their leadership and other help, even by establishing subgroups of singles to work out what it means to be single yet part of a family elsewhere as well as the family of God.

Ministering to Ailing Marriages

No Perfect People

"By reason of sin many a cross has been laid upon this estate . . . " says our traditional Agenda's wedding service. This the pastor will discover only too soon. Even before the wedding, families may fight over the nature of the service, the color of the apparel, or why their beloved is marrying someone perceived as not quite good enough. In only a few months, the newlyweds find themselves disagreeing over many issues, some of which seem so trivial, and they wonder what happened to their love.

For these reasons, the pastor should have long emphasized in his educational groups that there are no perfect people or relationships on earth. Adam and Eve left a legacy that tries to play God and gain the upper hand. Banished from the Garden, male and female find their love for each other giving way at times to self-love, their good intentions causing hurt, their prize communication twisted and turned to conflict. They take each other for granted, abuse one another physically and verbally, and perform a variety of offensive behaviors which corrode the binding vows of love. Frightened and confused, many withdraw and feel cheated. Although a few couples resolve to make the best of what they have, many others who start off enthusiastically end up bored, apathetic and uncaring—just existing with each other.

Sin is real, and it takes its toll. It cuts at the bond of two individuals as a harmonious unity. Do not be surprised if the "perfect couple" within the congregation eventually causes the most grief. Such is the reason for the cross.

In order to detect the early warning signals that a marriage is starting to shake apart, the pastor needs to keep his senses tuned; for preventive intervention and healing is more important than the "burial" of a divorce. He will help his people realistically identify the distortions that arise in the marriage process and, following confession and absolution, help them identify and practice behaviors that can bring healing and growth to their brokenness. While secular counselors speak of "maintenance and reconciliation factors" needed for ailing marriages, the pastor knows the true factor necessary: the forgiveness of sin, the power of God's Spirit to renew human relationships and interactions.

In order to personalize the application of Law and Gospel, the pastor should understand some of the common foundations of sand on which people build their marriages and why so many lament, "Our marriage ruined a perfectly good relationship." People marry for a variety of reasons which may have little to do with God's intention or with *agape*. The following topics (which have to do with one's whole view of life) touch lightly on but a few of the reasons for marital strife.

Marriage as Escape. People often envision marriage as the end of their problems—unwanted dependence, tyrannical (perceived or real) parents, loneliness, personally diminishing relationships, abusive environments. They hope that this new partner will provide the necessary nurture. In reality, this approach asks the spouse to be a therapist. While this can indeed take place to some extent, where great deprivation has been felt, great demands will be made—often crippling the marriage.

Marriage as Reworking of the Past. Remembrance of the past often provides a filter through which one spouse sees the other. This filter can distort the present so badly that it becomes necessary to seek help. That's because the argument is not with the spouse but with a father or mother, sister or brother. Spouses may berate one another with "Why aren't you as good as your father/mother/sister/brother" when they actually mean "I'm disappointed that you aren't better than *my* father/mother/sibling." Listen carefully to the standard marital reply to nagging (which is not the true battle being fought): "You're not my mother/father!"

Nor should the pastor be surprised when some marriages fail because they have "succeeded." For example, a very shy person may marry an extrovert in order to gain confidence and practice in reaching out. When successful, the ex-introvert may no longer feel a need for the spouse.

Consciously, people select spouses who excite them, who are similar to them, who have common interests. Unconsciously, people select spouses who enable them to correct old mistakes, to master old conflicts, to work out the old relationships that never got worked out, to pay off old scores. One psychiatrist stated, "Engagements may be made in heaven, but marriages are made in the land of neurosis."[6]

Marriage as Projection: Most if not all people marry their fantasy and do not actually know the person they wed. They project so many expectations on their spouses that they end up saying, "You never see me at all; you don't know who I am. We've been married x-number of years, but you still don't know me."

Most young people have little idea of what marriage is and therefore allow their projections to obliterate commitment. They believe that marriage will right every wrong, guarantee happiness, provide an escape from pressure, require no psychological or spiritual development, be easy to sever if things don't work out. Projection focuses on one's own needs, wants, and choices and not on the commitment (or work) necessary to build a strong Christian home.

A Ministry of Reconciliation

As people of God, Christians are encouraged to look at others not for what they are (sinners) but what God intends them to be (redeemed sinners who strive to live a sanctified life). (This could

---

[6] Source unknown.

be unhealthy if interpreted to mean that sin is ignored or abuse tolerated.) Jesus saw from the Father's perspective the meaning of creation and the work of redemption. He saw people's dignity, bestowed by the Spirit and meant to be recognized and respected by others.

Law-Gospel marriage counseling exposes the ways in which husbands and wives use each other to deal with the past or to act out fantasies. In so doing, the pastor helps people to be reconciled to each other as an extension of their reconciliation to God—to see beyond their own self-needs and perceptions and to recognize that the other exists in his/her own right as a created, redeemed and sanctified person.

The pastor can also help the couple understand and appreciate the Biblical view of why they are married. As James Atkinson summarized Luther's view in his sermon on marriage, "It is God who gives a man and woman to each other. . . . Marriage, then, is far more than mating. It is a matter of choosing and accepting the spouse God gives just as Adam chose and accepted Eve as his wife" (LW 44, p. 5). How a Christian treats a gift from God differs significantly from the expectations and advice of the secular world.

Conception and Technology

Most couples eagerly anticipate their opportunity to conceive, bear, and raise "flesh of my flesh." When some physical problem does interfere with normal conception, the couple may turn to the pastor for spiritual advice on various types of technology—clinical conception and/or (at least in the probable future) human genetic engineering. In either situation, the pastor ought not see his ministry as legalistically preventing sin but as leading God's people within Law and Gospel as the basis for a sanctified, joy-filled life. Toward that goal, some questions and principles need to be addressed.

How much may Christians involve themselves in those aspects of the conception process that heretofore were considered to be God's domain? Where is the line between using knowledge/ability with Christian wisdom and "playing God?" Just as the church has to evaluate the use/disuse of artificial means in the preservation of earthly life, the church also has to evaluate the use/non-use of artificial means within the establishment of life. Some procedures (e.g., abortion) are clearly contrary to God's will; others (e.g., genetic engineering) are not spoken of in Scripture. Total uninvolvement would be unfaithful stewardship of God's gift of the mind to be used in service to others as well as worship of him. Nor will the other extreme satisfy: acting as if there were no God or that he cares not about what we do. God is always involved in human life (though not as a puppeteer manipulating everything that happens); sometimes he blesses our plans and sometimes he frustrates them—but he is always present. Regardless of causation, basic and most important is keeping a right relationship to and with God.

As stated in chapter one, God created male and female to be in family and to participate with him in the ongoing creation of succeeding generations. Because of the Fall, however, sin has obstructed God's ideal. The existence of infertility and handicapped children reminds Christians that they live in a fallen world and that these conditions are manifestations of it. While the Lord continues to bless marriage with the gift of children (Gen. 29:31; Ps. 127:3; Is. 44:2), he also has allowed some marriages to be childless and in some cases has directed them so to be (Gen. 20: 17–18; 30:2; 1 Sam. 1:5). And, while the human perspective may think a handicapped child is evidence that God has withheld a blessing, the handicapped child is just as much a blessing from God as any other child; and the handicap itself is just another manifestation of sin's presence and power in the world.

In counseling the couple the pastor needs to determine (among other things) their attitude toward God and what they perceive to be God's will being worked out toward them.

- Would the use of technology be an act of defiance against God for what he has already done in their lives?
- Do they see themselves (or their spouse)—whether infertile or carrying a defective gene—as less than complete? As less than a "real" man/woman? As less than a true gift from God?
- Are they incapable of a sacrificial love which accepts God's decisions for children in their family?

Artificial Conception

Technology offers today's couples various types of clinical conception[7]—artificial insemination (by the husband or by an-

---

[7] Because new techniques are frequently developed and in order for the pastor to be of the greatest spiritual help, he will need to keep himself informed on the latest possibilities. Even more so, he needs to remain a man of God with "singleness of eye."

A very helpful report has been prepared by the Lutheran Council in the USA, entitled *In Vitro Fertilization: Study Material and Guidelines.* Cf. especially pp. 31ff. Equally helpful is *Human Sexuality: A Theological Perspective,* op. cit., especially pp. 36–39.

other male), the use of another woman's ovum, surrogate mothering (using the sperm and/or ovum from the infertile couple), or perhaps methods not yet developed. The increase in technology puts into new contexts the continuing question of how to live the sanctified life.

Behind the processes lie two important questions. 1) If the process involves the disposal of "unnecessary" fertilized ovum, does that constitute abortion? 2) If either the ovum or the sperm is donated from someone other than the couple, does this involve an anti-Scriptural intrusion of a third party into the one-flesh union of husband and wife?

The first question, about the disposal of fertilized ovum, may be answered relatively easily. Based on our understanding of Scripture that human life begins with the uniting of the ovum and sperm, disposal of any "extra, unnecessary" fertilized ova constitutes abortion of a human being.

A second objection to in vitro fertilization is that it frequently involves gametes that are not from a husband and wife united in marriage. While this may not constitute adultery, the question remains whether it is ethically and morally defensible as we seek to determine the will of God.[8]

Psychological and ethical questions are just as important, not because human issues are equal to God's Word (which they aren't) but because they intimately involve one's conscience—a matter that does pertain to one's posture before God. The parish pastor should be careful not to burden people's consciences unnecessarily but to help them sharpen their consciences under God's Law and Gospel.

Genetic Engineering

At this writing, the use of human genetic information is limited to the identity of paternity and the presence of defect in the unborn (usually with an eye toward possible abortion). So far, the church can easily respond: Information in itself can help a couple in Christ plan for the future; and abortion is sinful. The harder questions are at the door:

- May a Christian use the capability of genetic engineering

---

[8] Although the Scriptures do not deal directly with the subject of artifical insemination by a donor other than the husband (AID), it is our opinion that such a practice must be evaluated negatively; whatever the reasons offered in support of AID, whether eugenic or simple concern that an infertile couple be enabled to have a child, the process of fertilization is removed from the personal context of the one-flesh union of husband and wife in a way that not even their consent can allow. Cf. *Human Sexuality*, CTCR, pp.38–39.

to conceive a child without deformity and hereditary disease (assuming abortion is not involved), or must the couple decide that their potential child must "take its chances" (and the parents theirs) as did all generations from Adam and Eve to the twentieth century?

- Would their use of medical technology be an act of hubris or part of the human responsibility to subdue the earth (Gen. 1:28)?
- If Christian parents (through the medical technician) have the capability of ensuring their child will not be born with a handicap, are they morally irresponsible if they don't use that capability?
- If genetic engineering is used but brings about an unforeseen drawback, are the parents (and/or physician) morally culpable, or would this result be accepted as the providence of God just as handicaps have always been?

To restate, the pastoral task is to minister to the couple with Law and Gospel as the basis for their sanctified life in marriage—lived in the Spirit as happily as possible in this fallen world.

The Pastor's Marriage and Family

Pastors are discovering that they too are vulnerable to the pressures that confront other marriages and families. Sadly, many pastors do not accept this and pay dearly for neglecting their own humanity and the needs of their family.

Complicating such matters is the false notion that pastors are not to have needs—that there is something selfish about needs. Some people have said that the pastor's life is solely in the church, in "God's work," and that his family exists solely to support his ministry. (Implicit in this attitude is that the pastor can have no sexual problems. If they try to surface, the "godly" pastor will deny his needs and gallantly bear his burden.) So, most pastors bury their complaints, their hurts, their emptiness and try to go on. In time they are weighed down with neglected personal desires, uncommunicated violations, diminished dreams, unresolved conflict, and unfulfilled expectations.

The pastor's wife may also find herself feeling isolated, in a fishbowl, wondering who her husband is (much less her pastor). She may feel that he has no time or energy for her, considering the demands of his parish, numerous denominational and civic posts, preparation, teaching, counseling and all else that constitutes his calling.

Children of pastors complain of being in a box. Teachers and peers place "PKs" in certain categories that anger and hurt these children. Pastor's children have problems like anyone else—and may go too far to prove that sameness. Complicating this, some pastor-fathers overreact from guilt for providing the congregation a less-than-perfect family.

Seminarians have long argued which has priority: being a pastor or being a husband. The dilemma is false, for God established both offices—one at the foundation of the world, the other at the foundation of the church—and they telescope into each other (1 Tim. 3:2–5). If either is neglected, God's will is not done. Just as the pastor can spend too much time/energy in the church, so he can with his family.

The solution is found in balance (not juggling)—the balance of being the father/spiritual father of his earthly house and of the household of God in that place. On occasion, the pastor must immediately respond to calls from parishioners regardless of even special family observances. On the other hand, the pastor will learn through experience that some emergencies are false alarms. The pastor is a model for his people. If he is never home, spends little or no time with the family, he may receive applause for being a hard worker, but he also misleads his people concerning Christian living within families.

In addition to taking care of his family, the pastor must take care of himself, for all life in this world is in a physical body. The man who pays little heed to his own self will have little to offer to others. Every pastor needs time for spiritual development, a devotional life, hobbies, solitude, re-creation. Above all, he needs his own *Seelsorger* (as does his wife). Good family life requires support.

In all, the pastor needs daily to recall that nothing is up to him. Like his people, he is one of the forgiven ones. Not having to prove himself, he is daily empowered by the grace of God to live out the forgiven life. The pastor's willingness to commend himself and his family to the God who graciously forgives sins, flowing from faith in God's love in Christ-crucified (the essence of Christianity), is the hallmark of the pastor's future growth and present strength.

3
The Pastor Cares
for Those
about to Be Married

Courtship and Sexual Behavior

The concept and practice of secular courtship differs considerably from that of Biblical times. Some parents do not know or meet the "beloved" until the wedding date is set. In some cases, the couple may not be of the same ethnic background, economic status, or denomination/religion. Sexual intercourse during the dating process and living together has become accepted by the modern world.

In today's culture, many live-in couples (including those couples professing to be Christian) have already justified to themselves the moral acceptability of their arrangement.[1] If so, it usually takes some tragedy to open their hearts to a Law-Gospel ministry regarding this issue. However, in preparing the couple

---

[1] In counseling against this practice, the pastor should keep in mind Luther's pastoral comment "On Marriage Matters": "This lying together in secret in anticipation of betrothal cannot be reckoned as whoredom, for it takes place in the name and with the intention of marriage, which spirit, intention, or name whoredom does not have. Therefore there is a great difference between whoredom and lying together in secret with the intention of betrothed marriage." However, Luther does not equate sexual intercourse with marriage. For example, "When a girl's honor is taken away by force, which is called rape, [it] is not to be considered a marriage" (LW 46:293, 308).

to hear and live out God's Law and Gospel, the pastor can point out the failure rate of marriages begun with premarital cohabitation (some 80%). He also might ask the couple to forego sexual intercourse and focus on their ability to relate. Although this will be resisted, many young adults have found that removing the physical side allows the needed opportunity and time to work through relational needs, concerns, and expectations. If the couple agrees, the pastor may then find them more receptive to the Biblical teachings and ideals about marriage and the family.

Engagement and Premarital Counseling

Although today's engagement differs from the Biblical betrothal (with its binding legality), a public announcement is still in order. It helps set the tone of responsibility required of two becoming one, and it lets others know of the intention and asks for the support and prayers of friends and family. Engagement should not be taken lightly nor used merely to explore. In itself it is still a moral promise to be one, and it implies the commitment that is the essence of marriage.

Premarital guidance is a vital part of pastoral ministry. It directs the couple to the Word of God as the source for strength and help in years to come. Young premarital couples are idealistic and have distorted views of what their marriage will be. Sixty percent of marriages per year are second marriages; and counseling for them is often neglected even though so important. Therefore, the pastor will want to help the couple work through and practice dealing with the issues that frequently destroy marriages.

The pastor needs to do more than simply remind the couple of Christ's atonement and the presence of the Holy Spirit in their hearts. He, as the spiritual father, needs to help God's people uncover the specifics of sin in their lives and to practice using the power of the Spirit in sanctified living. In order to do so, premarital counseling often uses an open-discussion approach, the couple determining which topics within sanctification are most critical to them.

Premarital guidance can be very important for strengthening (or establishing) a bond between the couple and the church's ministry. The manner in which the pastor has helped the couple prepare for married life can influence them to think of a pastor as a person to whom they always can turn with confidence—a person who administers Word and Sacrament, God's powerful source of help, especially when troubles arise.

The amount of time to set aside for premarital counseling will depend partly on the pastor's own style and partly on the materials (if any)[2] that he uses. Many pastors set aside three to six hour-and-a-half sessions to establish and make use of the necessary rapport. However, effective premarital counseling is a combination of sessions before the ceremony *and* within the first year afterward. Securing the cooperation of the couple will be easier when the congregation and pastor publicly have established a set process and when previous participants attest to its validity.

Should the Pastor Perform the Ceremony?

The pastor is under no legal or moral obligation to solemnize every marriage. In some instances (an existing marriage, minors, and consanguinity as determined by the state), he is forbidden to perform the ceremony; and in others he will choose not to.[3] In any case, the pastor must know the state laws. At a bare minimum, this includes having in hand a marriage license. Also, some states require parental consent for youths between certain ages. Obviously, if the pastor knows of any false information on the license, he cannot proceed with the ceremony.

Before proceeding, the pastor will want to consider additional questions/issues. The Christian marriage service is written as though it involves *Christians*. It includes pastoral *blessings*. These are not light matters. Some people do not qualify. Especially when the prospects are strangers to the pastor, he will want to assess his participation (which involves, by implication, the congregation and the visible church on earth). These questions include

- Why has this couple come to ask him to conduct the wedding?
- Do they view the service as some type of magical act that will warrant their marriage against defect?
- Are they simply pleasing the "out-of-date wishes" of their parents?
- Is one or the other merely enacting a childhood dream of a picture-perfect event?

---

[2] The Family Life Department of the Synod has provided many excellent resources through the years. The newly-ordained pastor will have previewed various materials in his training and might ask for the assistance of the District office and Circuit counselor in selecting materials appropriate to his style.

[3] A few generations ago, the mentally handicapped were considered ineligible for marriage. To some extent, this has changed due to physical therapy, sexual training, and an improved understanding of the abilities and needs of the handicapped. The pastor who is asked to solemnize such a marriage should work with the responsible social agency to determine how he can best serve the needs of the couple.

- Are they coming out of guilt for an existing pregnancy?
- To what extent might drugs or alcohol be involved—enough for the pastor to say that either party is unable to make a lifelong commitment at this time?

In general, no pastor should allow himself to become known as a "Marrying Sam," thus disgracing Christianity and God himself.

Developing the Christian Couple's Communication Skills

This area of human interaction has a greater effect (positive or negative) on the marriage than any other. Even the "communication" of sexual intercourse will die unless husband and wife truly communicate and empathize with each other as Christian persons, in Christ. They need to be able to share their needs, fears, hopes and dreams—without fear of ridicule or reprisal. They need to be able to listen with their heart (i.e., to actively listen)—to confess their sins and hear forgiveness. In that context, couples will be able to resolve their differences by (1) understanding the emotions behind each other's wishes, and (2) finding a solution in Christ that will not hurt the other's self-concept. Because the sinful side of humanity cannot suffer emotional hurt throughout life, the submission and giving up on one's self of Eph. 5:22–25 may include putting aside his or her own defenses in order to truly listen to the hurts of the other.

Good Christian communication will help the couple deal with potentially destructive issues, will lead to acceptable and happy solutions, and will assist the couple in living out the fruit of the Spirit: "love, joy, peace, patience, kindness, goodness, faithfulness, gentleness and self-control" (Gal. 5:22).

Premarital Counseling Topics to be Explored

A Living Faith in the Home. The significance of a person's faith needs to be pointed out. From strong faith to indifference to antagonism, a person's relationship with God is as closely interrelated with self-image as is sexuality.

Sometimes people seek in marriage that which can come only in a relationship with God. The joy for which they yearn may be that which comes only in the Lord—for it is not joy *per se* but joy in being forgiven and receiving ultimate acceptance. However, humans need to experience that joy/forgiveness/acceptance *from* others in order to share it *with* others. That, in part, is why God put the lonely in families (Ps. 68:6) and in the greater family, the church. Couples will find the strength to withstand the trials of marriage when they have a faith that enables them to forgive and accept each other. The "family altar" of the Christian home, devotions that listen to and receive from God, will be a vital resource for unity and for achieving the promises of marriage.

Troublesome questions arise when the husband and wife do not confess the Christian faith with one heart and mind. Basic questions of life and the meaning and purpose of family all center around the answer one gives to the call of Christ. Mixed religion in the home often results in both becoming indifferent to (or rejecting) the Truth in order to avoid pressuring the other and building antagonism.

In some areas of the country, the mixed-Christian marriage problems will arise when the non-Lutheran comes from a Protestant denomination that promotes "a decision for Christ" or in some other way undermines the total and complete efficacy of the atonement, confusing sanctification with justification. Simply because most people lump Lutherans with all other Protestants, this danger (which may seem to young couples to be negligible) can be the most problematic. Jumping to the other denomination seems to be no problem at all.

Problems also arise in the marriage of a Lutheran to a Roman Catholic. Because the Roman Catholic Church equates itself with the *una sancta*, the one, universal church (and marriage as a Sacrament), the Catholic's parish pastor will pressure for two items: (1) the priest's involvement in the ceremony in order to ensure the "validity" of the marriage; and (2) that the Catholic spouse pressure (ever so gently) the non-Catholic to convert and/or at least to allow any children to be brought up in the Roman faith. The Roman Catholic Church no longer requires the signing of the nuptial agreement, but it does require its members to do whatever they can to achieve the same result (without, however, breaking the marriage). If the couple speaks with the priest (as is required), the non-Catholic will be urged to resolve the problem even before the wedding. Most young people, caught up in the passion and idealism of their love, do not understand the significance of such consent nor the implications which they later will regret.

When the pastor perceives a mixed-faith engagement to be firmly established, he will work gently in order not to put a stumbling block before either his own member or the other. He remembers that neither St. Paul (1 Cor. 7:16) nor St. Peter (1 Peter 3:1–2) forbid Christian/non-Christian (much less mixed-Christian) marriages,[4] and he understands the importance of pastoral

------

[4] Luther also noted, "Just as I may eat, drink, sleep, walk, ride with, buy from,

follow-up after the marriage and the value of modeling the importance of God's grace in Jesus Christ.

Long before serious dating begins, the church should help youth understand the problems of mixed-faith marriages. Sixth grade is not too early. Leaders (pastor, Sunday school teacher, etc.) may occasionally find children of such marriages sharing resulting unpleasant experiences. Tactfully handling such exchange of information, also by mixed-faith couples themselves, may help point up the disadvantages of mixed marriages and thereby provide helpful counsel. The leaders of the youth groups should be chosen to model the strength of a same-faith home. Sunday school and confirmation classes can study the main tenets of the most populous other denomination in the area. Whatever the approach, it should not be limited to a one-time event. Strengthening the faith in the next generation is an ongoing process.

A word of caution: Listen carefully to how the children respond in case the above is misunderstood to drive a wedge between the child and a non-Lutheran parent. Mixed-faith marriages can and do exist, even as strong families. Rather, the lack of a common faith will be just one less resource for overcoming difficulties, just one more obstacle to overcome, just one more missing factor for building a strong Christian home.

Role Expectations. Couples who desire to live under the Lord may in good conscience differ on *how* to live out the Biblical order within marriage. The pastor should not take the responsibility for deciding which spouse should do what around the house or how the couple divides child-rearing tasks. The helpful pastor will (1) lead the couple to realize that they come to the marriage with sin-filled expectations for themselves and for each other, and (2) help the couple practice active listening and planning as they work on mutual decisions that grow out of their relationship to God in Christ Jesus.

Finances. The use of money may seem to young couples to be relatively free of emotion, and they may be surprised to discover how closely their spending habits reflect personal values—and even their relationship with God. Financial pressures often find both spouses working outside the home to make ends meet, only to discover that a sizable portion of the double income is expended unexpectedly on double work clothing and personal grooming,

---

speak to, and deal with a heathen, Jew, Turk, or heretic, so I may also marry and continue in wedlock with him. . . . A heathen is just as much a man or a woman— God's good creation—as St. Peter, St. Paul, and St. Lucy, not to speak of a slack and spurious Christian" (LW 45:25).

quick foods, transportation, day-care for children, etc. "Planning the family budget" begins with a faith in Christ that understands the responsibilities of stewardship for the physical gifts entrusted to the couple by God.

Relatives. Because of sin, young Christian couples may have trouble leaving father and mother (Gen. 2:24) and, at the same time, honoring them (the Fourth Commandment), but they might not be able to identify the specific human occasions that give rise to sin's outburst. In order to encourage the couple's growth in sanctification as they relate to each other's family, the pastor might help them to explore their previous experiences in and current expectations of events such as contact with the extended family and attendant feelings, gift exchanges, birthday and holiday expectations, and the like.

Family Size. This is an anti-family time. Governmental policies along side of industrial and business procedures tend to work against the family. Those employed in the service sector may discover that they cannot have off from work for religious holidays or even for Sunday worship without endangering their job. To some extent, society inadvertently contributes to the breakdown of the family (and, in subtle ways, may violate freedom of religion). These realities need to be balanced with the other reality: Society and economics do not control who people are or what they do; their relationship with their gracious and protecting God does. It should be obvious that neither income nor family size determines family happiness.

Within this awareness, the young couple should discuss their plans for family size. Economics, time, and emotional maturity are but some of the factors involved. As persons whose every moment is passed in God's hands and under his eye, Christians make their way in humility, seeking to live as his faithful servants and stewards.

The pastor will include also a discussion of birth control methods, but within the context of the discussion on sexuality (Unit V, chapter 1). To be helpful to the couple, the pastor should be familiar with the different types of birth control. Some involve surgery; some use a "natural" method (e.g., abstinence), others on blocking the fertilization of the ovum (e.g., condoms, shields), and still others that use an abortive principle (e.g., the "morning after" pill). The matter is best discussed in the light of God's intention for men and women as his created and redeemed sexual beings. For example, the "morning after pill" is not a birth control device but an abortifacient and therefore contrary to God's will.

Social Background. A couple's differing social (as well as ethnic/racial) backgrounds present no spiritual problem for the pastor. However, he will want to help the couple think through and plan for a grace-filled life in the Spirit in the presence of the pressures (external as well as internal) they might face.

Testing for Sexually-Transmitted Diseases. Herpes, chlamydia, syphilis, gonorrhea, AIDS and other sexually-transmitted diseases raise serious questions of pastoral care. Given the prevalence of premarital sex and the persistence of severe sexually transmitted disease, the pastor may well raise the question of testing so that each can promise the other the gift of a sexually disease-free body. Some people have no idea they are carrying a particular disease. Either of the couple may have been sexually active with someone else, which geometrically increases the possibility of being infected. Shyness on the pastor's part will not serve the welfare of his people.

Planning for the Wedding Service

Most Christian couples choose to make their vows before God in a public worship service. There they are reminded that the Gospel of God's love is the root of their love; and they invite their fellow Christians to join them and their families in asking God's blessings on their life together. Certainly, Biblical teaching seems to support a worshipful basis for marriage.

Since Christian marriage rites are to be in a context of evangelical worship, it is appropriate to announce the wedding and to invite the congregation to join in a prayer for the engaged couple.

Shortly after his arrival in a new parish, the pastor should acquaint himself with the state's family laws, particularly where they speak on marriage and divorce. He will also acquaint himself with the congregation's customs and etiquette regarding wedding ceremonies. Some of the details of the service and accompanying events may be occasions for disagreement between the pastor and the couple (e.g., music selection, throwing rice, when to stand and not to, etc.). Many problems can be avoided if the congregation and pastor have established clear standards and explanations that direct the couple to God as the focus of worship as well as incorporate appropriate parish tradition(s).[5] When these (perhaps in printed form) have been used as part of the parish's education program and have been rediscussed during the premarital counseling sessions, many problems will be avoided. Printed or not, the church's rules should not become legalistic

---

[5] Sample guidelines from other pastors and congregations may be helpful in developing one's own.

procedures that force people into unwilling submission resulting in resentment, but helps in focusing on God's presence in Christ Jesus. Just as the Gospel is lost if the Law is lost, so also the Law with no Gospel destroys faith and the Christian life.

Though the state gives any pastor the legal right to solemnize any marriage, most often the bride's pastor is the officiant. Good order requires that a pastor serve nonmembers only with the knowledge and consent of their own pastor, who sometimes may have refused to perform the ceremony for good cause.

Planning the service can be a joy—or an agitation—to all involved. While the problem may be the immaturity of the couple or, e.g., the intransigence of relatives, the pastor has the responsibility to help all concerned to plan the ceremony as a service of worship. Planning the service itself, of course, is the pastor's responsibility (although he should feel encouraged to incorporate the couple's wishes when appropriate). Nonessential matters (such as whether the groom enters from the sacristy or escorts the bride up the aisle) need not provide an occasion for disagreement.

Approved orders of service for marriage are available in the Lutheran Agenda(s). Advance agreement with the couple concerning the particular rite (and any variations) should be sought.

The wedding address may be omitted in private ceremonies, but without question should be a part of a public marriage service in the sanctuary. The address need not be long, but the Gospel Word should be brought to all present. Sin and grace each have their effect in marriage, and the pastor will proclaim both Law and Gospel. The listeners should hear that the church is aware of the sin-caused difficulties people face daily as well as hear that *The Way* (Acts 24:14) through troubled times can benefit them too.

Wedding services generally include the use of the organ and perhaps some form of singing. Since the context is worship, secular music is to be avoided. The pastor will need to work carefully with the couple to choose appropriate music, especially when "their song" is an offense to Christian understanding and faith.

Video cameras, flash cameras and annoying photographers do not add to a worship atmosphere. The pastor, in charge of the service, has the right and responsibility to govern how people will behave during the service of worship.

The date and time of the ceremony may be set for any time of the year (although the joyful nature of the event does not harmonize with the solemnity of, for example, Holy Week). It is worth noting that some people are having their marriage vows take place during a Sunday morning worship service. This practice leaves no doubt about the worship context and helps prevent some of the more outlandish displays in vogue.

Along with the details of the service, the date of the rehearsal should be planned ahead of time. (The pastor and couple may want to rehearse their parts alone, before the others arrive, in order to assure their agreement.) Because most young couples will include non-Lutherans in the wedding party, the rehearsal can be seen as a brief introduction to Lutheranism—and sometimes to the Christian church itself. Here fun and seriousness blend together, revealing a Gospel-oriented people celebrating the fullness of life under a gracious God.

4
Pastoral Care
and the Cult of Self-Love

Promiscuity and Abortion

The Pursuit of Pleasure

Human self-love after the Fall finds the implications of the marriage-oriented, male-female duality too limiting. Centering on self as a sexual being from birth, humans love to justify non-marital sex, abortion, adultery, homosexual activity, and even incest. The problem is not simply that this behavior violates divine rules but that it grows out of an idolatrous self-love. Note Luther's comments on Satan's temptation of Adam and Eve:

> Satan has staked everything on this one effort to draw them away from the Word and faith, that is, from the true God to a false God.[1]

In order to appreciate the identification of self-love as idolatry, listen to Luther's Scriptural answer to what is a god: "A god is that to which we look for all good and in which we find refuge in every time of need" (LC I 2). Consider, then, Satan's tempting suggestions to Adam and Eve—and ultimately to each of their descendants: "You are able to make better judgments for yourself than God can; he wants only to limit human experience. You are able to establish yourself as a god and to look to yourself to determine what is good, trusting in your own strength for survival."

---

[1] LW 1:152.

The enticements to self-love constantly lure all, Christians and non-Christians alike. The media encourage as healthy full "testing" of experience and emotion. Ethics and values are based on absence of harm as subjectively measured. Power through sex is positive. Bodies and lives belong solely to the individual—even to the point of abortion—without any responsibility toward others. Commitment is to be avoided because it will cause inevitable pain—as will mutual service and support. The best sexuality is *eros*, an active sex life in whatever form desired. And *agape*, total self-giving love, is more out of date than "Father Knows Best."

> Having lost all sensitivity, they have given themselves over to sensuality so as to indulge in every kind of impurity, with a continual lust for more (Eph. 4:19).

Perhaps the church in every age considers its times to be more pleasure-oriented than any in the history of the world. At least this much is true today: Western civilization's promotion of pleasure is growing in geometric proportions. Mass advertising and global communications have given new impetus to the justification that "everyone's doing it."

Paralleling the growth of personal pleasure are the hurts that result from it: false guilt, loneliness and isolation, loss of meaning in life, insensitivity, jealousies, broken hearts and homes, the effects of prejudice, the loss of standards, the destruction of self-worth. These pains require more *Seelsorger* skills and time than any other of the pastor's duties.

Sexual immorality is not the exclusive domain of the young unmarried. It tempts everyone every time a story on screen or TV portrays sexual liaisons as acceptable/desirable. An advertisement that extols the body beautiful has the potential of enticing the consumer to separate the body from the soul. Every justification for a wandering mind excuses a philandering heart.

The pastor cannot isolate his flock from these attacks, nor will he ordinarily be at the side of a lamb when she or he has to make a moral choice. The pastor can, however, compassionately apply Law and Gospel in his preaching and teaching (formal and informal); he too can use the art of advertising and storytelling to help his flock remember the tender mercies of our God in Christ.

In addition to dealing with the hurts that arise out of specific situations, the pastor also needs to build up God's people in Christian self-giving. This attitude will help people overcome temptations as well as provide new impetus after repentance and absolution for some act of promiscuity.

The creation of a "suitable helper" for Adam (Gen. 2:20) points to the need for human companionship in general as well as to the intimate fellowship in marriage. "It is not good for the man to be alone" (v. 18).[2] Such close fellowship, however, cannot survive in the desert of self-centeredness; it requires the fertile garden of *agape*, of self-giving love.

The pastor's concern for souls realizes that a legalistic use of Bible passages (such as Eph. 5:1, 21; or Gal. 5:22; or the Beatitudes; or 1 John 3:16) motivates no one. Rather, the Law without the Gospel will turn the garden of God's *agape* into a desert. The compassionate pastor, therefore, is available when his sheep are hurting. He helps them understand the self-centered sin which has caused their pain, and he binds up their wounds with the forgiveness and love of God in Christ Jesus. At that point, when people are most thankful for what God has done, the pastor helps his people draw upon the power of the Spirit to be renewed for a life of self-giving. (Note that this "point of hurting" is not limited to the pain of some promiscuity. It occurs whenever people suffer from self-centered pleasure. And the weakness of the human heart requires repeated application of Law-Gospel for Christians to maintain growth in grace.)

Abortion

Were it not for an unrelenting scramble for privatized pleasure, abortion might not be an issue. Apart from occasional instances of the fetus threatening a termination of the mother's life and of pregnancies due to rape or incest, most unwanted pregnancies result from promiscuity and/or interfere with an individual's "right to pleasure" (America's heresy).

Even before the United States Supreme Court legalized abortions, they were available for the wealthy and those willing to risk back-alley sleaze. The Roe vs. Wade decision, however, was seen by many as making abortion moral by its legality—all in the name of freedom of choice and woman's right to privacy.

Pastors must speak out for life (Prov. 31:8). The LCMS itself has already done so in convention.[3] The organization *Lutherans for Life* also has addressed abortion and related issues. But for

---

[2] See also passages such as "God sets the lonely in families" (Ps. 68:6); "A friend loves at all times" (Prov. 17:17); "Better a neighbor nearby than a brother far away" (Prov. 27:10).

[3] The LCMS addressed the issue of abortion and the right to life and passed Resolution 2-39 in 1971. It has addressed these issues in succeeding conventions. Cf. the 1977 *Proceedings* of the convention at Dallas, p. 130. Subsequent conventions reaffirmed and expanded on the concern (St. Louis 1979, *Proceedings*, p. 117; St. Louis 1981, *Proceedings*, p. 155f.; St. Louis 1983, *Proceedings*, pp. 154f.; and Indianapolis 1986, *Proceedings*, p. 148).

the individual Christian facing an unwanted pregnancy, it is the fellow Christian and/or the pastor who must give direction and counsel. The laity of the church must hear their parish pastor as God's vocal and visible representative. Exceptional situations, of course, may arise. For example, a doctor's best medical judgment may suggest that a pregnancy be terminated in exchange for the mother's life. The parents' subsequent decision-making process should have the assistance of sensitive pastoral care. Some couples will be led to place the unfolding of these events completely in the Lord's hand. Other equally sincere Christian couples will see the Lord's hand at work through the doctor—and will do everything possible to save the mother's life. Weighed in divine scales, both mother and child are of equal value; but the realities of this world may determine a greater need to preserve the life of the mother for the sake of the family and/or community. Few choices in life so poignantly illustrate the fallen condition of our humanity in which the "best" decision, even for a strong Christian, may be a lesser evil. Luther's comment is apt: Sin boldly, but believe more boldly still.[4]

Apart from the therapeutic decision, there will be many hard cases—the high school senior, unmarried but pregnant; a fellow pastor unaware that his young daughter is pregnant; the mother on welfare whose husband just walked out, leaving her pregnant with a fourth child; the 45-year-old with an increased risk that her child could be born with Down's Syndrome or other genetic defects. Heartaches, disappointments and unhappy endings cannot be avoided. For the pregnant girl who has been pressured into marriage or abortion by boyfriend or parents, for the deceived and the misinformed, for the thousands of women who have been exploited by abortion (some of whom suffer significant psychological problems later), we must offer and demonstrate the compassionate love of Christ. While there is a place for righteous anger against those who advocate, promote, and practice abortion, the pastor must remember that he has a gospel ministry to exercise. Approval he cannot give, but acceptance of the penitent he cannot withhold. The God who accepts every repentant sinner in Christ is prepared to accept every woman who has ever had an abortion and every man who ever brought her to that point. The Father waits with compassionate and forgiving love for every prodigal son and daughter. Jesus' invitation has no restrictions: "Whoever comes to me I will never drive away" (John 6:37).

---

[4] LW 48:282.

Pastoral Care and Homosexual Behavior

Homosexual behavior, i.e., physical intimacies and affection-ate "love-making" between consenting people of the same sex, has gained a great measure of social—and legal—approval. Whatever the causes within the person[5], homosexual behavior is outside God's will for the expression of human sexuality by his creatures.[6]

If we consider homosexuality in the light of the total Biblical context regarding the purpose of marriage and the man-woman duality discussed above, . . . we may come to a clearer under-standing of why Christian thought has condemned and should continue to condemn homosexual lusts and acts.

The creation of human beings for covenant community finds its original expression in the fellowship of male and female. This fellowship, as we have stressed above, requires a commitment to the integrity of our sexual identity. The fellowship of male and female implies a recognition that we are male and female and that we should not strive to transcend that distinction. The ultimate fellowship for which God is preparing us, of which the man-woman polarity is an intimation, is not a merging of those who are alike into an undifferentiated openness. It is a har-monious fellowship of those who, though different, are united in love. From this viewpoint we may say that the homosexual relationship approaches too closely the forbidden love of self and minimizes the distinction between lover and beloved. The male-female duality as the created pattern of human fellowship re-quires of us fidelity to our sexual identity, a willingness to be male *or* female.

Second, and very obviously, a homosexual relationship is non-procreative, . . . Some, of course, may regard this as mere bi-ological fact, irrelevant when the possibility of deep affection and love in a homosexual relation is considered. Nevertheless, the Scriptures do not place love in such "splendid isolation". . . Furthermore, when we point to the fact that the homosexual relationship is nonprocreative, we do so against the background

---

[5] While competing theories abound, researchers have sketched possible back-grounds for homosexuality. For the male homosexual: a domineering mother and a detached, hostile father. For the female homosexual: a hostile, competitive mother and a father unable to express affection for his daughter.

[6] While the presence of AIDS and/or any other sexually-transmitted disease does not prove divine displeasure about any specific sin, their presence in the homosexual community is beyond question. In order to minister to homosexuals, the pastor must come to grips with his feelings about sexually-transmitted dis-eases and set aside any misconceptions and barriers. Above all, the pastor must keep in mind the privilege of his calling: an evangelical and evangelistic ministry, Law and Gospel ministry at its best.

of the significance we found in suggesting that the one-flesh union of a man and woman is ordinarily expected to be fruitful.

Hence, we can say on Christian premises that mutual consent or even genuine affection is not enough to justify a homosexual relationship. The human being is, according to the Scriptures, more than mere freedom to define what he or she will be. There are acts or relationships to which we cannot consent without stepping beyond the limitations our Creator has set for his creatures (Rom. 1:26ff.). . . .

It is important to realize that there are those persons who, apart from any deliberate choice on their part, have a predisposition toward homosexuality. . . . In order to offer such persons the compassionate help they need, the church, having condemned all homosexual acts engaged in by such persons, . . . must stand ready to offer its assistance to those who seek to overcome the temptations which beset them and who desire to remain chaste before God despite their homosexual orientation.

It must be said that a predisposition toward homosexuality is the result of the disordering, corrupting effect of the fall into sin, just as also the predisposition toward any sin is symptomatic of original sin. Furthermore, whatever the causes of such a condition may be, . . . [we are not] implying that such a person's sexual orientation is a matter of conscious, deliberate choice. However, this fact cannot be used by the homosexual as an excuse to justify homosexual behavior. . . . Such a person should be counseled to heed the church's call to repentance, trust in God's promise of deliverance (Ps. 50:15), and order his/her life in accord with the Creator's intent.[7]

Just as a recovering alcoholic can be a Christian and yet always consider him- or herself an alcoholic with a strong inclination toward that behavior, so also a nonpracticing homosexual may be a sincere believer. All Christians, like St. Paul (Rom. 7), struggle with the conflict of the old man/new man. The "recovering" (i.e., non-practicing) homosexual within the fellowship of believers needs the acceptance, nurture and care which the supportive ministry of Word and Sacrament extends to every member who is *simul justus et peccator.*

Finally, wisdom and genuine concern for the homosexual's welfare may urge the pastor to call for help from other professionals whose specialized training may equip them to deal more effectively with this very difficult problem. Homosexuality is so intertwined with personality, with the need for intimacy, with self-identity and self-justification that few pastors are equipped to

---

[7] *Human Sexuality,* CTCR, pp. 33-35. Italics original.

apply Law and Gospel in any meaningful way that will be heard by the homosexual. The pastor's best "art" may be as a resource person who shows the weary where to find rest (Matt. 11:28).

Pastoral Care and Power Sex: Abuse, Incest, Rape

If psychologists are correct, the desire to control another person through the use of power/pain grows out of a "fight/flight" response to a threatening situation. Perhaps because sexuality is integral to who a person is, using another person's sexuality against him or her seems to be almost as threatening (and effective) a control as murder. And in spite of popular perception, females as well as males use power sex, both sexes as soon as they learn its effectiveness. (Statistically, of course, males tend to use power sex more violently than do females.)

Although abuse and incest are problems within a family and rape (usually) an act of violence against a nonfamily member, the "threatening situations" which perpetrators use to justify power sex almost always relate back to the person's family situation. Therefore, the reader is urged to restudy and apply as necessary the discussion on "Abuse," Unit IV, Chapter 2: "The Pastor as Counselor."

5
Divorce and Remarriage

Divorce

The chapter on marriage (which should be studied prior to this discussion) has presented its Scriptural and theological bases.[1] That chapter provides the background for the following summary statements by the Synod's Commission on Theology and Church Relations concerning divorce. In presenting these statements to the church, however, the Commission noted the dangers of these becoming a law code that on the one hand might be used to find excuses for divorce or on the other hand might be used to condemn everyone involved in a divorce. Thus, the prefatory reminder is given "that the will to obey God's commandments is born not of the Law but of the Gospel of forgiveness."[2]

1. *When God instituted marriage at creation he intended that it be the lifelong union of one man and one woman. By its very nature the one flesh union of husband and wife will not permit the intrusion of a third party; therefore, what God has joined together let no man put asunder.*

2. *Divorce, destructive of what God has joined together, is always contrary to God's intention for marriage.*

3. *A person who divorces his/her spouse for any other cause than*

---

[1] Passages pertaining to divorce should also be studied: Deut. 24:1–4; Matt. 5:27–28, 31–32; 19:3–12; Mark 10:2–12; Luke 16:18; 1 Cor. 7:10–16.

[2] *Divorce and Remarriage: An Exegetical Study* (November 1987), The Commission on Theology and Church Relations (The Lutheran Church—Missouri Synod), p. 6.

> *sexual unfaithfulness and marries another commits adultery. Anyone who marries a person so discarding his/her spouse commits adultery.*
>
> 4. *When a spouse commits fornication (i.e., is guilty of sexual unfaithfulness), which breaks the unity of the marriage, the offended party who endures such unfaithfulness has the right, though not the command, to obtain a legal divorce and remarry.*
> 5. *A spouse who has been willfully and definitively abandoned by his/her partner who refuses to be reconciled and is unwilling to fulfill the obligations of the marriage covenant despite persistent persuasion may seek a legal divorce, which in such a case constitutes a public recognition of a marriage already broken, and remarry. . . .*
>
> In determining whether a person has been truly abandoned in a way that can be considered willful and definitive, the main factors are consent to live within the home and to carry out the commonly recognized obligations of mutual support and sexual cohabitation.[3]

While the above principles seem simple enough, the average parish pastor will spend an incredible amount of time and will experience a carload of heartache as he, the *Seelsorger*, applies them to husbands and wives who are hurting, angry, and perhaps vengeful. At times he will see the healing and renewing power of the Spirit in the lives of his flock. At other times he will be reminded that "marriage counseling" is often a euphemism for the death rattle of marriage. He will even note within himself a degree of confusion and doubt—praying that a particular marriage survive, yet feeling relieved when the spouses are freed from their destructive relationship.

What is the pastor's responsibility? Is it to save every marriage? To force people to remain in punishing relationships? To threaten damaged people for their inadequacies? To free people through "official forgiveness" to do what they're going to do anyway? Some clear guidelines can be given in answer to these questions.

Responsibility for the Divorce

Persons contemplating divorce (as all people) make their own decisions, yet some will try to manipulate the pastor rather than take social (much less spiritual) responsibility for the failure of

---

[3] Ibid., pp.37–39 (italics original). Luther comments on this point in reference to 1 Cor. 7:4–5: "When one resists the other and refuses the conjugal duty she is robbing the other of the body she had bestowed on him. This is really contrary to marriage, and dissolves the marriage" (LW 45:34).

the marriage. The pastor, however, is unable to take their accountability from them or to make decisions the people do not want to make for themselves. His responsibility—to the couple and to God—is to provide a Law-Gospel ministry.

Innocence and Guilt

Under most circumstances, the pastor should avoid taking sides or seeking to determine who is "the innocent party." A clearly-drawn picture will exist in some instances; however, in most situations, the intricacies of human relationships are such that even those within the divorce cannot see the real truth behind actions and attitudes.

Luther sees the problem as resulting from not grounding the marriage within true faith.

> To recognize the estate of marriage is something quite different from merely being married. He [or she] who is married but does not recognize the estate of marriage cannot continue in wedlock without bitterness, drudgery, and anguish.[4]

To recognize the estate of marriage is to see the spouse as a gift from God to be accepted and treated as such. And, while every married person since the Fall has various self-centered needs that he or she expects the spouse to fulfill, the Spirit-empowered believer in Christ who recognizes the estate of marriage sees the needs of the other as having priority over self. When a couple comes to the pastor to discuss their divorce, he may wonder if either spouse ever understands this or puts it into practice.

Therefore, rather than pronouncing one spouse innocent and the other guilty, the pastor must help both individually to discover their own guilt and to work through repentance with an eye toward patience, forgiveness, hope, and change.

A Pastoral Presence

The pastor can help the couple think through the past, present and future. He can join them in reconsidering commitments, responsibilities and consequences. He can "be there" as God's ambassador for his people—not just as a caring person but as one who ministers with God's power. He can walk with them through the valley of the shadow, encourage them in their weakness, challenge them in their doubt, confront their self-destruction. He may also assist them in calling in professional help for problems of a specialized medical/psychiatric nature outside his professional expertise.

---

[4] LW 45:38.

His overarching role is to teach God's will with respect to marriage and divorce. The pastor can help the couple pray (as well as pray for them). Prayer with the couple, when approved by them, may also help open the door toward a renewed effort on their part.

The pastor can help the couple understand their sin and, when they are ready to hear with open hearts, surround them with God's love in Christ. The pastor may at times be as perplexed as they, but he can model hope with the prayer that God will provide a way and that even in the breakdown of relationships they will find healing in the Lord.

A person can (re)learn how to love the spouse and forgive. Often making an effort to understand the feelings and needs of the other and showing an effort to change will cause the love to reappear. Practicing new behaviors, redefining complaints, seeking new "contracts," and a variety of other techniques may help a couple experience enough hope that, with God's help, they will work to improve their marriage.

However, when reconciliation is not possible, the pastor will spend much time counseling individually, helping in the process of redefining oneself on the basis of the Gospel as a single, worthwhile person. This process includes grieving. The loss of a relationship is, in many ways, similar to a death—except that the church has few overt symbols or rituals to mark or close a marriage. The pastor will look for the signs of grief and help the individual move through the various stages toward a changed life under God.

Conflicting Behavior

The pastor should understand that couples in the process of separation and divorce exhibit conflicting behavior that reflects the couple's vacillating emotions. Personal possessions may be left in the home, which necessitates coming back to claim. They make "how are you doing" calls. One spouse may be called to help the other repair something, and the two might end up in bed. The pastor ordinarily should not understand such contact as attempts to reunite. Rather, many people find it difficult to break psychological dependence on the spouse and so reaffirm themselves with occasional contact with each other.

The Presence of Children

If young children are involved, the pastor needs to minister to them too. Typically, children believe they have the power to bring the parents back together. Some believe that they were the true cause of the divorce. Some will be manipulated by one or both parents in order to hurt the other. The pastor's ministration to the children includes his support for both spouses in their role as parents. Some research has shown that the long-term detrimental effects of divorce on children is minimized when they spend healthy, creative, and meaningful time with both parents. The pastor needs to encourage the parents to formulate and maintain a mutual, workable policy of structure, nurture, and discipline for their children.

The Christian Community

The pastor can help those divorcing to sort through and then share what happened. Openness with the important people in a person's life renews people-connections, resolves some of the discomfort about who knows what, and begins the definition of new relationships independent of the former spouse. Such openness can also help puzzled friends know how to relate.

The pastor can help the rest of the congregation (and, perhaps, the community) sort out its response to the divorce. He must give a continual witness indicating that divorce is contrary to God's will. Divorce can be a difficult time for all who know the parties involved. Friends and family feel the need to choose—which spouse was right/wrong? Who will be friends with which spouse? Which spouse will be invited to what events? This problem will be particularly acute in small, intimate congregations. And in every congregation, the pastor certainly will work with his elders, both giving and receiving direction and prayer.

The congregation might also play a valuable role in the renewing process for the divorced, who now face new functions and obligations, who may need to learn new skills, find a place to live, develop new ways to relate to their children, overcome the challenge to develop new intimacy, learn to forgive one another (and self), and even allow the other to forgive. Some congregations provide group opportunities for working through feelings and needs. Specialized singles ministry can reach out with creative programs, social events, and a helping network for coping with practical problems.

The Other Man/Woman

In cases of adultery, the pastor must be concerned also about "the third party" (if known and if willing to be ministered to). It is not uncommon, e.g., that "the other woman" discovers she has been used when the wayward husband doesn't marry her. Guilt, anger, a sense of betrayal, bitterness, and distrust are not unusual responses. Clearly, God's Law-Gospel message is needed to heal here also.

Remarriage

This difficult subject has not had the attention it deserves (from the church) within the context of contemporary practice. The Commission on Theology and Church Relations, however, has touched on some of the basic theological concerns.

> What response is to be given to those who after an unscriptural divorce desire to remarry, declaring that they are unable to restore a previously broken marriage and expressing their intention to amend their sinful lives? . . .
>
> Obviously, no answer can be given which will cover the circumstances of each individual case, but some general observations may be helpful. . . .
>
> Divorce for unscriptural reasons, and remarriage involving such persons, are plainly contrary to God's will. . . .
>
> The question remains, however, whether the pastor may announce God's forgiveness where genuine repentance appears to be in evidence. To deny such persons the assurance of God's pardon would be to limit the atoning work of Jesus Christ, in whom there is forgiveness for all sins. . . .
>
> True repentance would presuppose a genuine desire to reconcile with one's estranged spouse. . . . Where the refusal to reconcile and to seek healing is judged to be absent—insofar as such a judgment is possible—the pastor will be constrained to deny a request for remarriage.
>
> There are circumstances, however, where there are reasons to believe that true repentance is indeed present but where reconciliation and restoration of a broken marriage simply are not possible, either because the former spouse has remarried or is unwilling to be reconciled. In such cases, remarriage becomes a possibility.[5]

Having stated the above, the pastor might ask if a divorced person can be genuinely repentant for the brokenness of a marriage and yet know that reconciliation is not possible. We live in a sinful world. In our weakness, some people are too difficult to live with. Beside the obvious psychopaths, some men and women tend to hurt or constantly exploit their family for reasons they may not even understand. Their intransigence may become an insurmountable barrier to reconciliation. By the time the pastor is called upon for pre-remarriage counseling, the previous marriage may be (humanly speaking) as impossible to reconstruct as

---

[5] *Divorce and Remarriage,* CTCR, pp. 39–41.

Humpty Dumpty, no matter how Christian the people see themselves.[6]

On the other hand, the pastor also will discern some individuals who don't care at all about God's Word or will, who live only for themselves. Where the pastor legitimately discerns such behavior, let him not participate in any marriage (and that requires strength of character on the part of the pastor). Play not the fool nor the insensitive clod.

If the pastor has determined that he can participate in a remarriage, premarital counseling is in order. He should not be put off by the excuse that the couple has been through all this before. The fact that the previous marriage failed increases the "baggage" brought into the remarriage. The couple needs to understand that this counseling is not a lecture by the pastor but a way to help them discover more deeply who they are, in relationship to each other, under a forgiving Lord, whom they say they desire to have as a party to their marriage.

---

[6] Luther, pastorally concerned for people beset with their humanity, suggests that "the adulterer may betake himself to a far country and there remarry if he is unable to remain continent. . . . Between two evils one is always the lesser, in this case allowing the adulterer to remarry in a distant land in order to avoid fornication. And I think he would be safer also in the sight of God" (LW 45:32f).

UNIT VI
THE PASTOR AS EQUIPPER

1
Mission/Evangelism: Communicating God's Graciousness

The term *mission* should encompass everything the church is about, for the term describes not only the church's activity but also God's. *Mission* (from *mitto*, to send) is used in the Latin translation of Jesus being sent by the Father (John 17:8), of Jesus' promise that the Father will send the Spirit (John 14:26), and of Jesus sending the disciples (John 20:21). Because the church's *doing* of what it is sent to do grows out of what God himself is doing and has done, the church needs to rehearse God's activity from the beginning in order to construct a *theology of mission*.

In Eden, God created humanity for perfect fellowship with him—and, together in him, in fellowship with each other. Though that perfect relationship was broken in the Fall, our gracious God quickly mended it in view of Good Friday—and communicated that restoration to Adam and Eve (Gen. 3:15). While the subsequent communication of the restored fellowship was to be shared by the people themselves, God sometimes spoke it directly (as to Noah and Abraham) and mediately (as through Moses and the prophets). The restoration *per se*, however, was not words but the action of God when he communicated himself in the flesh, in Christ Jesus the Word, to atone for the sins of all, which had broken the relationship.

God himself continues to communicate this restoration to fellowship. The relationship we in Christ have with each other is "the body of Christ"—not just in terminology but by his creation. We are (Rom. 12:3–13) both *en Christo* (in Christ) and *hen soma* (in one body). And his promise to the Apostles extends to us, "Surely I am with you always, to the very end of the age" (Matt. 28:20). And he assures us that the mission of all three Persons of the Trinity is to be with us (John 14:23–26). We are people in the Father's love, with the Spirit's power, as the body of Christ.

Therefore, the term "mission" describes

- the joint activity of God and His people;
- communicating to each other and all peoples of the earth (by proclaiming, by loosening and binding, and by baptizing and teaching); and
- their renewed fellowship because of the sacrifice of Christ and the forgiveness of sins (realized only in part now, but perfectly in the eternal Eden).

Ways to Speak of Mission

From within this theological construct, the Great Commissioning text of Matthew embodies something more than a charge of a sovereign Lord; it offers to the Apostles (and, ultimately, to all[1] who proclaim God's restoration in Christ) the promise of God's presence and his success as they go among all peoples. Matt. 28:19–20 serves as a summary for everything the *laos* do as the people of God, empowered by the Spirit of God. As Luther emphasized,

> "The Holy Spirit carries on his work unceasingly until the last day. For this purpose he has appointed a community on earth, through which he speaks and does all his work. For he has not yet gathered together all his Christian people, nor has he completed the granting of forgiveness (LC II 61f.).

This mission of communicating the restored fellowship in Jesus' blood can be summarized or focused in a number of ways.

Mission as the Mind of God. Behind all the promises of God lie the active and creative mind and heart of God which said, "Let

---

[1] While the Commission in Matthew is directed to the disciples, Luke (24:46–49) includes other disciples in addition to the designated apostles (vv. 33–35). In the first epistle of Peter (2:9; 3:15; 4:11), telling others about Christ is the work of the *laos* and not just those called as evangelists. The many New Testament examples of witnessing encourage all believers to do the same: the shepherds (Luke 2:17); the woman at Sychar (John 4:38–30, 39), the Jerusalem believers (Acts 8:1, 4); Priscilla, Aquila and Apollos (Acts 18:26–27); and the saints in heaven (Rev. 6:9).

us make man," thereby signaling his communal and communicative nature. He expressly willed to create Adam and Eve, who, in God's own likeness, could readily communicate and be in full, perfect, and harmonious fellowship with God and with each other.

Mission as the Grace of God. In the crisis immediately following the Fall, God demonstrated that his thoughts are not like human thoughts, that his ways are not like ours (Is. 55:8–9). Instead of shelving the mission, the *originator* of the mission creatively carried on in love and grace, for "God wants all men to be saved and come to the knowledge of the truth" (1 Tim. 2:34). He willed that so strongly that he promised, "I myself will search for my sheep and look after them" (Ezek. 34:11). Therefore, "He gave his one and only Son. . . . " (John 3:16). He loved the world that much!

Mission as Promise. The commissioning action of the Great Commission grows out of the covenant promises of the Old Testament in which God clearly revealed to Abraham the essence of his mission: "All peoples on earth will be blessed through you" (Gen. 12:3). All are justified by the grace of God, not because they are the biological children of Abraham but because they received God's grace by faith just as Abraham did (Rom. 4:1–17).

Mission as Communication Incarnate. The Old Testament records God's continuing communication with mankind for renewal of the fellowship relationship which was broken at the time of the Fall. When the Word was made flesh, however, the mission of God became more intimate and direct (John 1:1, 14; Heb. 1:1–2). God the Father communicated his own intention concerning his mission through the incarnate Christ at the time of the baptism of Jesus (Matt. 3:13–17 *et al.*) and particularly at the time of the transfiguration (Matt. 17:5 *et al.*). As both *message* and *message bearer,* Jesus truly is the seeking and finding shepherd (Ezek. 34; cf. also John 10:30).

Mission as the Body of Christ. With the arrival of God in the flesh, the God/humanity separation was broken down in the perfect life, death and resurrection of the Messiah. Though he reconciled the whole *world* unto himself (2 Cor. 5:19—objective justification[2]), yet he also works faith in the *individual* heart (John 3:5–6; 1 Cor. 12:3—subjective justification), recreating the Christian as part of the *body of Christ* (Gal. 3:26–29). As Paul described that new existence: "I have been crucified with Christ and no longer live, but Christ lives in me. The life I live in the

---

[2] However, see also FC EP XI, 11.

body, I live by faith in the Son of God who loved me and gave himself for me" (Gal. 2:20).

Mission as the Body of Christ *in Action*. The body of Christ properly functions as the result of the internal relationship for which Jesus prayed in his high priestly prayer (John 17:23a). Thus, God's mission moves out as his body responds to the creative direction of Jesus, the head.[3]

Jesus modeled the mission, and he could not be contained—not by calling him a blasphemer (Matt. 9:1–8), not by claiming he was in league with Beelzebub (12:22–28), not by the tradition of the elders (15:1–14), not by the threat of death (16:21–23). Not even death itself could contain him (27:40, 50, 28:5–6). Rather, throughout his ministry, Jesus communicated in deed and word God's restoration of his people. Such activity[4] did not stop with his ascension but continued through his Apostles—so effectively that they "turned the world upside down" (Acts 17:6 RSV).[5] And the activity will continue till the end of the age through God's blessings and gifts.

> It was he who gave some to be apostles, some to be prophets, some to be evangelists, and some to be pastors and teachers, to prepare God's people for works of service, so that the body of Christ may be built up until we all reach unity in the faith and in the knowledge of the Son of God and become mature, attaining to the whole measure of the fullness of Christ (Eph. 4:11–13).

The three specific actions delineated in the Great Commission—*matheteusate*, *baptizontes*, and *didaskontes*—are not three distinct activities, nor are they presented in any chronological sequence. Rather, Christ charges his sent ones to one task: to make disciples through the work of God in Word and Sacrament (baptizing and teaching).

Mission as Witness. Scripture frequently uses the court imag-

---

[3] Eph. 1:22–23; 4:15–16; Col. 1:18–23; 2:18–19.

[4] For additional examples, see Peter (Acts 2:14–43, 3—4; 9:32; 11:18; 12:1–18), Stephen (6:5–60), Philip (6:5–7; 8:4–8), Saul-Paul (9–28), and the believers in general (4:32–35; 5:12b–16; 6:1–4).

[5] Note that the activity is not limited to verbalizing the Gospel but includes all that God calls "good works." The Confessions also, while admittedly contrasting different issues from today, extol for the laity "the works that God commands, like the tasks of one's calling, the administration of public affairs, and the rearing of children" (AP XV 25). The Confessions hold up the servant girl who can boast, "If I do my daily housework faithfully, that is better than the holiness and austere life of all the monks" (LC I 146). The Apology summarizes, "All men, whatever their calling, ought to seek perfection, that is, growth in the fear of God, in faith, in the love of their neighbor, and similar spiritual virtues" (AP XXVII 37).

ery of a witness who gives personal testimony to establish God's truth: the rainbow (Gen. 9:12–17), the written words of God (Deut. 31:26), stones (Joshua 22:34), a heavenly being (Job 16:19), and his people (Is. 43:10–13). The act of bearing testimony to the truth takes on added importance in the New Testament as the Father witnesses for the Son (Matt. 3:17; 17:5; John 8:16–18), and as certain individuals were chosen to be eye witnesses (Acts 1:21–22), which became the basis for spreading the Gospel (Acts 2:32). The importance of the latter, however, lies not merely in the Twelve giving their eyewitness testimony but in the charge to all believers to give evidence of *salvation* (Luke 24:48; John 20:29) in word as well as in deed (Matt. 5:13–15; 1 Cor. 11:26; 2 Cor. 3:2; 9:12–13; 1 Peter 2:12).

Mission as a Prayer Concern. In Luke's presentation of the mission of God in Jesus, prayer occupies a primary place for our Savior (e.g., 3:21; 4:42; 6:12; 9:28; 22:41). When Jesus sent out the disciples two by two to proclaim that same mission, he encouraged them to pray (10:2)—and in prayer rejoiced on their return (10:21). In the prayer above all prayers that he gave us, he urges all his followers to pray for that mission (11:2; cf. also Matt. 9:38).

Mission as the Whole Body. While it may have seemed (and may still seem) to some that the mission of God belongs only to him and those specially set apart for the task[6], the Reformation reemphasized the Biblical concept that the spread of the Gospel involves the whole people of God.[7] As Luther wrote, the first office, that of the ministry of the Word, is common to all Christians, and therefore when we grant the Word (of God) to anyone, we cannot deny anything to him pertaining to the exercise of his priesthood.[8]

On the other hand, the Confessions emphasize also the office of the pastor:

> In his boundless kindness and mercy, God provides for the public proclamation of his divine, eternal law and the wonderful counsel concerning our redemption. (FC SD II 50).

In the Confessions, the pastoral office does not usurp the priesthood of all believers; rather, the pastor takes responsible leadership in teaching and proclaiming the Word of God so that the laity have a full understanding of their benefits and responsibilities. Ideally, lay Christians are so repentant, forgiven, taught,

---

[6] Cf. Matt. 28:16; Luke 24:48; John 20:21; Acts 2:4; 6:5–6; 13:2–3.

[7] LW 40:7–44.

[8] Ibid., p. 21.

inspired, admonished, and encouraged that they joyfully carry out their integrated life as living stones (1 Peter 2:1–9) and active members in the body of Christ (Eph. 2:1–10; Rom 12:1–21). Such outreach (which is but one of the Christian's good works of which all are equal) grows out of the Gospel, not "shoulds" or "oughts."

> We believe, teach, and confess further that all men, but especially those who are regenerated and renewed by the Holy Spirit, are obligated to do good works.

> In this sense the words *necessary, ought,* and *must* are correctly and in a Christian way applied to the regenerated and are in no way contrary to the pattern of sound words and terminology.

> However, when applied to the regenerated, the words *necessity* and *necessary* are understood as involving not coercion but the due obedience which genuine believers, in so far as they are reborn, render not by coercion or compulsion of the law but from a spontaneous spirit because they are "no longer under the law but under grace" (FC Ep V 8–10).

If the spiritual leader of the flock becomes discouraged because this doesn't produce his desired "fruits" (e.g., a significantly growing membership roster), he ought not give into the temptation of Law-inspired programs but remember,

> In the elect children of God this spontaneity is not perfect, but they are still encumbered with much weakness, as St. Paul complains of himself in Rom. 7:14–25 and Gal. 5:17.

> Nevertheless, for Christ's sake the Lord does not reckon this weakness against his elect, as it is written, "There is therefore now no condemnation for those who are in Christ Jesus" (Rom. 8:1; FC Ep V 13–14).

The pastor's task is to be a *Seelsorger* and to guide and teach his people for their part in God's mission, not to browbeat them into it.

Mission as World Wide. During his short ministry, Jesus had sent his apostles ("sent ones") to the lost sheep of Israel[9], but in the Great Commission as recorded in Mark 16:15–16, he sends them *eis ton kosmon hapanta,* into all the world, to *pase te ktisei,* to all the created ones (above the animals). Luke adds (in Acts 1:8), to *eschatou tes ges,* the remotest part of the earth. These terms echo the promise to Abraham that through him all *peoples* (*mishpecot,* all divisions or subdivisions of the world's population—groups, tribes or nations) would be blessed. Taken together, the texts portray God as emphasizing that his mission extends

---

[9] Matt. 10:6; Luke 10:1.

beyond Israel, beyond ethnocentricity.[10] The supposedly (to some in Jesus' day) *ex*clusive grace of the Old Covenant is again revealed to be *in*clusive. If the disciples had any doubts, they were erased on Pentecost when the Gospel was heard in everyone's own tongue (Acts 2:8), an emphasis reaffirmed by God in the Peter-Cornelius events (Acts 10).

Mission as God's Priority. Keeping in mind God's will for humanity (that it worship him in perfect fellowship), his drawing all mankind unto himself in Christ Jesus leads to the inescapable conclusion that mission has priority over the things of this world. The disciples questioned this even as late as just before the ascension: "Lord, are you at this time going to restore the kingdom to Israel?" (Acts 1:6). Jesus' reply moved their preoccupation with power and the physical kingdom out of first position: "It is not for you to know the time or dates the Father has set by his own authority" (v. 7). Having opened the top position, Jesus immediately filled it with God's priority: "You will be witnesses in Jerusalem, and in all Judea and Samaria and to the ends of the earth" (v. 8).

Just as Jesus always put the eternal mission of God first, fulfilling God's righteousness (Matt. 3:15), so he gave his disciples a new vision of the world as he commissioned them to "go and make disciples of all nations."

---

[10] See also Dan. 7:14 and Zech. 14:9.

239

2
The Pastor as Administrator

Administration and the Body of Christ

Secular and Ecclesial Models Compared

Today's pastor bears a host of particular responsibilities: preacher, counselor, teacher, leader, financial advisor, comforter, and student—and administrator. For many, the latter means the pastor sits behind a desk as he successfully manages the business of the organization (as compared to a *Seelsorger* who deals personally and primarily with people, God's people). At times, methods of secular administration do bring about outward success in a congregation and please the people well. Unfortunately, these methodologies usually are adopted without being adapted to the specific and unique concept of Christ's church.

The pastor as administrator needs to take his cue from the Scriptures. First Corinthians uses *kubernesis* for "administration": a steering, a piloting, a directing. The pastor as administrator oversees and guides, pointing people always to Christ. 2 Cor. 8:20 uses another word, *diakoneo*: "to serve," (literally, "to wait at table"). Therefore, the pastor as administrator serves by guiding and guides by serving, ministering to the body of Jesus Christ. While the secular world may distinguish between *leading* and *administering/managing*, Scripture does not. Therefore, *Parish administration* is concerned with

- the action of God's people at work,
- individually and corporately,
- in the mission of the church,
- arranged coherently and comprehensively,

- to bring the Gospel in Word and Sacrament to one another and to the world and
- in a manner that is salutary and effective (using all resources and personnel and serving the purpose).

In this definition, parish administration has its roots in what God is doing through Word and Sacrament in the lives of all his people, and in how they are growing up in every way into him who is the head, and being filled with him who fills all in all.

Thus, the pastor as administrator functions in a way totally different from an administrator in any other endeavor. He is not a dictator or private kingdom builder. His administration has relatively little to do with building construction, attendance at Christmas services, sociological surveys, budgets, and down payments on a new parsonage. Rather, when asked about goals, means, and resources, the pastor knows that all are wrapped up in Christ and his Gospel, in his grace and power, in his life flowing out through all the members of his body, the church. In everything the church does, it trusts completely in what Christ has done and in what he will do through his Word and Sacrament. The Holy Spirit is the one who nourishes faith and service; he is the one who creates the new man to come forth daily to live out the Word of God with joy. The Spirit is the one who has called them together by the Gospel to be the body of Christ, who is the head of the body and in whom centers all service and action. The church is always the church because of what God does, never because of what the people are doing.

As a result, enormous differences separate secular from ecclesial models and philosophies of administration.

1. Parish administration serves people more than programs; and the programs it uses (when rightly designed and administered) provide opportunities for God's people to use their God-given gifts (1 Peter 2:5).

2. Since Christ is the head of the church and exercises his authority through the Word of God, the question of Who's the decision-maker in the church? is already answered. Under his headship, all others are servants of each other (cf. Mark 10:43–45, John 13:1–5).

3. The unity of the church is in Christ. The individual believers live in *koinonia* with each other because each is in fellowship with the risen Christ. In other words, the *corpus* of Christ is corporate, not a collection of individualistic relationships based on convenience, common interest, human enjoyment, or economic privilege.

4. The church in a strict sense is a living organ*ism*, not a static organi*zation*. Christ is alive, and he speaks clearly to the

church through his Word. His body, the church, also is alive—a dynamic body moving with the ever-present activity of the Holy Spirit and the living Christ.

5. Values also differentiate the secular from the ecclesial concepts of administration. Secular values are self-defined, whereas the church has Biblical values. In contrast to business' self-interest (the "bottom line," salaries, etc.), the body of Christ values service to God and neighbor (with the highest service being the proclamation of the Gospel).

The secular world values coercion for motivation; in the church, God transforms people through his Word. The values differ so greatly that Christians speak of their jobs and careers as their vocation (calling) from God.

The very nature and mission of the church requires pastor and people to work together in service under the Word of God. The pastor's own person sets the tone of life in the congregation. The way he relates himself to people shapes the interrelationships of all the members as they fulfill their vocations together as the people of God. If the pastor views the people he serves as parts of a large machine, making it run successfully usually takes priority over people and their needs. The pastor's primary consideration always should be, Are the people I serve growing in faith and service? How may I honor them for what Christ has done for their salvation, see them for what they are, hear them for what they are saying, and lead them to live as the body of Christ in the world?

To reiterate: the pastor as administrator emphasizes mutual interaction and responsibility, not well-poisoning obedience to his office. After the pastor and people together have ascertained from God's Word the essential nature and function of the Christian congregation as well as the office of the pastor as servant/guide, they then arrange the responsibilities and plan how to carry out the God-given duties and privileges of a Christian congregation— i.e., to witness Jesus Christ to the world as they await joyfully the final rescue. Their lives of good works attract unbelievers to the faith that Christians confess (Matt. 5:16) and of which they speak as opportunity arises. When God's people live by faith active in love (which is "the only thing that counts" for the believer, Gal. 5:6), the only "administration" necessary is that which frees and enables Christians to carry out their true nature and task in a salutary and effective manner, "in a fitting and orderly way" (1 Cor. 14:40).

The Basic Principles of Pastoral Administration

The specific administrative activity of the pastor depends on his principles—and these, in turn, depend on his goals. Therefore, the goals are reemphasized here in order to focus on the principles.

The pastor as administrator will lead God's people, by means of his Word, to fulfill their calling as the people of God,

1. by believing and trusting in Christ, the head of the body, presenting their own bodies as living sacrifices;
2. by being enriched in Christ in every respect, including for a life of service (rather than for just getting the work done);
3. by understanding their mission as church, i.e., as bringing the Gospel to one another and to the world;
4. by understanding the world and testifying effectively to it, letting their light shine and being salt; and
5. by involving the other members, with everyone's resources, in the Gospel ministry, because the Spirit has given differing gifts for the common good.

In order to achieve these goals, the following seven basic administration principles should guide the pastor as administrator.

Principle One. Word and Sacrament, in worship and study, undergird all else the church does.[1] There the church gains an understanding of its true nature and mission. Without Word and Sacrament, a congregation may become a great institution, a builder of monuments, a popular gathering place, or a center for the community with social activities, but it won't be a *true* Christian church. Christian worship is the significant center of the church's life; there God comes to his people, bringing salvation in forgiveness of sins and bestowing his blessings in abundance. Therefore, the pastor as administrator responsibly leads corporate worship[2] and the study of God's Word[3] with great care and attention.

Principle Two. The pastor and congregation maintain fidelity to the teachings of the Holy Scripture and to the Confessions as the correct exposition of God's Word. Such faithfulness is freely given because both are convinced in heart and mind that this Law-Gospel emphasis blesses God's people. It is the pastor's responsibility to lead and teach the laity so that they can remain faithful.

---

[1] The principle applies to the pastor as well; he too needs a vital personal worship and study life (which is not accomplished merely in sermon preparation). A seminary education achieves success when, beyond the teaching of the minimums, it has motivated and enabled the student to carry on fruitful study and worship throughout his lifetime.

[2] See Unit III for additional discussion on worship.

[3] See Unit VI, Ch. 4 for additional discussion on Christian education.

Principle Three. The New Testament mandates no particular structure or polity for today's congregation. Some of its descriptions and arrangements have survived the trials of time, but they are not binding. The only "structure" mandated is that the office of the holy ministry oversee the spiritual life of the flock (cf. Acts 20:17–28; 1 Peter 5:2). (Other auxiliary/facilitating offices, though not mandated, can be helpful in "organizing the body" under the serving leadership of the pastor.) Congregational polity and organizational structure, however, should be accommodated to the cultural and social patterns of the people (but without compromising Scriptural principles). This is especially important in an increasingly transcultural ministry in North America so that the Gospel "may not be bound but have free course and be preached to the joy and edifying of Christ's holy people, so that in steadfast faith [they] may serve [God] and in the confession of [his] name abide to the end" (Collect of the Church).

At the same time, it should be noted that the congregational structure should permit, preserve, and promote the universal priesthood of all believers and should not hinder members from individually fulfilling their calling and responsibility as God's people in Christian mission. (This, rather than "efficiency," should be the overriding criterion for selecting a structure.) All members have the individual responsibility to *do* mission and fulfill their Christian calling according to their gifts and abilities, both within and outside of the local parish. Some will be indifferent or reluctant, feeling inadequate or that the opportunity for service is trivial. Others want to do something worthwhile for and through the church; they feel their importance to the mission. In either case volunteers usually need proper encouragement, motivation, and trust. The pastor should expect to spend many hours in recruiting and/or appointing, in giving specific assignments (job descriptions) as he matches gifts to responsibilities, and in training others to serve under the motivation of the Gospel.

The pastor, however, sees his primary concern to be the ministry of Word and Sacrament.

> The distinctive task of the pastoral office is not that of organizing other people to do the "real ministry" but is that of serving them faithfully with the preaching of the Gospel and the administration of the holy sacraments.[4]

"Accordingly, he will be sensitive to the need to preserve a

---

[4] *Evangelism and Church Growth, with Special Reference to the Church Growth Movement* (September 1987), The Commission on Theology and Church Relations (The Lutheran Church—Missouri Synod), p. 40.

proper balance between reaching out to the lost and nurturing those who are in the church."[5]

A growing understanding of the mission of the church and of the implications of the lay person's vocation have brought into focus once again the importance of the *whole* church's witness to the world.

Principle Four. The church is free to select any of its members for various lay leadership offices, within Scriptural limits for women, to carry out its activities in a harmonious and effective manner, salutary for all. Effective leaders expand their efforts by training and enabling others for service within and beyond the congregation (John 8:31; 1 Cor. 12; Rom. 12; Eph. 4). Those who are chosen assist the pastor in leading the rest of the members in the mission and ministry of the congregation.

Principle Five. The example of the New Testament church emphasizes the importance of pastor-to-person relationships that exhibit mutual cooperation, interdependence, loving concern, forgiveness, and the relationship of the flock to the undershepherd, who leads it. Whether that is achieved in a congregation today depends heavily on the pastor's integrity, competence, humility, awareness of his sinful nature, faith, and genuine love for his people. While the Table of Duties (SC IX 3, which should be taught to the *laos*) calls for respect, obedience, and the willingness to be admonished, this should be motivated by the Gospel and faith, not legalism.

The church exists as a group by incorporation into Christ; yet each person is touched with water and Word individually. Therefore, the pastor will get to know personally the individuals and families of the congregation, opening the door to minister to their unique needs, conveying God's love and the church's concern through the *personalized* ministry of Word and Sacrament.

Principle Six. Because all parts of the body need each other (1 Cor. 12:14–27), the lay leaders work together along with and under the guidance of the pastor. In congregations with little or no careful planning, subgroups and activities may compete with one another and even duplicate or overlap their efforts. Or, if the planning is not coherent, subgroups may come to feel that they are ends in themselves and lose their sense of being in relation to the church. Therefore, leaders who skillfully develop and carry out short-term and long-range, comprehensive plans help all parts of the church see themselves as part of the larger whole with a single goal: the mission of God.

---

[5] Ibid., p. 43.

Principle Seven. Christ's resources and personnel beyond the parish also are used in moving toward the fulfillment of the mission of the church. The congregation recognizes that, by itself, it does not contain all the knowledge, insight, or resources required to meet the opportunities and needs of the church. Each congregation profits from the other's life and experience. Thus, congregations have joined together in the Synod; and the Synod serves congregations today in much the same way as when its first president, C. F. W. Walther, spoke on "Duties of an 'Evangelical Lutheran' Synod" in 1897[6]: To support fidelity to the Confessions and, thereby, to Scripture; to defend and protect congregations; to promote growth in the knowledge of Scripture and its teachings; to promote peace and unity in the church; and to seek the glory of God. To that end, the Synod (and its districts) provide a wealth of resources with which the pastor ought to be acquainted and use when appropriate for the congregation.[7]

Congregations and pastors also need to keep in mind that the Synod is able to provide its benefits only insofar as the congregations that have joined together as the Synod carry out their responsibilities to it. In essence, the Synod is nothing more (nor less!) than an expression of the commitment of its congregations and pastors to support each other.

Congregational Membership

Strictly speaking, congregational membership is comprised of all those in a given locale who have voluntarily joined together in a common belief in and confession of all that Scripture has revealed. Because the Spirit in Holy Baptism works faith in children as well as adults, congregations usually include among their numbers the small children of their adults. However, congregations often distinguish between baptized and communicant members.

Depending on their legal arrangement chosen for self-government, some congregations further designate as *voters* those communicants (usually over a designated age) who participate in the formal organization. Some congregations structure themselves under a type of council that carries out the formal administration,

---

[6] Walther's essay at the first Iowa District Convention, tr. Everette W. Meier. Excerpts: *The Heart of C. F. W. Walther* (St. Louis: Concordia, 1989), p. 3–9. The full essay will appear in a collection of essays to be published by Concordia Publishing House, St. Louis, in 1990.

[7] For a full listing of the departments of the Synod and the types of resources offered, see the current *Lutheran Annual.*

the council being elected by and reporting to all the congregation's members, meeting only periodically.

Whatever the formal/legal structure, the aforementioned principle must be maintained: that the congregational structure should permit, preserve, and promote the universal priesthood of all believers along with the office of the public ministry.

Membership In and Out

Christian congregations in general (and especially those in the same confessional fellowship) have the obligation to one another to support their members as they relocate in other locales and begin a fellowship with Christians in that area. Normally this includes (1) letting the departing member know which confessionally Lutheran congregations serve that area, (2) encouraging the relocated member to join such a congregation, and (3) transferring to the other congregation the responsibility for the person's spiritual welfare. While The Lutheran Church—Missouri Synod has no formal policy on terminology, the following definitions are often used:

Transfer denotes the move of a member in good standing from one congregation within the Synod to another.

Received by (Re)Affirmation/Profession of Faith generally designates the reception of those from Lutheran congregations not in pulpit and altar fellowship with the Synod, and for the reception of those who previously were dropped from membership in a synodical congregation.

The Rite of Adult Confirmation is generally conducted for those who come from unchurched or non-Lutheran backgrounds.

A Peaceful Release is generally given to those members who are joining a Lutheran congregation not in fellowship with the Synod or joining a non-Lutheran congregation that, nevertheless, publicly teaches salvation by grace, through faith, for Christ's sake.

Dropped from Membership is applied to those former members who give evidence of retaining their faith, but no longer wish to be associated with the original congregation and/or have joined an organization that severely compromises or rejects the Biblical way of salvation.

Excommunication is reserved for those situations in which a member steadfastly refuses to amend an openly sinful and impenitent life, rejecting the congregation's ministry of Word and Sacrament. This cannot be pronounced by an individual but is the action of the entire congregation—and then only after every effort to restore the fallen brother or sister has been exhausted. However, in keeping with the injunction of Matt. 18:17, the congregation then continues to relate to the excommunicated as "a mission prospect" (to use common parlance).

Multistaff Administration

The pastor as administrator often enjoys ministry in a multi-staff congregation. An effective team ministry, of course, does not happen simply because the congregation calls more workers. It takes time, effort, the constant evaluation of everyone's responsibility, and especially a scripturally sound understanding of the ministry of the church based on God's service, forgiveness, and leadership. The Synod's definition of *auxiliary offices* will be of great assistance in keeping this understanding clear:

> These are offices established by the church. Those who are called to serve in them are authorized to perform certain of the function(s) of the office of the public ministry. These offices are "ministry" and they are "public," yet they are not *the* office of the public ministry. Rather, they are auxiliary to that unique pastoral office, and those who hold these offices perform their assigned functions under the supervision of the holders of the pastoral office.[8]

Whatever the office held, every Christian leader is first a servant. Yet, aware of the pitfalls rooted in fallen mankind's nature, some general suggestions for team ministry can be made.

1. The church needs to understand its mission. When pastor(s), staff, and lay leaders agree on and are committed to Christ's purpose for the congregation, useless conflict and tension which lead to sin are avoided. To that end, many congregations are writing mission statements, clarifying and individualizing God's purposes in the congregation's particular context—and through the statements encouraging one another to work together under pastoral guidance/leadership (Heb. 13:17) toward the common good.

2. The servants need to agree on the purpose of the office of the ministry and their individual responsibilities/functions within or under it. When two men jointly occupy the congregation's office of the public ministry, their relationship is one of function. Persons active in the body of Christ are so as complementary members one of the other; invidious comparisons are out of order. Clear position descriptions, based on a proper understanding of the office of the holy ministry and spelling out

---

[8] *The Ministry: Offices, Procedures, and Nomenclature* (September 1981), The Commission on Theology and Church Relations, (The Lutheran Church—Missouri Synod), p. 12.

relationships and responsibilities, will help achieve this guideline.

3. Communication should be reciprocal and decision-making participatory. Staff members who feel uninformed and/or outside the decision-making process will not be able to carry out ministry as a team.

4. Everyone, beginning with the pastor, operates from a clear awareness of personal limitations due to the Fall.

5. Multiple staff relationships must be motivated *by* the Gospel and *for* the Gospel. Since Christ is the foundation of all relationships, all staff members see themselves in fellowship with each other in him. That view allows for and promotes the fruit of the Spirit (Gal. 5:22) which makes their ministry possible and a blessing to the church.

Ministering in a Multicultural World

Few congregations in North America consist solely of one-culture members and call same-culture pastors. Given the mobility of society, most churches include members from many cultures/subcultures. Therefore, every pastor (not just the overseas missionary) should enter his call recognizing the need for awareness of and sensitivity to other cultures.

Culture Defined

Although the term has been used as a synonym for a given society or people, the term "culture" properly is better defined as the integrated pattern of what a given group of people does and believes and what it transmits (by other means than heredity) from one generation to the next.[9] It binds people to each other and separates them from others. It defines the behavior the group considers acceptable or deviant. Culture is the model of reality that governs a people's perception of what is real and right. It teaches a people-group how to think and live; it is an organizing principle of life. Culture is not neutral but simultaneously helpful and harmful. Culture is not static but something that the group can add to or change. Culture is a second skin that all people wear wherever they go. Culture is like an onion, with outer layers of artifacts and behavior, and inner layers of values and beliefs. At

---

[9] According to Winter and Hawthorne (*Perspectives on the World Christian Movement*, Pasadena: William Cary Library, 1981, p. 321), an estimated 22,200 people-groups inhabit the world, each different and each subdivided into subcultures. To compound the problem, each person (at least in some features) has his own way of life, his own "ideo-culture."

the center is the view of reality that makes sense of and gives meaning to the culture's way of life.

Christians, who have the Gospel of Jesus Christ at the heart of their culture, want to share the good news. They look forward to the Holy Spirit creating faith in Christ through the Word, which they communicate to the world. But therein lies a problem; for the way Christians communicate the Word is intimately tied to their culture; and the way it is heard is intimately tied to the hearer's culture.

The problem is not limited to the overseas missionary but affects the North American pastor as well—perhaps more so because, being familiar with his own culture, he may be lulled by it.

Communication Defined

Communication is
- the art of transmitting a message
- from one individual to another
- in such a way that the message is received with a minimum of distortion.[10]

Although the communication process may seem natural and simple, the following five-step diagram illustrates its complexity and delicacy (with a sixth step to verify the accuracy of what was received).

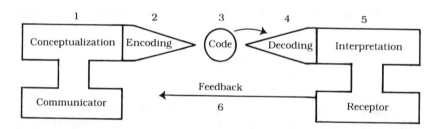

The key, of course, is in the coding and decoding processes; and clearly the communication process affords a large potential for failure at each step. The task requires our best efforts.

Culture and Communication

When the communicator and the receptor live in different cultures—different thinking patterns, beliefs, values, behavior, and supporting physical surroundings—the pastor should assume that the receptor will not automatically receive the same

---

[10] Pentecost, *Issues in Missiology*. (Grand Rapids: Baker, 1982), p. 3.

message sent. And the greater the cultural distance, the more barriers there are.

Consider, for instance, the phrase "to be born again." In the mind and mouth of a Christian, it stands for God's gift of a blessed life with God from the time of Baptism into all eternity. For the Hindu receptor, however, steeped in reincarnation, the phrase signals going through yet another life until enough good works liberate one from the burdensome cycle of rebirth—in other words, a condemnation instead of a blessing. Illustrations could be drawn also from multiethnic congregations (for example, German-Lutheran churches into which former non-Lutherans have married).

The Christian pastor, therefore, must take the initiative to find a way around/through the barriers. First, he must identify the differences in thought patterns, ways of life, and language that make the communication difficult—and do so without being judgmental or critical. And he must realize that many (but not all) of these differences are not tied to Biblical morality or Christianity *per se.*

Second, the pastor must understand how the differences are integrated into the receptor's cultural weave that provides meaning and understanding to life.

Third, the pastor needs to focus his communication on issues that are important in the receptor's culture (e.g., one's view of reality and morality)—and do so in ways that will be meaningfully decoded by the receptor.

Language, of course, plays an important part in this (cf. Acts 2:6–8.) Since one's mother tongue is a dear possession, it is the best language for study of the Word (and for worship), for God's Word is the power of God for salvation to everyone who believes (Rom. 1:16).

In short, the pastor's communication takes seriously language differences, psychological "noise," and cultural patterns of thought that raise barriers. All this because he understands the eternal significance of calling upon the name of the Lord for salvation (Rom. 10:13–15).

Cultures and Faith Connections/Fellowship

Because a person within a culture usually can communicate God's message better to others within the same culture than an outsider can, the outsider-pastor ideally supports the insider-receptor to begin his own process of communicating Law and Gospel. The pastor also strives to help the insider build fellowship and faith connections with same-culture Christians in order to resist temptation and in order to confess his sins and receive absolution, comfort, counsel, and advice.

When the Samaritan woman at Sychar recognized Jesus as the Messiah, she immediately became involved in telling others (John 4:29)—and many of them believed because of her witness (v. 39). One of the greatest gifts the pastor can give to a new believer is the opportunity to witness, to learn to participate with the encouragement of a mentor, and on his own to guide others to their Savior, who transcends all cultural boundaries.

3
Equipping for Stewardship

Biblical Stewardship

To many people, stewardship means giving of one's time, talents, and treasures. However, such volunteerism is not the right way to consider the matter. Being a steward means *ordering the household, managing.* And the household that is managed is built by Christ by grace; there is no stewardship except through and under the cross. There our gifts (of time, talent, and treasure) mean nothing, for there we can only receive the gracious gift of life in Christ by which there can be a household to manage—a gift made ours in Baptism. Therefore, properly speaking, stewardship refers to the distinct mission of the body of Christ, not to largess.

The term *oikonomia* (stewardship or administration) derives from *oikos* (house) and *nemo* (to distribute, manage) or *nomos* (that which is assigned). Twenty times the New Testament uses the term or some variation of it, and these only in the works of Luke, Peter (only once), and Paul.[1]

Stewardship in Luke's Gospel

Two pericopes in Luke refer to *oikonomos:* 12:32–48 and 16:1–13. In the first, the word is used in its secular, technical sense to denote the occupation of a household or estate manager

---

[1] *Oikonomia* (stewardship, administration)—Luke 16:2, 3, 4; 1 Cor. 9:17; Eph. 1:10; 3:2, 9; Col. 1:25; 1 Tim. 1:4. *Oikonomos* (steward[s], manager[s])— Luke 12:42; 16:1, 3, 8; Rom. 16:23; 1 Cor. 4:1, 2; Gal. 4:2; Titus 1:7; 1 Peter 4:10. *Oikonomeo* (to do stewardship, to manage)—Luke 16:2.

(v. 42), also called (vv. 37, 43) one of the servants (*douloi*) "whose master finds them watching when he comes" home from a wedding feast. The application of the parable (vv. 40–49, showing the need for readiness and responsibility before the *parousia*) describes the household as consisting of people who simultaneously are managers and servants. Indeed, they are his *oikos*, his house. He enlarges his house(hold) through the work of those to whom he entrusts the stewardship of the house. Thus, Christians are stewards of the people and the possessions God gives to them in their lives—especially the spiritual treasure that abides forever. Furthermore, this stewardship is judged on the basis of wisdom and faithfulness (v. 42) to what has been given (v. 48).

A similar identification of manager with servant is given in Luke 16:1–13, the "Parable of the Shrewd Manager." The point of the Lord's comparison lies in the prudence by which one behaves now in such a way as to prepare for the day of the great reversal. Christians are to exercise shrewdness and foresight in the use of their possessions for God's kingdom just as the "people of this world" exercise the same in their world of business. Indeed, the emphasis is not upon how much has been entrusted to them but on their fidelity in using it. (Cf. also passages such as Matt. 25:14–31 and Luke 19:11–27).

To summarize stewardship in Luke: *Oikonomos* (steward) refers to all those *douloi* of God who receive into their trust his responsibilities in his house for his people and possessions. Stewardship (*oikonomia*) is their management of the trust with faithfulness and wisdom (shrewdness) because they will ultimately give an account of their stewardship (16:2).

Stewardship in Peter's Letter

Stewardship in 1 Peter 4:10 also draws on the root word *house* (in context, God's people, his church). The stewards, the members of Christ's church, serve the house(hold) with varieties of "God's grace in its various forms." The gifts differ, but all equally find their source in God and his grace. And the steward is evaluated on how he responsibly manages his gifts "to serve others" to benefit the whole house. While in Luke *steward* is associated with *servant*, in Peter it is identified with *service*. The similarity is pronounced.

Stewardship in Paul's Letters

In many instances Paul uses the term *oikonomia* in a way similar to that of Luke and Peter. In 1 Cor. 4:1, Paul introduces himself and his fellow workers as "those entrusted [*oikonomoi*, stewards] with the secret things of God" (cf. also Eph. 3:2–4 and

Col. 1:25), in order to win others for Christ (1 Cor. 9:19). His strength for carrying out this stewardship comes from God's power (Col. 1:29), and his motivation from God's grace (Eph. 3:7). Although freely motivated, he describes the preaching of the Gospel as a stewardship from which he cannot withdraw (1 Cor. 9:17). Thus, again, stewardship is tied to faithful servanthood and service (1 Cor. 9:17; Eph. 3:7; Col. 1:25; Titus 1:7).

However, Paul introduces a significantly broader usage when he refers uniquely to *God's administration* of his plan of salvation. In Eph. 1:9–10 and 3:9, God is shown to be the administrator of the fullness of time, the administrator who has now revealed to all his *mysterion* (his hidden plan) for the world: that through the atonement of Jesus Christ (1:7), both Jew and Gentile would be the sons of God (2:14), united in him who brings "all things . . . together under one head, even Christ" (1:10).

To summarize stewardship in Paul: The term includes both God's plan of salvation throughout history as well as the Christian's task of making known this plan—the latter deriving from the former. Thus, stewardship is God at work within his house; for the Christian it is a life of service with Christ at the center.

A Theology of Stewardship

The Department of Stewardship of The Lutheran Church—Missouri Synod defined stewardship in this way:

> Christian stewardship is
> > the free and joyous activity
> > > by the child of God and
> > > God's family, the church,
> > > > as a response to God's love in Christ
> > in managing all of life and life's resources
> > > in a God-pleasing manner and
> > > in partnership with Him,
> > towards the ultimate purpose of glorifying Him
> > > by making disciples of all nations.[2]

Note the way in which this definition touches the three articles of the creed.

The First Article—Creation and Stewardship. "The earth is the Lord's, and everything in it, the world, and all who live in it" (Ps. 24:1). The passage immediately takes us back to Genesis 1 and 2 and Adam and Eve's ideal management of creation before the Fall. As Luther explained the First Article of the Apostles

---

[2] Original printing unknown.

Creed, God graciously allows people to use his possessions for their physical needs as well as for the advancement of his kingdom.

The Christian differs from the unbeliever in three respects. (1) The Christian knows that God is the owner of all things and that he calls for responsible management of his property. As Luther says so aptly, all that God gives comes without any merit in the steward. (2) The believer is empowered by the Spirit to live out the management under God. (3) The Christian is empowered by the Spirit to respond in thanks, praise, service, and free obedience.

The Second Article—Redemption and Stewardship. For the sake of his Son, the redeemer of the world, God is gracious to sinners in order that we (as Luther explains) "might be his own and live under him in his kingdom and serve him in everlasting righteousness, innocence, and blessedness."

Among all the gifts that God has given us to administer, the Gospel is foremost. Thanks be to God for "his indescribable gift" (2 Cor. 9:15) of "the gospel of Christ" (v. 13)! Of this message God's people in Christ are stewards, and they "no longer live for themselves but for him who died for them and was raised again" (2 Cor. 5:15).

The Third Article—Sanctification and Stewardship. This article focuses on the work of the Holy Spirit, who has brought us to faith and has enabled us to be stewards of the gifts of God. "We are God's workmanship, created in Christ Jesus to do good works, which God prepared in advance for us to do" (Eph. 2:10). And, by the Spirit's work in us through the Gospel, enlightening us with his gifts, we are freed to be good stewards of those gifts.

Principles of Stewardship

Paul, in 2 Corinthians 8 and 9 (referring to a collection of money for the saints), delineates a number of principles of the stewardship life. Although he is not presenting a sequential outline, his progression offers much to Christians in every age. In these chapters, the pastor will find many practical suggestions for strengthening the congregation's total stewardship of the household of God. How these are applied will vary from congregation to congregation, but they should be kept in mind—especially when evaluating and/or participating in a fund-raising effort so that it is not thought of as the congregation's total stewardship effort.

Chapter 8:1–2, Principle One. God's grace provides the base for all Christian stewardship—"the grace that God has given,"

God's grace in sending his own Son for us. This should be the motivation for the Christians in Corinth as it was for the Christians in Macedonia who, in response to God's grace, gave toward the collection with "overflowing joy" and "in rich generosity" (vv. 1–2).

Verse 3, Principle Two. Christians give according to their means, just as the Macedonians "gave as much as they were able and even beyond their ability" amid great affliction and poverty, yet with joy."

Verses 4–5, Principle Three. Christians give themselves "first to the Lord" just as the Macedonians did, to be governed by his will. They were so committed as his servants that they even begged to be allowed to have a part in this service to their fellow Christians. God's grace moves Christians to surrender to God and not to worry about self.

Verses 6–7, Principle Four. The grace to give is firmly predicated upon all that God has graciously worked in the Christian (e.g., a strong faith, lively witnessing, and a growing knowledge of God).

Verse 8, Principle Five. Christian love shows itself in action, just as justification springs joyfully into sanctification. Stewardship is never predicated on the Law.

Verse 9 (Principle One revisited). The Christian's love breaks into action because it grows out of the gracious and self-sacrificing love of God in Christ. He emptied himself of his riches so that "through his poverty" we "might become rich."

Verses 10–12 (Principle Five revisited). Christian love springs out of justification willingly as well as joyfully. Paul does not emphasize the amount but the readiness to give, even as the widow gave her two coins (Mark 12:41–44).

Verses 13–15, Principle Six. Stewardship is a joint venture in the church, a mutual give-and-receive (equally) so that all people, particularly fellow Christians, may be helped in their need whenever it may occur.

Verses 16–23 (Principle Three revisited). The participation of Paul, Titus, and the other two "brothers" (vv. 18, 22) also grows out of commitment to the Lord, "to honor the Lord himself and to show our eagerness to help" (v. 19). Therefore, no one (and especially not Paul) may give the slightest suspicion of wrongdoing, for to do so might jeopardize the witness of the Gospel "in the eyes of men" (vv. 20–21).

Verses 24–9:2 (Principle Five revisited). Paul invites the Christians at Corinth to show their love breaking into action, not for self-aggrandizement but as a witness to others.

Chapter 9:3–5, Principle Seven. Christian stewardship re-

quires preparation. Paul praised the Corinthians for many good qualities, but he does not want his boast to come up empty in this matter of the collection. Not that the Corinthians will refuse to give, but Paul fears that they may lack the preparation and organization to carry out their plans.

Verse 5, Principle Eight. Christian stewardship involves promise, commitment. Paul reminds the Corinthians of their promise as a way to remind them more importantly of the joy out of which the promise was made. He is concerned lest they think of his urging in this letter as legalistic and, as a result, give grudgingly.

Verses 6–15, Principle Nine. Christian stewardship results in blessing heaped upon blessing. These include
1. The certainty of harvest, which comes with giving in the right spirit (v. 6).
2. God's love, extended to the cheerful giver (v. 7).
3. The grace to give (v. 8).
4. An abundance of "seed" to give (vv. 8–9).
5. A multiplication of the seed as well as the blessings of the scattered gifts (vv. 10–11), increasing the results of liberality.
6. Praises to God and prayers for the steward by those blessed with the generosity (vv. 11–14).

Summary

"Thanks be to God for his indescribable gift!" (v. 15), the gift of his grace in his own Son—a gift that, when handled by God's stewards, explodes into an unselfish demonstration of loving concern for others. Is that demonstration one of time, talents, and treasures? Yes, but those three are too small to contain all that a steward of God's household does and is. Rather, one should speak of the steward using everything in his Master's house to carry out his now-revealed plan of salvation to enlarge the household (cf. Matt. 25:14–30)

4

The Pastor
and Christian Education

In its broadest sense, *teaching* in the church occurs in every type of setting in which the Word of God is shared (apart from the celebration of the Sacraments and Absolution): formal class settings, sermons, one-on-one help so that another person understands/applies some point of doctrine, parents setting devotion and worship habits before their children, mutual consolation, etc. In fact, the term can be stretched to include almost everything that the church (as a group as well as individuals) does to "make disciples of all nations, baptizing . . . and teaching . . ." (Matt. 28:19–20)[1]

That emphasis on using every opportunity comes through warmly in Moses' instructions to the Israelites at the end of their exodus. Even though the words focus on a vertical generation-to-generation education as compared to a horizontal Christian-to-Christian-to-unbeliever teaching, they establish some excellent guidelines for Christians: begin and end with God's grace; use every opportunity; be patient, persistent, and personal.

Love the Lord your God with all your heart and with all your

---

[1] Note that the verb is *discipling*, which is done through baptism and teaching. The terms are not pitted against each other as though the Christian can disciple others apart from teaching or that teaching might result in something other than discipling. But it is also not a matter of teaching in the purely human sense, for it involves God's power through His Word, of which the pastor is a steward.

soul and with all your strength. These commandments that I give you today are to be upon your hearts.

Impress them on your children. Talk about them when you sit at home and when you walk along the road, when you lie down and when you get up. Tie them as symbols on your hands and bind them on your foreheads. Write them on the doorframes of your houses and on your gates.

In the future, when your son asks you, "What is the meaning of the stipulations, decrees and laws the Lord our God has commanded you?" tell him . . . (Deut. 6:5–9, 20f.).

That same warmth may be seen in John's description[2] of Jesus as the Good Shepherd, who tenderly leads and feeds his sheep (10:7–18), a picture that carries over to Jesus' personal, one-on-one instructing of Nicodemus (3:1–21), of the Samaritan woman at Sychar (4:7–26), of the man born blind (9:1–41), of Martha at the raising of her brother (11:5–27), of Thomas after the resurrection (20:26–29), and of Peter at the seaside (21:15–18). And he is, after all, called Rabbi. "You call me 'Teacher' and 'Lord,' and rightly so, for that is what I am" (John 13:13).

Some of Jesus' teaching, of course, occurred in group settings. The so-called Sermon on the Mount begins with the words, "He began to teach them, saying . . . " (Matt. 5:2). Most of the recorded education of the Twelve was conducted as a group. But whether in groups or with individuals, Jesus continually laid before his hearers both the convicting law and the good news of God's forgiveness and redeeming love. This chapter focuses on the education functions of the Christian congregation other than the sermon, realizing that both have the same focus and source and the same goal and objectives.

Focus and Source

The focus of Christian education is ever on Jesus, "for in him we live and move and have our being" (Acts 17:28). The pastor says with Paul, "I resolved to know nothing while I was with you except Jesus Christ and him crucified" (1 Cor. 2:2). Even though Christian education has to do with the individual's relationship with God, individuals *per se* are not the focus; rather, they are taught to focus their attention on God, who is revealed through Jesus Christ.

---

[2] The synoptics also relate similar events; e.g., Jesus teaching the Canaanite woman whose daughter was healed (Matt. 15:22–28), James and John (Mark 10:35–40), and the teacher of the law who heard the parable of the Good Samaritan (Luke 10:25–37).

The source of *Christian* education, therefore, is the revelation of Jesus Christ, which today is given only through Holy Scripture—all of which is inspired to teach people who they are, who God is, and what he has done for them—"to make [them] wise for salvation in Christ Jesus . . . thoroughly equipped for every good work" (2 Tim. 3:15, 17). Without Scripture, one simply cannot conclude that the depravity of humanity, begun at the Fall, has been overcome by the incarnate Son of God on the cross, who was raised again so that his people might have new life through a faith created and sustained by the Spirit of God. Although human concepts rightly help a person understand, e.g., how original sin exhibits itself or how the mind transmits truth to the next generation, only God himself can teach the truth and reality of his own heart. As the Confessions state,

> Without the grace, help, and activity of the Holy Spirit man is not capable of making himself acceptable to God, of fearing God and believing in God with his whole heart. This is accomplished by the Holy Spirit, who is given through the Word of God, for Paul says in 1 Cor. 2:14, "Natural man does not receive the gifts of the Spirit of God" (AC XVIII 2–3).

At the same time, the church recognizes that knowing/believing in God as revealed in Christ does not preclude using the mind to understand the how and what of the world. God created the human mind with a potential to be used to perceive, analyze, and reason. Granted, the mind is tainted by the Fall; it is and must be used nonetheless; otherwise the Christian will not be able to make use of natural history, science, psychology, etc. The church wants its members to be educated citizens in the world so that they actually can "give an answer to everyone who asks you [about] the hope that you have" (1 Peter 3:15) and can "encourage one another and build each other up" (1 Thess. 5:11). Therefore the pastor as well as his people have a responsibility to learn all they can about the world, confessing that its ultimate meaning is understood only by faith in Christ Jesus.

Goal and Objectives

"I have come that they may have life, and have it to the full" (John 10:10). In these words (as well as others) Jesus summarizes the goal, the purpose of God ever since the Fall—and, therefore, the overall goal of Christian education. Luther said it well in his explanation to the Second Article of the Creed:

> That I may be his own, and live under him in his kingdom, and serve him in everlasting righteousness, innocence and blessedness.

Although people sometimes forget or wish it were not so, all of life (including the mundane such as personal grooming) has been claimed and reclaimed by God; and the goal of Christian education is to apply Word and Sacrament through which the Spirit creates a living faith that expresses through every thought and act of life what God has done.

The objectives (i.e., the *measurable steps* toward the goal) of Christian education, therefore, can be grouped as follows:

Cognitive
> Knowledge of God and his grace in Christ, taught in Scripture.

Faith
> Belief and trust in God for life and salvation.

Affective
> Christian character—Christian love toward others and an attitude of forgiveness, even when outward sanctification falls short of God's plan (i.e., *thinking* as a Christian, not dividing between the secular and the religious, the empirical and the transcendental).

Behavioral
> The fruit of the Spirit (Gal. 5:22) lived out in private life, in the family, in the community, in the church—through worship, evangelism, witness, service, and fellowship.[3]

The Role of the Pastor

Given the nature of Christian education, the responsibility belongs to all believers as they are able. All are teachers. In certain circumstances, however, Scripture places the responsibility on certain people: on parents for the training of children (e.g., Eph. 6:4), and on the called pastor (and teacher) for the official, public training on behalf of the congregation (e.g., Acts 20:28, 1 Tim. 4:13; 2 Tim. 4:2).

Christians themselves are free to determine how to carry out these responsibilities. For example, even though the Scriptures (and human research) show that parents are the most influential people in a child's training, few are equipped to provide *all* education. Similarly, even though the pastor has the charge to oversee the use of the Word among the members, he may not have the

---

[3] For another expression of the objectives of Christian education, see *Patterns of Performance: Standards and Requirements 1968—1969*, Section 1 (The Board of Parish Education of The Lutheran Church—Missouri Synod, 1968), page 13.

time (or, in some cases, the ability[4]) to do the teaching himself. He, together with the elders/board of Christian education, may (and sometimes should) select and train assistants who can join him in teaching the Word: lay volunteers, called teachers, directors of Christian education, deaconesses, lay ministers, etc. With deep concern for the flock, the pastor might draw on professional Christian educators who can impart effective teaching methods to the assistants and/or pastor.[5] He can draw on the resources of the church at large (i.e., the denomination) for various media to help explain Christian doctrine to assistants and/or students. He can and should enlist assistants who can establish rapport with those being taught (e.g., very young children, teenagers, adults with special needs such as a congregational Al-Anon group, those with learning disabilities, etc.). And, given the laws of the land, he certainly will ensure that the teaching in a parochial day school will be done according to those laws (insofar as they do not contradict the Word of the Lord).

Whether or not the pastor uses assistants, the role of the parish ministry can be clearly seen in Peter's words:

> Be shepherds of God's flock that is under your care, serving as overseers—not because you must, but because you are willing, as God wants you to be; not greedy for money, but eager to serve; not lording it over those entrusted to you, but being examples to the flock. (1 Peter 5:2–3)

He is *the* representative of the Lord to administer the means of grace and to provide the community of believers with leadership in Christian living.

The Learning Process

Distinguishing between teaching and learning is more than a matter of semantics; it is the difference between hearing and believing. While the Holy Spirit alone creates and sustains faith, he uses people as they are created by God. Scripture affirms the learning process when it talks, for example, about being *fully convinced* (Rom. 14:5), *hearing* which is more than listening (Matt. 13:13), and *maturity* as compared to *elementary teachings*

---

[4] The directive in 1 Tim. 3:2 that pastors should be "able to teach" does not confer on them the ability to do so, much less in every teaching situation. Some pastors may be excellent teachers from the pulpit but ineffective with, e.g., four-year-olds.

[5] The pastor himself should seriously consider taking college classes in teaching methodology.

(Heb. 6:1). It happens *inside* a person. Therefore, the focus here is on *learning*, defined as

- processing new information/ideas/attitudes;
- relating it to what has been previously learned; and
- responding in some relatively permanent way as a result of what was processed.

Before that happens, the learner first receives the new information/ideas/attitudes by

- sensory input (observation, listening, etc.);
- imitation;
- sensory experience;
- trial and error;
- associations/relationships made; or
- any combination of these.

Effective teaching, therefore, works for internalized learning as appropriate to the learner's ability, and it understands one of its major tasks to be the removal of roadblocks to learning and faith through

- getting and keeping the learner's attention through a variety of media and methods;
- providing positive feedback;
- aiding memory through meaningfullness, familiarity, and/ or a recognized pattern or sequence; and
- freeing the learner to enact/practice the content.

How a teacher applies the above will vary according to the age/ developmental stage of the student as well as to the student's previous experiences. The pastor as teacher will want to understand and apply the best in theories of learning (and moral development) so that the work of the Spirit is not hindered.

The Pastor and the Educational Agencies of the Congregation

Teaching in the Home

Strictly speaking, the home never should be thought of as an "agency" of the church. Still, the church will assist parents and other adults as families grow in learning to live out their faith. Two temptations stand in the way, both based on the same premise that "Christian education" is limited to the transmission of Biblical information. (1) People are tempted to think of devotions and general Christian conversation as teaching-neutral; and (2) only the extremely Biblically-literate are qualified to transmit the information.

In reality, the church needs to support the home with encouragement, training, and resources.[6] Long before sociologists "proved" the significance of the home, Solomon reminded parents, "Train a child in the way he should go, and when he is old he will not turn from it" (Prov. 22:6).

Agencies for Teaching Children

Elementary and Secondary Day Schools. From its very inception, the Synod has emphasized the importance of integrating all learning under the Word of God. Today the Synod bylaws still affirm that

> The most effective education agencies available to the church for equipping children and youth for ministry are the full-time Lutheran elementary and secondary schools.[7]

Outside the home, no other program can devote the time and expertise available through trained teachers, assisting the learner to live all of life in the context and under the blessings of the Word. In spite of the schools' value, the pastor cannot require the congregation to establish such schools any more than the congregation can insist that its members send their children to such day schools. He can, however, help congregations and parents appreciate the schools' value and long-term benefits to the children.

As a general rule, the supervision of the school is delegated through divine call to an administrator/principal.[8] However, the pastor remains the *Seelsorger* who feeds and leads the students and staff. This he carries out, in part, through the staff but especially as he ministers directly to them in their calling. He is needed also to prevent a rift between the school and the church, to promote its support and use by the families of the church, and sometimes to teach the religion classes in the upper grades (usually considered to be the student's confirmation class).

The congregation should view the Christian day school also as an excellent agency for the spread of the Gospel. As of this writing, 50 percent of the children enrolled in Christian day schools come from outside the denomination; and in a recent two-year period (1986–88), more than 10,000 people have joined The

---

[6] In addition to excellent Bibles, devotional materials, personal Bible-study materials, and parenting programs, the Synod's Board for Parish Services through Concordia Publishing House also offers the *Nursery Roll Packet*, with resources and helps for parents of children ages one through three.

[7] *1989 Handbook: The Lutheran Church—Missouri Synod*, 3.233, p. 61.

[8] See Unit VI, Ch. 3 for a discussion on the pastor in team ministry.

Lutheran Church—Missouri Synod as a result of the congregational day school. On the other hand, gainsayers will claim that those statistics still do not warrant the expense of a day school.

The purpose of Christian training, however, is not simply to expand a congregation's rolls. God calls his people to fellowship with him in the one body of Christ, not mentioning any particular part or vision of it. And whether or not reflected on the membership roster, the Spirit works where and when he wills (John 3:8; Is. 55:10-11).

(A word of caution: In North American society, some families will try to use the private—i.e., nonpublic—Christian day school as a way to circumvent desegregation. Even the suspicion that the church allows such ungodly action vitiates the church's reason for existence. Lutheran elementary and secondary schools must do everything in their power to serve all people with the best God has to offer in his Son.)

Part-Time Agencies. All congregations, including those with a day school, can benefit from the varied opportunities and approaches available through part-time programs such as midweek/Saturday classes, release time classes, Sunday school, vacation Bible school, day-care[9], and preschool/early childhood programs. Compared to the time available in a Christian day school, any one of these comes in a distant second place; but cumulatively, they afford the church excellent opportunities to support parents in nurturing and training children in the Lord.

They have disadvantages. Because they are part-time and staffed by volunteers, parents and sometimes the church itself expect these programs to provide only minimal value. However, because some of these are recognized and accepted as a part of church life in North America, the pastor will do all he can to make the most of the opportunities they provide.

Trained teachers are the most significant ingredient. In spite of the view that almost anyone can teach children and that teaching ranks at the bottom of the congregational structure, the pastor understands the power of the Spirit and can envision the distinct benefits of quality Christian learning. Therefore

- Instead of accepting any and all volunteers, he seeks out and personally invites as teachers those who are able to teach and who already are well-versed in Scripture.
- Instead of spending an entire teachers meeting imparting Bible story facts, he provides opportunity for them to grow

---

[9] Day-care programs currently are the fastest growing educational agency in the LCMS.

in their teaching skills, knowing that how a person teaches affects the content and attitudes learned by the students.

• Instead of allowing the congregation to relegate the part-time agencies to a nonstanding status, (e.g., by insisting that they be self-supporting), the pastor holds them up at every opportunity as the best the congregation has for reaching many of the students. He promotes the agencies' high value by persuading the congregation to pay for equipment, teacher magazines, and other resources. He also visits the classes regularly in order to get to know the children and to say by his presence, "You are important to the church"—a statement reinforced whenever the children are asked to participate in the congregation's corporate worship.

• Instead of allowing these agencies to degenerate through a take-it-or-leave-it attitude, the pastor and congregation together establish high levels of professionalism, including punctuality and attendance by teachers as well as students, by proper accounting procedures and record keeping.

• Instead of hoping that the teachers are growing in their own faith, the pastor pays particular attention to them as individuals; they are, after all, his personal assistants in nurturing his flock.

Confirmation Classes. Popular piety has relegated confirmation classes to the status of drudgery that must be endured as a prerequisite for Holy Communion, the latter used as a crowbar to pry children into attendance. The reputation of confirmation classes is such that, for teaching adults, many congregations rename the classes to create a better image.

Originally the Christian church understood confirmation as the work of the Holy Spirit, confirming the faith expressed at the time of Baptism. This view soon led to the establishment of a ceremony (eventually a sacrament) connected to Baptism and later separated by time. By the 16th century, it had been so abused that the reformers discarded the extra-Biblical rite[10], calling for a simple, private examination by the pastor when he or the parents thought the child capable of the self-examination required for the reception of Holy Communion. The rise of Pietism in Germany soon emphasized self-examination to such an extent that instruction in Lutheran doctrine outshone everything else. An effort in the 1960s to adjust this direction accomplished little in the LCMS, perhaps because many pastors could not agree with an early-age

---

[10] Cf. Ap XIII 6 and SA Tractate 15f., 73.

first communion separated in years from formal confirmation classes.

However one evaluates the past, the parish pastor should understand and apply a few principles:

1. Properly speaking, the term *confirmation* should be limited to the ceremony itself. The classes leading up to the ceremony should be so designated.

2. Children and adults should meet the same criteria for participation in the Sacrament of the Altar. The course contents differ, for children see their role as "students" and are willing to study more concrete information than most adults, who see themselves dealing primarily on a conceptual level that relates to daily life. However, the "key" to the door to the Sacrament must not be withheld from a child for any reason not also applicable to adult. Nor should the reason be any other than the total inability/unwillingness to examine one's self under Law and Gospel.

3. The course content should cover the basics of Biblical, Christian faith, understood and expounded in the Lutheran Confessions (which includes Luther's Small Catechism), in order that the person is able to give public witness to the faith. The use of the Catechism *per se* does have precedence.

4. The rite of confirmation in the Lutheran church generally has consisted of three parts: the public confession of faith by the confirmand; the prayers of the congregation for those being confirmed; and the blessing from God symbolized by the laying on of hands. Three emphases should be avoided: (1) That the rite marks the completion of the study of God's Word; (2) that the rite of confirmation moves one into "real" membership in the body of Christ, the church; and (3) that the rite marks a transition from baptism-as-responsible-for-faith to the-individual-as-responsible. Rather, the rite marks only one stepping stone along a life-long path under the grace of God as one grows in sanctification.

Agencies for Teaching Youth and Young Adults

While the goals and objectives for these remain the same as those for any age groups in the church, youth and young adults present the church with unique challenges.

High schoolers, beginning to think abstractly, are working on the transition from an external-rule-oriented to an internally-incorporated way of life, and, therefore, test external authority (especially that of parents). From about ages 17 to 20, many begin to work on and make life-decisions (e.g., life partners, life-styles, vocation, commitment to God/church, etc.). And throughout these years youth and young adults are looking beyond their families for alternative models.

One very significant point: Youth are hurting (though they do not reveal their hurts readily). Older adults may think that the high school and college years are the most care-free in life. But study after study (particularly those conducted by Strommen, et al, in the 70s) uncovers the truth: Youth feel uncertain about their abilities to handle the tremendous pressures that face them; they make serious mistakes that threaten to dog them for the rest of life; they've been hurt enough by temporary friends that they are afraid to open up their inner selves to very many people (and especially not to authority figures who may use the information against them); and they are simply too unsure about themselves to completely trust that God can love them in spite of their sins and inadequacies. In addition, youth raised in the church often feel an unhealthy, unchristian guilt because they have not learned to trust the cleansing power of the Gospel. Openly they may insist that they are free from culpability, but inside they are panic-stricken about being caught at being themselves.

The church, therefore, needs to help those in this transitional stage to process and apply the knowledge and relationship they already have by grace with God in Christ. New information needs to be presented as usable by the youth/young adults in their primary tasks. The focus has to be on grace.

The pastor should not assume that an organized youth group in the congregation is capable of meeting the needs of all those eligible. He should not assume that youth are interested *only* in social activities. They also need serious use of the Word and Sacrament where God will find them. He should not assume that he automatically has the capability/patience/sensitivity to listen to and help the youth to learn (that is, to put faith into practice). Nor should he despair or abdicate his responsibility to be their *Seelsorger*. Instead, he will use every resource available to the congregation in presenting Word and Sacrament to youth as they learn what it means to be adult Christians.

Older, single young adults (e.g., in their 20s and early 30s) also present the congregation with unique needs—wondering why they've "fallen behind" their contemporaries in finding a spouse; working to be accepted in a society that focuses on them as what they are not (i.e., not young marrieds with small children); somewhat lonely because they do not have a life-partner with whom they can share themselves and who can accept them "as is." Again, the educational process will focus on helping these children of God to apply God's grace and strength in their lives.

Agencies for Teaching Adults

In many congregations, the only official agency is the Sunday morning adult Bible class; however, the pastor should view as an educational opportunity almost any adult gathering in the congregation—men's and women's organizations, mother's clubs, the altar guild, seniors, the opening of the voter's assembly and other congregational boards and committees, etc. (In fact, one might question a church organization's validity if it refuses to use the Word.)

Popular perception may suggest that the Sunday morning gathering should be devoted to the dissemination of Biblical information, which many adults want and enjoy. The pastor, however, knows that the primary task of the adult's heart is not collecting information (even about God) but applying God's grace to the difficulties and joys of a particular stage and situation in life and providing mutual support (spiritually as well as physically/emotionally).

The use of a lay teacher for adults in a particular setting needs to be thought through carefully. In the pluralistic society of North America with many people marrying across denominational lines and with high exposure to non-Lutheran "media religion," the most enthusiastic volunteer teacher may be the one most in need of learning the Law-Gospel emphasis of Scripture's theology of the cross. And the Bible class that focuses on Bible information may be the very group most able to be led by a conscientious volunteer. The pastor and elders/board for Christian education will want to plan carefully in order to support all adults (including those with special and/or age-specific interests/needs) in their continual growth in Word and Sacrament.